To Shipmate Ray
With best wishes
Don
9/9/01

IN PEACE and WAR

The Story of HMS Glasgow

1937 – 1958

G. D. Oliver

Copyright © G.D. Oliver

First Published 2001

Published by:
G.D.Oliver
2,White Hart Cottages
Wickham Market.
Woodbridge
Suffolk IP13 0RA

Edited by:
Lieutenant Commander P. Hinton, MBE, RN, (Retired)

ISBN 0-9540782-0-9

**British Library Cataloguing-
in-Publication Data**

A catalogue record of this book
is available from the British Library.

Printed by:
PRINT WRIGHT LTD
6, Boss Hall Business Park
Ipswich. Suffolk IP1 5BN

Contents

*This Book is Dedicated to all those who served in
the Royal Navy and Royal Marines aboard
HMS Glasgow 1938-1956*

The production of this book would not have been possible without the support and encouragement of Brenda who patiently endured my frequent absence upstairs working at the computer; the kind assistance of Geoff Dewing who undertook, on my behalf, research in the PRO and at the Imperial War Museum; Mr. D. P. Crowley for proof reading the manuscript and making suggestions relating to the narrative, Lieutenant Commander P. Hinton, MBE, RN who kindly undertook the editing, my son-in-law Darren Baker, who provided the required computer support; my son David; Commander T. Horton, RN, Warrant Officer C. Cole HMS *Sultan*, The Lord Provost of Glasgow and the following Shipmates: A. Acton, Don Aldridge, Darby Allen, R. J. Ayres, Eric Baker, J. Behan, Arthur Beards, Geoff Breading, Geoff Briggs, Clifford Bygate, Doug Carter, Richard Cameron, John Chiverell, Mike Cobbold, Guy Cook, Ron Condy, Bob Craig, Lt. Ken Davidson, RNVR Les Darnell, David Dixon, Roy Dixon, Bill Gates, David George, Ted Goodhall, John Goodyear, Reg Gossage, Bill de C. Hastie, Sir Hugo Huntington-Whiteley, Bt., Miles Huntington-Whiteley, VRD**, Fred Leach, Dennis Le Marquand, John Morgan, Bill Newman, Allan Mercer, Len Nicholl, P. Nicholls, Gerry Nugent, Roy Palmer, Jack Parr, Admiral of the Fleet Sir Michael Pollock, GCB, LVO, DSC, Derek Rawlings, Sam Rowe, Vic Smith, George Stemp, Roy Tinsley, Charles Trevellion, Irvin Walker, John Waters, Ron Walsh, Drummond "Spike" Window MBE, RVM, OPR., Harry Winward, William Wright, Derrick Woodcroft, Fred Yates, E. Young, and Jock Young all of whom provided photographs and information relating to the history of HMS *Glasgow*.

I also wish to thank the following: Mr A. Credland, curator of the Maritime Museum in Hull, who assisted me to obtain a copy of a photograph of HMS *Glasgow* held by the museum, The Imperial War Museum, The National Maritime Museum, The Fleet Air Arm Museum and The Royal Naval Museum for granting permission to reproduce photographs used in the book, Mr. Matthew Sheldon - Curator of Manuscripts at the Royal Naval Museum, Mr. G. A. Smith of the Naval Manning Agency – Portsmouth, and North Down Borough Council (Bangor) Co. Down, N. Ireland.

In some cases it has not been possible to trace the copyright holder and I offer my apologies for any breach of copyright which may have occurred in this book. I shall be happy to make amends in any future edition.

Nowhere is man more conscious of his mortality and his transience than at sea, where the sailor can hear the movement of the water along the ship's side, sometimes gentle and almost melancholy and sometimes hammering away through an excess of strength.... like the devil playing an organ with all the stops out.

Foreword

It is a privilege to be asked to contribute to Don Oliver's history of HMS Glasgow. My own connection with the ship was quite slight - I was the Sub of the Gunroom during the last commission and therefore responsible for the socialisation of a number of young midshipmen during their first tour of sea duty. During the 1956 Suez crisis I recall that all the close-range anti-aircraft gunnery armament was de-cocooned and set to work through a series of sleeve shoots. Glasgow's back end was fairly prickly with Bofors and pom-poms - as Quarters Officer of the After Close Range my command 'Open Fire' was a terrific success but 'Check Check Check' a complete disaster due to the thunderous noise. Although the sky was speckled with puffs, we didn't actually shoot down the target towing aircraft. Or the sleeve, as I recall. Otherwise I remember various educational visits to European ports - we were young then!

There is an enormous amount of research here and Don is to be congratulated on his thoroughness. As a graduate historian, I particularly like the way that the Glasgow story is so well supported by accounts of surrounding events and by descriptions of the strategic context. Because of this educated approach, we can see clearly the influence of international arms control agreements upon the decision to build a Glasgow in the first place and, subsequently, the contribution to the war effort made by this fine ship. Those who fought in the war realise already that it was not entirely a sequence of famous battles but also contained long periods of inactivity - or, indeed, activity of a pointless, sometimes dangerous and often unsuccessful sort. Despite striving for realism in pre-war exercises and tactical games, there is no doubt that the Royal Navy - and the nation as a whole - got much better at fighting the war as it progressed. The early stages - and one can cite the melancholy Norwegian campaign described here - were pretty much groping in the dark and some of this comes across very well in Don's pages.

In retirement I have been very privileged to be the Royal Navy and Royal Marines obituary writer for The Times newspaper for about the last seven years and this brings one into contact with many diaries and other memoirs kept by people who have not only participated in famous events but who have also recorded the humdrum aspects of their lives . It is extremely important that these types of records are not lost - "old men forget" is the quotation. Once forgotten, these memories cannot be retrieved. I therefore believe that Don Oliver's Glasgow story is a significant and worthy contribution to the archive of naval knowledge - not only because of the great events depicted here but also because of the small ones.

I served in fourteen ships - the most *beautiful* was Glasgow.

Guy F Liardet
Rear Admiral CB CBE
May, 2001

Commanding Officers
HMS Glasgow 1937-1956

Captain F.N. Attwood, RN	8th September 1937
Captain C.G.B. Coltart, RN	20th January 1938
Captain F.H. Pegram, RN	1st July 1939
Captain H. Hickling, RN	6th June 1940
Captain J.W. Cuthbert, RN	28th February 1942 - 22nd May 1942
Captain Evans-Lombe, RN	5th August 1942
Captain C.P. Clarke, RN	25th November 1943
Captain A.G.V. Hubback, OBE, RN	13th January 1946
Captain C.L. Firth DSO, MVO, RN	1st August 1948
Captain W.J. Yendell, RN	26th April 1950
Captain J. Holmes, RN	18th September 1951
Captain B. Bryant, DSO, DSC**, OBE, RN	6th April 1953
Captain P. Dawnay, MVO, DSC, RN	19th May 1954
Captain C.D. Bonham-Carter, RN	10th November 1955

In Memoriam 1938-1956

Ordnance Mechanic Roy W. Andrews

Royal Marine A.H. Bragg Po/x 100314

Chief Stoker Percy John Bowers P/K66148

Ordinary Seaman Robert Walter Burrows P/SSX 23322

Boy Seaman Cheverton

Petty Officer A.E. Davey P/JX127182

Able Seaman William James Dawson P/SSX 840160

Able Seaman L.N.Goy C/JX138693

Stoker Second Class Arthur Gudger P/ KX 97026

Boy Seaman Archibald P.J. Jeffries

Royal Marine A. Johnson Po/x 104059

Able Seaman L. Keilty.

Midshipman E.J.M. Lucas, R.N.

Engine Room Artificer Mansfield.

Surgeon Lt.G. R. E. Maxted RNVR.

Ordinary Seaman Donald A. Pitt P/SSX 27397

Chief Petty Officer Richards (Shipwright) P/MX52868

Acting Leading Signalman Eric William Sizer P/JX 138361

Able Seaman John Smith

Royal Marine G. Wymer Ch/x 4302

The Sailor's Prayer

Almighty and everlasting God, by whose grace thy servants are enabled to fight the good fight of faith and ever prove victorious: We humbly beseech thee so to inspire us, that we may yield our hearts to Thine obedience and exercise our wills on thy behalf. Help us to think wisely: to speak rightly: to resolve bravely: to act kindly; to live purely. Bless us in body and in soul, and make us a blessing to our comrades. Whether, at home or abroad, may we ever seek the extension of Thy Kingdom. Let the assurance of Thy presence save us from sinning: Support us in life, and comfort us in death.

O Lord God accept this prayer for Jesus Christ's sake.

Amen.

Prologue

This book has its origins in an autobiographical account of the service life of the author, who served aboard HMS *Glasgow* during the period of the ship's last Commission between November 1955 and November 1956.

Recollections of ex-shipmates and places visited stimulated an interest to record, for posterity, the complete history of this Southampton class cruiser, from the date when her keel was laid in 1934 until she went to be broken up in 1958, after a long and distinguished career.

The term 'cruiser' goes back to the days of sail when large frigates could be detached from the main fleet to maraud independently to attack and destroy enemy ships that preyed on commercial vessels. In the nineteenth century, when sail gave way to steam and those built of iron replaced wooden ships, the cruiser became a powerful warship. Such ships patrolled the trade routes of the Empire and protected those merchant vessels belonging to friendly countries.

At the end of hostilities following the First World War, cruisers were designated according to the size of their main armament. HMS *Glasgow* is therefore referred to as a six-inch cruiser and this is an account of the ship's actions during the Second World War 1939-1945.

Every attempt has been made to produce a complete and accurate account of the ship's history in chronological order. The account includes recollections from those who served aboard the ship during the Second World War and in those peacetime periods, pre- and post-war, until the ship was finally paid off and withdrawn from service.

Memories of wartime experiences often evoked powerful feelings because for the Royal Navy there was no phoney war. Those who served in this branch of the armed forces were plunged into action within hours of war being declared. Many witnessed, for the first time in their young lives, the pain and destruction associated with armed conflict.

HMS *Glasgow* engaged in the invasion of Norway, the evacuation of His Majesty King Haakon from his country, Norway, to prevent him, together with members of the Norwegian Government and the country's bullion reserves, from falling into the hands of the German invaders. The ship also played an important role in providing protection of convoys of merchant shipping to Russia, the interception of 'Blockade Runners,' the destruction of the German Brest and Bordeaux flotillas in the Bay of Biscay, the Normandy landings on D-Day 6th June 1944 and the bombardment of Cherbourg.

She had a distinguished career in peacetime, first of all when serving with the Second Cruiser Squadron of the Home Fleet before the Second World War. In May 1939 she was chosen, in company with HMS *Southampton* to escort R.M.S *Empress of Australia,* with their Majesties King George VI and Queen Elizabeth aboard, to Canada and America.

After the war, following a major refit the *Glasgow* sailed to the East Indies where she became the Flagship to the Commander-in-Chief 1946-1947. A year later, after a short spell at home she sailed again, this time to the West Indies where she relieved HMS *Sheffield* to become Flagship of the Commander-in-Chief, America and West Indies Station. In October 1950, on completion of her tour of duty HMS *Glasgow* returned home.

Twelve months elapsed before she became Flagship of the Commander-in-Chief, Mediterranean, Admiral The Earl Mountbatten of Burma. KG, GCSI, GCIE, GCVO, KCB, DSO, PC.

The ship was also accorded the great honour of acting as escort to Her Majesty the Queen Elizabeth II and HRH The Duke of Edinburgh, upon their return from the Commonwealth Tour in 1954, as they visited Malta and later returned to England.

Her final commission was to act as Flagship to Vice-Admiral R.G. Onslow, CB, DSO***, Flag Officer Flotillas Home Fleet, from November 15th 1955 – November 12th 1956. Shortly after completing this last tour of duty she was "mothballed," before being put on the disposal list in March 1958, after which she was handed over to BISCO (British Iron and Steel Corporation) and allocated to Hughes Bolkov.

On 4th July 1958 she was towed from Portsmouth to the yard of Hughes Bolkow at Blyth for breaking up on July 8th later that same year.

All proceeds arising from the sale of this book will go to a Royal Naval Charity and a local Children's Hospice.

The Ship's Crest

The people of Lanarkshire adopted HMS *Glasgow* and visitors to the ship were often puzzled to see two entirely different crests in and around the cruiser.

"MEMOR ES TUORUM"
(Be mindful of your ancestors)

The ship's crest reproduced here was taken from the uppermost section of the armorial bearings of the city of Glasgow. The half-length figure represented is Saint Kentigern, also known as St. Mungo, the patron saint of Glasgow, born 518 A.D. It shows the saint mitred and vested, his right hand raised in the act of benediction, his left hand carrying a crozier.

Below is the Ship's Motto:–
"Memor Es Tuorum"

"Be mindful of your Ancestors"

The origin of St Mungo stems from the sixth century A.D. when the east of Scotland was mainly Celtic and inhabited by fierce warriors, the Picts. It is unclear who these people were but they are thought to have been of Teutonic extraction.

For some centuries before the sixth century A.D. the pagan Picts had been subject to invasion from another pagan race, the Scots who hailed from Ireland. It is worthy of note that these two races gave a good account of themselves in the first four centuries of the Christian era, against the Roman invaders.

St Mungo's mother was Princess Thenew, whose tribe lived on the southern shores of the Firth of Forth, where there was a fortified neck of land. This was known as Traprain Law and formed what is now known as East Lothian.

The people of this region were undoubtedly seafarers, borne out by the fact that in 1919 a collection of Roman silverware and pottery was unearthed there. This treasure trove is thought to have been part of a collection of goods looted from the neighbouring continental coast. It is also highly probable that the tribe were aware of the tribal customs present in Scandinavia at that time, where wrongdoers were subjected to a rigid code of behaviour and frequently punished.

When Princess Thenew was found to be with child, fathered by Urien, Prince of Cumbria, she was cast out from the tribe on to the inhospitable waters in the Firth of Clyde, in a coracle, to die from the effects of hunger and cold. The coracle drifted out to sea before being swept back up the Firth, eventually grounding on the shore at what is now Culross, near Dumfermline. Inside the coracle Princess Thenew was found, cold and wet, by local shepherds who gave her sustenance.

Shortly after giving birth to a boy, she and her new born son were taken to a local monastery run by Saint Serf. Here mother and child were both baptised into the Christian faith with the boy taking the name "Kentigern", which means "chief lord." Kentigern grew up in the monastery where, because of his friendly disposition, he was often called Mungo, by St. Serf, meaning "dear friend."

On reaching manhood and after finishing his training he left the monastery, around 550 A.D., and made his way westwards to embark on missionary work, before building his own monastery.

Soon after leaving Saint Serf's monastery he went to the house of a holy man named Fergus at Kernach where legend has it that the holy man died the night of Mungo's arrival.

Mungo placed the body of the holy man on a cart yoked to two wild bulls and commanded them to take it to the place ordained by the Lord. The bulls stopped at Cathures where Fergus was buried and it was here that Mungo established a church, referring to the spot as "Glasgu", the beloved green place.

A cluster of huts and houses sprang up around the monastery to form the beginnings of what has become known as the City of Glasgow, and the monastery into Glasgow Cathedral.

During his life St. Mungo had to flee from Scotland, because he had antagonised one of the kings, and it was while in exile in Wales he met St. David. One of his disciples is St. Asaph, after whom the present place and monastery are known. The parish church in Llanelwy, North Wales, which was built in 1524 is dedicated to Saints Kentigen and Asaph. Within the church is an acknowledgement to the fact that whilst Kentigen (or Mungo),was exiled from Scotland, he founded a missionary college there in the local settlement in 560 AD. Before returning to Scotland in 573, to become Bishop of Glasgow, he left the college in the care of his favourite pupil St. Asaph. St. Mungo lived to be about eighty-five years of age. He died in 603 A.D., and was buried on the south side of the High Altar of his monastery. He was later canonised and became the patron saint of Glasgow with a feast day on January 13th.

Armorial Bearings

The devices on the Armorial Bearings of the City of Glasgow, namely an oak tree, a robin, a salmon swimming upside down with a signet ring in its mouth and an old fashioned hand bell are all symbols of the miracles allegedly wrought by Mungo during his lifetime. Originally these were used on the seals of the Bishops of Glasgow but were later incorporated into the Coat of Arms of the City.

Although the City is so old and the Bearings quite ancient, they were not registered as the official Armorial Bearings until 1866.

The stories behind the tree and bird are as follows:
when Kentigern was a youth he was put in charge of the Holy Fire, which St. Serf was supposed to have got from Heaven. One day he fell asleep, and some of his envious companions crept into the Refectory and put the fire out. On awakening, Kentigern, seeing what had happened, plucked some frozen hazel twigs from a nearby tree and, by praying over them, caused them to burst into flame, thus restoring the Holy Fire. Although in the legend it started as a hazel branch, an oak tree now represents the tree.

The bird is a robin, which was a pet of St. Serf who had tamed it. Some of his disciples accidentally killed it and apportioned the blame on St. Mungo who, taking the bird in his hands, prayed over it and restored it to life, whereupon it flew chirping to its master. Stories connected to the bell and salmon relate to the Saint's later life.

4

Although there is no definite information as to how he obtained the bell, St. Mungo may have brought it home from Rome having been given it by Pope Gregory the Great.

By the fifteenth century "St. Mungo's Bell" had become a notable institution in Glasgow. In 1450 John Stewart, "the first provost that was in Glasgow", left an endowment to have the bell tolled throughout the City to call the inhabitants to pray for his soul. Others did the same and the City treasurer's accounts for 1578 show an entry of two shillings "for one tong to Sanct Mungowis Bell." The bell disappeared and its fate is unknown. However, in 1641, the Magistrates purchased a replacement and this bell still exists in the People's Palace.

The fish story concerns the Queen of the area in which St. Mungo worked, Queen Languoreth. Her husband King Hydderch Hael, King of Cazdow, gave the Queen a signet ring that she subsequently gave to a Knight of the Court. Suspecting that she was having an affair the King, on finding the Knight asleep during a hunting party, took the ring and threw it into the nearby river.

On his return home the King asked the Queen for the signet ring to be returned, threatening to have her killed if she failed to do so. The Queen made an appeal to the Knight who could not help and she then went to enlist the help of St. Mungo, for which she promised to do penance. St. Mungo thereupon sent one of his monks to fish in the river, giving him strict instructions that he was to return immediately with the first fish that he caught. This turned out to be a salmon with a ring in its mouth, which St. Mungo extracted and handed to the Queen.

The fish that appears to be handing up the ring is represented on the counter seal made in around 1271, belonging to Bishop Robert Wyschard.

Associations with the City of Glasgow

HMS *Glasgow* was the seventh ship of the Royal Navy to bear the name of the Scottish ancient city. The ship was ordered on December 17th 1934, with construction commencing on April 16th 1935 at the shipyard of her builders Scotts Shipbuilding and Engineering Company Limited (Greenock).

It was a natural conclusion that she should bear the name of the nearby City of Glasgow, after her launch on 20th June 1936.

The ship was launched and named by the wife of the then Prime Minister, Stanley Baldwin. To mark the occasion the builders presented a silver cigar and cigarette casket to the ship which, under the terms of the dedication agreement, had to be kept in the ship while she was in commission in the Royal Navy. Should the ship pay off, the casket was to be placed in the care of the Commodore of the Royal Naval Barracks at the port where she paid off.

The casket is to be passed down to all ships bearing the name of HMS *Glasgow* until there is finally no ship so named. At such time it is to be put in the care of the Commodore at the port at which the last ship called HMS *Glasgow* is finally paid off. Furthermore, Admiralty approval is required before the casket may be loaned to another ship.

The people and Corporation of the City of Glasgow always expressed a great interest in the cruiser, the subject of this book, and generously provided much of the silverware that was held by the ship, some of which had been passed down from its predecessor.

Included in the silverware presented to the sixth ship in 1911 was a Gunnery Shield which was competed for each year, a large silver bowl, and two other pieces: a centre- piece consisting of the armorial bearings of the City of Glasgow guarded by two sailors and a silver galleon, both of which were given by the Ladies of Glasgow.

Other trophies held on board HMS Glasgow included:

1) The battle ensign flown by her predecessor at the battle of Coronel, 1st November 1914, and the battle of the Falkland Islands, 8th December 1914.

2) A pair of silver mounted carvers presented by the 6th Duke of Portland. These were made from the trotters of a pig, known as 'Tirpitz,' rescued from the German cruiser *Dresden* as she sank at Juan Fernandez Island in 1915.

3) A life buoy from the *Dresden* was also among the trophies aboard the *Glasgow*.

4) Silverware presented by His Majesty King Haakon in commemoration of his safe evacuation from Norway in 1940.

Conception, Birth and First Commission

In mid-July 1921 America, concerned about the increasing strength of Japan's navy and the shift in the balance of power, convened a conference between the world's leading naval powers to consider ways and means of limiting the arms race then in progress.

At the conference, which was held in Washington DC in November that year, it was agreed that the size of cruisers should not exceed 10,000 tons and that the size of their armament should be limited to a maximum of 8 inches.

Soon after the conference Japan made it known that it was planning to construct a number of cruisers to comply with the agreed criteria. The Admiralty responded by making preparations for the Royal Navy to be supplied with "County" class cruisers, which were also to be built to the required displacement and armament standards.

Two years later, in 1923, the Admiralty put forward, for Treasury approval, a proposal that the Royal Navy's obsolete cruisers and destroyers should be replaced, over a period of ten years, as part of a structured programme of construction. The plan provided for eight of these "County" class cruisers to be laid down the following year.

However, before a decision could be made the Government of the day fell, to be replaced by a Labour Government committed to a programme of disarmament, which caused the Admiralty to reconsider its proposals.

In 1927 under the auspices of the League of Nations, a further conference was convened, in Geneva to enable the major powers to agree mutually on disarmament. This was seen as the way forward to achieve a lasting peace by preventing arms races, which could lead ultimately to another Great War. Britain and America were unable to agree on the limitations concerning cruiser construction and the conference disbanded.

Three years later, early into the New Year of 1930, a third conference was convened and, at its conclusion, Britain was compelled to accede to America's request that the Royal Navy's cruiser strength be reduced in terms of numbers and tonnage. These imposed limitations led to the design of the "Leander" class of cruiser, which were of 7,000 tons displacement and armed with 6-inch guns.

In 1933, by the time the Treasury had presented the estimates for approval, America and Japan had already resorted to constructing cruisers of 10,000 tons displacement with 6-inch armament.

Responding to this knowledge, and to keep pace, the Royal Navy cancelled orders for one of the proposed "Leander" class and two of a smaller "Arethusa" class cruiser design. This action was to permit the building of two 6-inch cruisers which, although based on the "Leander" design, bore little resemblance to it upon completion.

These cruisers were enlarged to allow extra turrets to be fitted, their armoured protection to be improved, and hangers provided amidships to enable spotter planes to be serviced and maintained ready for action.

Although originally it had been intended that the class should receive classical names this was changed and they were named after towns.

HMS *Glasgow*, one of eight cruisers built in response to the Japanese cruisers *Mogami* and *Mikuma*, which had twelve six inch guns fitted as part of their armament, was ordered on December 17th 1934, with construction commencing on April 16th 1935 at the shipyard of Scotts Shipbuilding and Engineering Company Limited, Greenock.

The following year, on 20th June 1936, she was launched, by the wife of the then Prime Minister Stanley Baldwin.

On 8th September 1937 the first Royal Navy crew to board HMS *Glasgow* arrived at Greenock. First to arrive on board was her captain, Captain F. N. Attwood, closely followed by his fellow officers: Commander C. I. Horton, Commander (E) C. A. Shaw, Pay Commander H.C.H. Vaughan, Lt. Commander A. B.Usher, Lt. Commander E. L. Pemberton, Lieutenant E.J.S. James, Lieutenant K. M. Woods, Lieutenant J. Y. Thompson, Lieutenant P.B. North-Lewis, Lieutenant (E) C. B. I. Havergill, Lieutenant (E) Dormatt,

HMS Glasgow launched at Scotts' Yard Greenock by Mrs Baldwin, wife of the Prime Minister Stanley Baldwin, 20th June 1937.

Lieutenant (E) C. W. Russ, Pay Lieutenant E. S. Sherbourn, Pay Sub-Lieutenant C. J. Grist, Commissioned Gunner E. Cove, Commissioned Gunner L. C. Devoil, Gunner R. Eccles, Commissioned Shipwright J. G. James and 66 ratings.

Later that same day another 340 ratings arrived with the Navigating Party and the newly formed ship's company exercised 'Fire Stations.'

The next day a pilot came aboard and the new cruiser made passage to Portsmouth. During the voyage the ship was swung to calibrate her compasses and her armament was tested to enable the captain to formally accept the ship from the builders.

Following her arrival in Portsmouth on 14th September 1937, the Royal Marine detachment led by their commanding officer, Lieutenant B. B. Keen, RM, went aboard.

The month of October was full of incidents which included: an explosion in an auxiliary boiler room due to an accumulation of fuel oil in the furnace, a visit from C-in-C Portsmouth, the christening of the daughter of Lieutenant J. Carson on the Quarterdeck, and on the 12th, an unfortunate accident during provisioning, involving a Boy Seaman, A.P.J. Jefferies, which tragically resulted in his death. Furthermore the ship was subjected to a force nine south-westerly gale, went to the assistance of a trawler aground near Stack Island, and went aground herself at Portland.

Towards the end of this eventful month the *Glasgow's* two Supermarine Walrus Spotter-Reconnaissance Amphibian Biplane Flying Boats were taken aboard, and the catapult crews worked hard to perfect the techniques used for launching the planes from the ship and their subsequent recovery aboard.

Early in November the Spotting Table and 6" gun crews were also subjected to numerous exercises to familiarise them with the new equipment and armament. As the month drew to a close the ship went to Portland where full calibre firing tests were undertaken, which were successfully completed on the 29th November. The remainder of the year was spent with the crew engaged in working up exercises to hone them into a disciplined and efficient fighting force, punctuated on 11th December 1937, when the ship was dressed with masthead flags in honour of the first anniversary of His Majesty King George VI's accession to the throne.

1938 Commission

On 20th January 1938 Captain C.G.B. Coltart, assumed command in Portsmouth, where the *Glasgow* was victualled in preparation for a passage to Gibraltar.

HMS Glasgow at anchor 1938 (NMM)

The cruiser slipped on 5th February and proceeded across the Bay of Biscay where two days later, ironically in view of what was to come, greetings were exchanged with the German pocket battleship *Deutschland* at 8.30pm at 41° 05' N, 09° 32'W.

Four days after leaving England *Glasgow* arrived in her destination port to meet up with HM Ships *Nelson*, *Rodney*, *Royal Oak*, *Revenge*, *Amora*, *Sheffield*, *Guardian*, *Nanwhal* and *Porpoise* in the Straits of Gibraltar. Shortly after her arrival *Glasgow* engaged in gunnery exercises with her sister ships *Sheffield, Southampton* and *Newcastle* in the waters adjoining Gibraltar.

On 25th March 1938 HMS *Glasgow* returned to Portsmouth where she hoisted the flag of Admiral Sir Charles Morton Forbes, KCB, DSO, before it was subsequently transferred to HMS *Nelson.*

During April and May that year the ship was engaged in exercises in the waters near to Portsmouth and Portland.

On 20th June the cruiser was dressed overall as part of the welcome extended to His Majesty King George VI, as he visited the Fleet at Weymouth, and a twenty one gun salute was fired in his honour.

During her stay at Weymouth the Navy League and the Naval Association made presentations of silver bugles to the Captain, who accepted them on behalf of the ship. Stavanger was the next port of call as the ship made a series of courtesy visits in Norway. In Stavanger the ship was open to visitors and a number of the local inhabitants, including twenty-five Rotarians, were able to go aboard and meet the ship's crew, as the cruiser lay in harbour. When all the planned courtesy visits had been made the warship returned to Pompey where she remained for the month of August. Later that year HMS *Glasgow* was attached to the Home Fleet as part of the Second Cruiser Squadron operating in the North Sea. Here she was frequently engaged in exercises, which included the recovery of her Walrus aircraft, by the "Slick Method," between Invergordon, on the East Coast of Scotland, and Scapa Flow.

On 22nd September that year Richard Cameron, who had joined the *Glasgow* after completing his training as a Signal Boy at HMS *Ganges* in Suffolk celebrated his 17th birthday. While the ship was exercising the transfer of communications with flags, one of the signals halyards became unstopped and trapped on the yardarm. Someone reminded the "Bunting Tosser" that it was the lad's birthday and, as a present, the Yeoman told Richard to climb the mast and retain the clip. The young man successfully completed his duty and had good reason to remember his special day!

The year ended uneventfully with the ship's return to Portsmouth.

Royal Tour of Canada

In January 1939 HMS *Glasgow* sailed from Portsmouth, making her way via Portland, to Gibraltar to join the Mediterranean Fleet for exercises with her sister ships *Sheffield*, *Newcastle* and *Southampton*. This not only gave many of the crew their first experience of travel to foreign parts but caused many of them to be very seasick as they made passage through a rough Bay of Biscay. Recovery was assured when the ship reached her destination, where the crew was able to go ashore and relax. This relaxation was cut short, however, when orders were received requiring the cruiser to return to the U.K. for special duties.

Following her return from Gibraltar the *Glasgow* was cleaned from top to bottom in preparation to escort, in company with her sister ship HMS *Southampton*, the RMS *Empress of Australia* carrying H.M. King George VI and Queen Elizabeth, across the Atlantic to visit the World Fair Exhibition in New York.

Departing from Portsmouth on 6th May 1939 the three ships ventured out to Spithead, where HMS *Repulse* was already at anchor. As the liner, with her royal passengers, passed Clarence Pier the assembled warships fired a 21 gun Royal Salute before forming up as the Royal Squadron. All the ships then proceeded out of harbour in single line ahead, in order: HMS *Southampton*, HMS *Glasgow*, *Empress of Australia* and HMS *Repulse*, four cables apart.

Before heading out into the Atlantic the ships proceeded to rendezvous with the Home Fleet, hampered as they did so by the presence of merchant ships. The liner, upon completion of ceremonial protocol, flanked by the cruisers on either quarter with the *Repulse* astern, steamed out into the Atlantic, at 17 knots, towards America. Three days out into the passage visibility deteriorated to barely five miles and soon there were indications that a gale was approaching. By 2.00 pm the wind had freshened to blow at gale force eight from south by east. HMS *Repulse* detached from the Squadron and the liner, with her escorting cruisers, sailed westwards. An hour and a half later the wind rose rapidly from the southwest and the sea became very rough forcing the Squadron to reduce speed to 12 knots. Between 6.20 pm and 7.00 pm both warships were forced to heave to temporarily; *Southampton* because a sea had stoved in the Wardroom ports, and the *Glasgow* to secure wooden fenders, which had become adrift on deck. At its height the storm blew squall reaching force twelve and the cruisers rolled heavily, and just before 5.00 pm *Southampton* rolled 43 degrees to port losing her sea boat as she did so. Not to be outdone *Glasgow* rolled to 45 degrees! The ship was hammered and hurled about, first in one direction then in another. The ship pounded and rolled, heaved and pitched, labouring heavily in the terrible seas and life on board was no joke for either officer or rating. The constant effort of giving at the knees to counter the rolling of the ship and that of stopping the body being hurled about in one direction or the other was as arduous as climbing a mountain, except that the unwilling mountaineer aboard *Glasgow* had nothing to show for his efforts nor was he able to take a breather. Having regard to the fact that the cruisers were "equally comfortable" at a higher speed *Glasgow's* captain, Captain Coltart, rang down to increase speed to 15 knots. The following day the storm blew itself out and the weather cleared enabling visual contact to be maintained with the *Empress of Australia*. As night fell *Southampton*, making use of her anti-submarine equipment to detect ice went ahead of the liner.

On the 11ᵗʰ May, mid way through the Morning Watch, the sea temperature dropped 14 degrees, bringing with it the formation of a widespread fog which reduced visibility. *Southampton*, having detected the presence of ice using her Asdic, fired a warning gun and the Squadron hove to, remaining virtually static all day. That night a vain attempt was made to make passage, using searchlights. However, with little progress being possible the plan was aborted.

The Empress of Australia, shrouded in fog, passing through an ice field   (PRO)

Conditions remained much the same the next day although the occasional clear patch permitted the ships to make sporadic progress.

Eventually the fog cleared from the northward to reveal numerous "Growlers" ahead that appeared to have come from an iceberg seven miles distant to the northwest. The respite was short lived and the fog returned, bringing with it the inevitable delays, relieved only when breaks occurred and visibility improved.

On 13th May, at the end of the Forenoon Watch, an iceberg appeared close to the starboard bow of the *Empress of Australia*. The warships, astern of the liner at the time, were unaware of anything unusual happening until they heard the liner signal with three short blasts on her siren and the Squadron slowed.

This was in some way fortuitous because aboard the *Glasgow* one of her crew was suffering with a suspected perforated appendix. Surgeon Captains J.A. Maxwell, and H.E.Y. White, were transferred by boat from the liner to the cruiser where they successfully operated on the patient, in the warship's sickbay. Four days later when the ship reached Quebec, the patient was removed to the Military Hospital.

As daylight dawned on the 14th May, in the limited available poor visibility, sludge ice could be seen about five miles distant, through a sector stemming from due north clockwise around to west. The sun, climbing steadily upwards in the sky, gradually burned away the fog, albeit to leave isolated patches, which enabled the Squadron to turn and steer southwestward to avoid the worst of the ice, although during the Afternoon Watch the ships passed through fields of sludge and pack ice.

HMS Glasgow making her way through sludge and pack ice   *(PRO)*

The early evening wind freshened to clear away the remains of the fog and the liner, with her escorts, increased speed and resumed the passage at 18 knots.

The next day *Glasgow's* sister ship catapulted its aircraft to reconnoitre ahead of the steaming vessels, and when it returned to circle the ship the pilot reported that no ice had been sighted within 60 miles. While it was still airborne, and before the aircraft was recovered, both cruisers carried out height finding and barrage procedures exercises. Upon the successful completion of these the cruisers launched their Walruses to reconnoitre the Cabot Strait, in the vicinity of Cape Ray, before positioning themselves on either side of the liner to simulate depth charge attacks. Midway through the Dog Watches HM Canadian Ships *Skeena* and *Saguenay* joined the Squadron which, with their ship's companies fallen in as for entering harbour, passed down the starboard side of the *Empress of Australia*, the men cheering as they did so. The destroyers then took station before all the ships made their way towards Orleans Island where they were due to anchor. Two days later, on 17th May, the cruisers and destroyers weighed anchor five minutes before the Forenoon Watch in preparation to make passage to the first port of call, Quebec, on the St Lawrence River. Twenty minutes later the destroyers positioned themselves on port and starboard bows of the *Empress of Australia* each two and a half cables distant, with *Glasgow* and *Southampton* respectively four and eight cables astern of the liner.

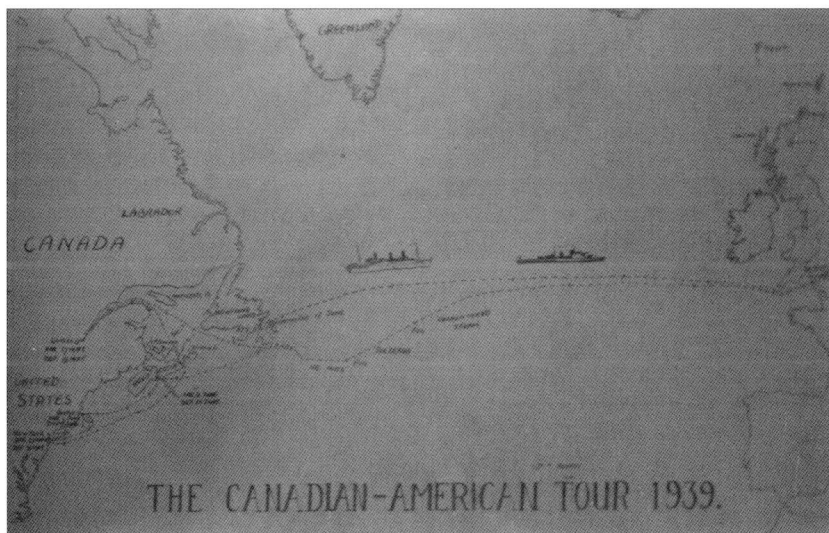

Postcards issued to crew members, which portrayed the tour, were sent home. (RC)

On arrival at Quebec the ships anchored in the river below the Heights of Abraham. Ashore, the Canadian Royal Mounted Police (Mounties) assembled to provide the welcoming party for the Royal Family. For the younger members of *Glasgow's* crew, many of whom had never been abroad before, the spectacle created a memorable sight. That evening, between 9.45 pm and 10.15 pm the British cruisers provided a searchlight display to entertain crowds of well wishers on the quayside. The cruisers and destroyers were illuminated and, set against the backdrop of a firework display on the other side of the river, they created an effective and memorable image. Two days later, on 19th May 1939, *Southampton* and *Glasgow* set sail for their next port of call, New York.

In the forenoon of the 20th May, following their departure from Quebec, *Glasgow's* aircraft exercised launching and recovery methods during the course of which one of them, L2308, crashed. Midshipman John Knox Laughton, RN who witnessed the incident recorded that Petty Officer R.B. Lunberg, the new rating pilot, under the Admiral's orders was practicing landing in a chop using the "Slick" method. This was a method whereby a ship altered course to create an area of calmer water into which a reconnaissance aircraft could land prior to its recovery.

Class Photograph of No.41 Course taken after   (FAAM)
PO. R.B. Lunberg completed his training.

During the exercise the Walrus circled *Glasgow* twice before coming down low onto the formed "slick" without landing. The pilot then circled for a third time, this time bringing his plane down onto the "slick," As the Walrus hit the water it bounced three times and took off again. [Whether this was an attempted landing or not Midshipman Laughton did not know].

Once again the Walrus circled *Glasgow* and the pilot brought it into the formed "slick." As it landed heavily on the starboard float, the strut collapsed to push the float through the starboard lower wing effectively destroying it. The plane tipped on its side, with the wrecked wing partly submerged, to be propelled round to starboard in small circles. The engine, being heavy, forced the nose down into the sea. As the plane made its second circle the tail came up and the plane slowly capsized with the pilot able to sit on the wreckage.

The crash whaler's crew, under the command of Midshipman Boyall, was launched to rescue the crew. Two occupants were seen to climb out of the hull but one soon disappeared from view. Petty Officer Lunberg, who had managed to sit on the wreckage, was rescued by those in the whaler but the state of the sea prevented Able Seaman L.N.Goy from being found quickly. Fifteen minutes later he was found floating in the icy water. By the time he was picked up by the whaler he was dead from shock and exposure. Within seven minutes the plane sank below the icy water. Able Seaman Goy was buried at sea, in a snowstorm, in the early evening that same day with *Glasgow* stationed on the weather beam of *Southampton.*

The ships continued to make passage to New York during which they encountered fog, which forced them to reduce speed. However, at times the fog cleared and they were able to proceed at 22 knots to make landfall at New York on 23rd May.

Here, the Statue of Liberty and a skyline of skyscrapers greeted the crew. *Glasgow* moored in the Hudson River off 72nd Street in company with HM Ships *Berwick,* flying the flag of C-in-C, America and West Indies, *Exeter,* flying the broad Pennant of the Commodore, South America, and the Argentine cruiser *La Argentina.*

On Empire Day 24th May 1939 Vice-Admiral G.F.B. Edward-Collins, CB, CVO, was accorded a fifteen-gun salute as he left the offices of Rear Admiral C.H. Woodward, USN. This salute was rather unusual in that the saluting battery was too far away from the Admiral's office in the Navy Yard to be heard and loudspeakers had been placed outside the office building, where the ceremonial guard was mounted, to relay the sound! At 4 pm that day the liner *Queen Mary* sailed from her berth. This enabled *Southampton* to proceed to moor alongside pier 90, leaving *Glasgow* out in mid river.

Statue of Liberty 1939   *(RNM)*

Empire State Building 1939

The following day *Berwick* and *Exeter* sailed for other American ports leaving *Glasgow* and *Southampton* behind and open to visitors. Although an estimated 15,000 Americans visited *Southampton* few were able to reach *Glasgow*, which was still moored in mid river. On Friday 26th the ships were dressed overall in honour of HM Queen Mary's birthday and *Glasgow* fired a Royal Salute, whereas *Southampton*, being alongside, was not permitted to take part. The next day *Glasgow* was able to go alongside and she moored alongside pier 54.

Two days later, on 29th May, the body of Leading Stoker James Healey surfaced between *Glasgow* and the pier. He had been reported as an absentee from the *Berwick* when it had it sailed three days earlier. After *Glasgow's* Executive officer, whose responsibility it was to make the necessary arrangements, had incurred considerable expenditure, the funeral took place on Tuesday 30th May. The weather improved dramatically during the warship's stay, reaching a maximum of 85°F, and tropical uniforms were the order of the day. To enable the crews to visit the World Fair, leave was granted from 9.00 am to the off duty watches of both ships for two days. For a member of the crew coming from a small fishing village back home this was an exciting time, with visits being made to Long Island, Coney Island, Central Park, the Empire State Building and the World Fair. Many of the shows were free to those in uniform and understandably the crew were saddened when it was time for *Southampton* and *Glasgow* to leave, at 6.00 am, on 31st May.

Two hours later, when they were three miles apart, both cruisers launched their aircraft to engage in launch and recovery exercises. Two American aircraft arrived in the vicinity and engaged in machine gun practice using a sleeve target. The aircraft from the British cruisers were quickly recalled!

As the Afternoon Watch was completed *Glasgow* parted company with her sister ship and made passage to St. Johns, New Brunswick. Nine days later *Glasgow* rejoined *Southampton* and both ships made passage together to Halifax. Here a number of social and sporting events were arranged which included a boxing match against a Canadian Services team. Out-classed in both fitness and skill, the British seamen were beaten decisively 11-3.

On Tuesday 13th June 1939 the *Empress of Britain*, under the command of Vice-Admiral Sir Dudley North, berthed in the port. Two days later Their Majesties arrived in the city, by train, to be greeted by Royal Salutes fired by the British warships. Journalists were permitted to travel aboard the two cruisers to cover the Royal Tour during the trip to Newfoundland. Those from the Times and the Daily Express went aboard *Southampton* and those from the Sunday Times sailed on *Glasgow*. At 6.30 pm that evening Their Majesties embarked on board the *Empress of Britain* and soon afterwards the liner put to sea, escorted by HMC Ships *Skeena* and *Saguenay*, with *Southampton* and *Glasgow* astern. Shortly before dark the Canadian warships were detached.

On the advice of Canadian Pacific *Berwick* preceded the *Empress of Britain* to patrol the proposed route to be taken between Halifax and

Conception Bay and report on ice conditions. The passage was uneventful and the ships arrived safely at Conception Bay where they anchored overnight.

At dawn on Saturday, 17th June the liner, with the royal party aboard, and the escorting cruisers weighed anchor and proceeded to Newfoundland, where they anchored four miles off Holyrood Pier. Just before 10.00 am His Majesty left the liner, aboard the Admiral's Barge, to go ashore and The *Empress of Britain* weighed anchor to return to her previous anchorage off Bell Island. As the liner was anchoring a seaman working on one of her boats fell overboard and, although a life buoy was dropped close to him, he slipped under the water. In spite of the fact that one of the liner's lifeboats arrived at the spot where the seaman disappeared within two minutes, and boats from the two British cruisers were launched to assist in the search, no trace of the man could be found and the attempted rescue was in vain. After a period of three-quarters of an hour the search was called off.

Their Majesties gave notice that they intended to visit *Glasgow, Southampton* and *Berwick.* Shortly after making their intentions known a moderate westerly wind sprung up, making Portugal Cove a dead lee shore and *Glasgow* was ordered to proceed to embark them. Some difficulty was encountered when the Royal Barge, as it conveyed Their Majesties the King and Queen from the shore, became entangled in some fishing nets. This caused a minor hiccup, forcing the young royal couple to transfer to another barge in the middle of the Bay before they finally arrived alongside *Glasgow* at 5.45 pm to the cheers of the assembled Divisions. The King and Queen were welcomed aboard by Captain Coltart and invited to tour the ship. On completion of the tour *Glasgow's* captain was conferred with the CVO by His Majesty before the Royal couple departed for the visit to HMS *Southampton,* in the *Berwick's* barge.

At 10.30 pm the *Empress of Britain,* with *Southampton* and *Glasgow* as escort, set sail for the return journey to England. Speeds of up to 24 knots were maintained during the daylight hours to enable them to pass quickly through the iceberg region in which ten isolated icebergs were sighted. As the ships approached the English Channel on Tuesday 22nd June the strong north-easterly wind increased to gale force strength, causing the cancellation of the planned RAF fly-past and reception by the Home Fleet. As the Royal Squadron proceeded up the Solent visibility increased, and on reaching a position off Yarmouth on the Isle of Wight, the *Empress of Britain* stopped to enable Their Royal Highnesses the Princesses Elizabeth and Margaret Rose to transfer from the destroyer HMS *Kempenfelt* to the liner by Royal Barge.

Southampton and *Glasgow* passed ahead of the *Empress of Britain* before heaving to with engines stopped and their ship's companies assembled on their foc'sles. The liner then passed the stationary cruisers to the sound of cheers for the Royal Family. Having completed the required protocol the Squadron reformed with the cruisers taking up station astern of the liner. With the ships safely back in home waters the escorting vessels *Southampton*, *Glasgow* and *Kempenfelt* were detached, and as they parted company the following messages were exchanged as Royal Salutes were fired.

From HM the King

To CS2 Southampton and Glasgow

On parting company with my cruiser escort I wish to thank officers and men for the efficient way in which they carried out this duty, at times under most difficult and trying circumstances. I have been much impressed with the smart appearance and good station keeping of Southampton and Glasgow. The Queen and I wish you all the best.

From CS2

To VAC HMY ® S and G

Will you please convey the following message to HM the King.

Your Majesties' most gracious message is deeply appreciated by all. It has been a great privilege to have the honour of acting as your escort on such an historic occasion. With humble duty all officers and men in Southampton and Glasgow wish Your Majesties a very happy homecoming.

The *Glasgow* returned to dock in Portsmouth on 1st July where Captain C.G.B.Coltart, handed over command to Captain F.H. Pegram, nine days later.

On 27th August 1939 the ship sailed for Invergordon during which passage the log entry records "Hands preparing for war".

The Storm Clouds Gather as
Hitler Prepares for War

Adolf Hitler consulted with his Naval Chief of Staff Admiral Raeder as he prepared to wage war in Europe. Both had learned lessons from the battles of Jutland and the Falklands, during the First World War, and abandoned any thoughts of taking on the might of the British navy. Instead they formulated a plan to use the German battle-cruisers and pocket battleships, which had been built as powerful, sophisticated commerce raiders, to roam the seas independently to strike at merchant shipping wherever, and whenever, it presented itself.

On the 21st and 24th August 1939 respectively the German battle-cruisers *Admiral Graf Spee* and the *Deutschland* departed from the German port of Willemshaven, each accompanied by a supply ship.

Under the cover of fog both ships were able to escape detection as they made passage north of Scotland, before making their separate ways. The *Admiral Graf Spee* headed towards the East Coast of South America, while the *Deutschland* steamed towards the mid Atlantic. Each ship was to await further orders.

By the end of August 1939 all ships of the Home Fleet were at or on the way to their pre-designated war stations, and aircraft from Coastal Command were flying reconnaissance missions over the North Sea. That same month a detachment consisting of two six inch cruisers and the 7th Destroyer Flotilla from the Home Fleet combined to form the Humber Force which, under normal conditions, was to be under the control of the Admiralty. However, for the purposes of planned operations and emergency situations it would come under the orders of the Commander in Chief, Home Fleet, who was authorised to act without previous reference back.

Immingham was the main base of the Humber Force, although occasionally the anchorage was changed, within the area defined by the Thames to the south and the Firth of Forth to the north, to prevent the enemy from knowing its whereabouts.

The tasks to be fulfilled by the Force were to:
1) protect shipping on the East Coast of England;
2) intercept enemy light forces in the act of invading the East Coast;
3) undertake offensive operations in the Heligoland Bight as required by the C-in-C, Home Fleet;
4) afford cover for convoys of merchant shipping moving through the designated areas.

For the Royal Navy, in the autumn of 1939, there was an air of déjà vu, with conditions very much resembling those which existed at the outbreak of the First World War. A number of the senior Admirals in service had served as captains in the Grand Fleet of the "Great War." When the signal, advising the Fleets that Britain was at war with Germany, was transmitted on 3rd September 1939 what followed bore more than a resemblance to that which had gone before. Battleships again assembled at Scapa Flow and cruiser squadrons throughout the world ensured that enemy merchant shipping vanished from the seas. Although Germany did possess heavy cruisers, which had been specifically designed for commerce raiding, (in fact the *Graf Spee* had already been dubbed a pocket battleship), the Royal Navy dwarfed Hitler's Kriegsmarine in numbers of available ships.

Aware that a war with Germany was imminent, measures were put in hand to ensure that merchant shipping sailed in convoys. Furthermore, the Admiralty warned British Ships, on 1st September 1939, that German warships might move into Icelandic waters to await the outbreak of hostilities. To counter this perceived threat, Admiral Sir Charles Morton Forbes, KCB, DSO, Commander-in-Chief, dispatched a considerable force out from Scapa Flow to patrol the seaways between the Shetland Isles and Norway. The search was in vain because the intelligence reports issued by the Admiralty proved to be incorrect. However, two German pocket battleships, one of which was the *Deutschland*, were in fact in the Atlantic awaiting orders.

While the force from Scapa Flow was searching northern waters for the enemy the Humber Force patrolled the north-east coast of Britain.

28

Declaration of War

HMS Glasgow at sea 1939   (NMM)

On 2nd September 1939 HMS *Glasgow*, under the command of Captain F. H. Pegram, (Later to become Vice-Admiral F.H. Pegram, CB, DSO, Fourth Sea Lord) set sail from Grimsby on passage to Rosyth. While off the Norwegian coast, at 11.00 am on Sunday 3rd September her captain received a signal that war with Germany was declared. The entry in the ship's log records quite simply "Great Britain at war with Germany." At 1.13 pm that day the ship went to "Action Stations" when those aboard the cruiser were convinced that gunfire had been heard, to the southeast. This proved to be a thunderstorm and at 1.53 pm the order to assume "Defence Stations" was given.

Following the declaration of war, measures were introduced to prevent the movement of war materials by the interception of enemy merchant ships. While the main body of the Home Fleet patrolled the waters some four hundred miles west of the Hebrides in search of the German liner S.S. *Bremen,* known to be on passage home from New York, the British cruisers *Glasgow* and *Southampton,* with eight destroyers in support, were instructed to cruise off the coast of Norway. In response to information that the German fleet was leaving Schillig Roads, Admiral Forbes turned his force eastwards to the Fair Isle Channel, where he intended to lay in wait for the enemy. Here the weather closed in dramatically and a thick fog descended to enshroud the searching ships, thereby thwarting them in their task. It was alleged at the time that two torpedoes had been fired at the ship only to pass harmlessly forty yards astern of her. The ships returned, unsuccessful, to Scapa Flow on 6th September 1939 where, towards the end of the month, the Second Cruiser Squadron was reinforced by the inclusion of the cruisers *Sheffield* and *Aurora.*

On 22nd September the Cruiser Squadron, under the command of Vice-Admiral Sir G. Frederick. B. Edward-Collins, KCVO, CB, sailed from Scapa Flow intent on carrying out a raid in the Skagerrak. However, as the result of a collision, which occurred between two of the accompanying Humber force destroyers, as they carried out manoeuvres, the plan was aborted. The ships returned to base next day. Three days later news reached Admiral Forbes that the British submarine HMS *Spearfish* had been badly damaged off Horn Reef and was unable to dive. This required immediate action to be taken and *Glasgow* sailed in company with the cruisers *Sheffield, Aurora* and *Southampton,* with six destroyers acting as screens, to extricate the stricken vessel. This was successfully concluded and, supported by the Eighteenth Cruiser Squadron, the rescue force and submarine safely reached Rosyth on 26th September 1939.

The next month, on 6th October, Poland fell to the German assault and on land the rest of Europe was at war with Germany, albeit stopping short of active aggression, with the RAF bombarding the enemy with threatening leaflets. This gave rise to the expression the phoney war, which was aptly named. However, at sea, in the wilderness of the North Atlantic, the war was real enough with no long drawn-out prelude to the hostilities. In fact, the killing began barely nine hours after war had been declared when the *U-boat U30* sank the British passenger liner *Athenia,* with the loss of 112 lives.

This action triggered off a series of attacks, carried out by other U-boats, with the result that over 300,000 tons of Allied and neutral merchant shipping was sunk during the first two months of the war.

Adding to the enormous threat to commercial shipping posed by the U-boats it was also known that a powerful enemy raider was at large somewhere in northern waters preying on unescorted merchantmen.

Air Attack

It was while serving with the Humber Force that *Glasgow*, in company with the cruisers *Southampton* and *Edinburgh*, was subjected to an air attack on 9th October 1939. At eight o'clock that morning a strong sun shone in a blue sky partially covered with cumulus clouds, at six thousand feet. The sea was roughened by a fresh south-easterly wind. Two unknown aircraft were sighted and, as they approached the ships from the east, one fired two Very's lights. Initially the planes were thought to be friendly but they soon proved to be enemy reconnaissance aircraft. During the next hour two of these aircraft were engaged by the *Glasgow's* gunners, one at maximum gun range and the other at a range of 10,000 yards, without success. Just before 11.30 am a Junkers 87 dive-bombed the *Southampton* before being engaged by *Glasgow's* close range weapons as it approached and by the four-inch armament as it flew away. An hour later, at 12.30 pm, three more enemy planes, thought to be either Junkers 88's and/or Heinkel 111's flying at an estimated 230 knots were sighted, this time from the south, out of gun range. Although they could be observed as they worked their way towards the sun they were lost to sight when they broke formation near it and, being virtually totally obscured by the brilliant sun, they were not sighted again until a few seconds before the bombs were released. Almost over-head they dropped bombs on *Edinburgh's* port bow while being engaged by guns at maximum elevation. For the next forty-five minutes half a dozen aircraft in succession, making use of the sun to confuse the gunners below, attacked the ships. All were engaged by retaliatory fire after they had dropped their bomb loads!

Five minutes later, at 1.15 pm, seven or eight aircraft were seen heading south-west, out of gun range, making towards the sun. At 2.00 pm five aircraft were seen approaching the ships, compass bearing 240°, at a height of 10,000 feet. The ship's guns engaged them at a range of between 11,000 to 6,000 yards and the formation broke up to take refuge in the clouds. The enemy aircraft were re-sighted five minutes later as they made their way back towards the sun, again out of range of the guns. Twenty minutes elapsed before two enemy planes passed overhead in formation at a height of 15,000 feet. These were immediately engaged by *Glasgow's* four-inch H.A. guns' crews. A minute later, at 2.24 pm, bombs fell on the cruiser's port side, closely followed by others falling on her starboard quarter.

During a prolonged bombing attack engine and boiler rooms resemble the inside of a giant kettle against which a sledge-hammer is being beaten with uncertain aim. Sometimes there is a clang, as more speed is called for when bridge telegraphs call for "emergency full speed ahead" and the rudder indicator would go to port or starboard at the moment of the bombs release.

The enemy aircraft continued to launch attacks on the ships below, during which bombs fell; first off *Glasgow's* port bow, then off her starboard one, followed by one ahead and two more astern of her. The pattern of attacks remained the same, with more bombs dropping ahead off the cruiser's port and starboard bows, before they ceased at four o'clock in the afternoon. At 4.15 pm a shadowing Dornier flying boat approached the ships from the north. This would have presented the gunners on board *Glasgow* with a relative easy target had *Edinburgh* not fouled the range. The German plane continued to shadow the Humber Force cruisers, flying outside gun range until well into the Dog watches.

It was estimated that during the attacks 120 bombs, of between 100-300lbs, were dropped in salvoes of 3, 4 or 5 at a time. Each salvo had a spread of 30-150 yards, with the majority falling within 50 yards of each other. During that day-long attack HMS *Glasgow* engaged 31 aircraft with her four-inch H.A. armament, as these made direct approaches, passing runs or retired from the scene, expending 668 rounds of ammunition in the process.

Valuable lessons were learned that day. It was later suggested by *Glasgow's* captain that a squadron of ships subjected, as they made passage, to heavy high level bombing attacks should maintain a one mile gap between them to:
a) prevent bombs that missed other ships resulting in hits being made on those close by;
b) ensure that only the ship under attack by planes approaching from the direction of the sun would be "blinded" ;
c) enable warships to manoeuvre freely to bring their armament to bear.(This was particularly important to *Glasgow* because her H.A. Director would not bear forward of Red/Green 30°)

Furthermore, Captain Pegram recommended that ships should not proceed in single line ahead, thereby denying attacking enemy aircraft a target line. He also advocated that the steaming speed be maintained as high as possible to afford more rapidity of manoeuvre to avoid falling bombs.

32

Convoy Protection and the Search for Commerce Raiders

Following attacks carried out by commerce raiders orders were issued for British shipping to be suitably protected from this threat. On 12th October 1939 HMS *Glasgow* sailed from Rosyth to exercise with her sister ship, HMS *Newcastle,* at Scapa Flow. Here, the cruisers' captains received orders to provide protection for unescorted convoys passing through the area, extending from 45° N 30° W to 53° N and 20° W, while maintaining mutual support for each other. Each ship was to patrol independently in specified areas, and rendezvous daily at noon, while maintaining wireless silence except in the case of an emergency or when the enemy had been sighted. The ships duly sailed from Scapa Flow and on 13th October 1939, the same day that news was received that the *Royal Oak* had been sunk, *Newcastle* reported that a submarine periscope had been spotted. Both ships immediately took evasive action although there was no confirmation of the report.

Next day on 14th October the French cruiser submarine the *Surcouf* was met on the surface in company with convoy KJ2. The submarine identified her but neglected to reply to any of *Glasgow's* other signals! That same day the commerce raider *Deutschland,* marauding in the North Atlantic, had sunk the Norwegian S.S. *Lorentz W. Hansen* and another merchantman. It had also, rather embarrassingly, captured an American ship, the freighter *City of Flint.* This information only came out when the rescued Norwegian crew identified the enemy ship as the *Deutschland* on being landed at Kirkwall on 21st October. The following day news was received that the *City of Flint* with a prize crew aboard had reached Murmansk. After leaving the North Russian port the *City of Flint* endeavoured to make its way back to Germany by choosing to take the inshore route, hugging the coastline inside neutral Norwegian territorial waters. HMS *Glasgow,* with accompanying destroyers, was sent to intercept it but the mission was unsuccessful.

It was at this juncture that the Admiralty decided that the activities of this heavily armoured commerce raider should be curtailed and drew up plans to bring this about. Aware that the *Deutschland* had been at sea for almost three months, and believing that she might make a dash for home by the northern route, a substantial

33

British force was positioned across her likely path to prevent the ship's successful return to the safety of a German port.

The cruisers *Norfolk* and *Suffolk,* supported by three armed merchant cruisers patrolled the Denmark Straits. Four smaller cruisers and another armed merchant cruiser covered the area between Iceland and the Faeroes. A further three "C" class cruisers were positioned to the south of these islands, while *Glasgow*, in company with two destroyers was to the northeast of the Shetlands. HMS *Sheffield* accompanied by three more "C" class cruisers and five submarines provided further support to the force. Standing by in the Clyde, on the West Coast of Scotland, at an advanced state of readiness, were the battleships *Nelson, Rodney,* the cruiser *Devonshire,* and seven destroyers. At the same time in Rosyth, on the East Coast of Scotland, the cruisers *Southampton, Edinburgh* and *Aurora* with two destroyers in support were also ready to put to sea. All this frenetic activity was in vain because the *Deutschland* had returned to Germany a week earlier and was safely tied up in Kiel.

On the same day that the Norwegian crew from the S.S. *Lorentz W. Hansen* were landed at Kirkwall, the Admiralty received intelligence reports which indicated that two enemy pocket battleships were at large marauding along the trade routes serving Britain. In response to this information Admiral Forbes ordered *Glasgow* and *Newcastle*, still operating in their patrol zone, to search for and escort into port a high value convoy KJ3, which included nineteen oil tankers, in-bound from the West Indies. Some difficulty in finding the convoy was experienced and the *Glasgow* flew off her "Walrus" in an attempt to locate it. Early in the afternoon of the 22nd October 1939 the cruisers received a signal giving the convoy's amended position and the search continued to the north and west of the patrol area.

At 4.05 pm the convoy, escorted by HMS *Effingham,* was sighted to the west, approximately fifty miles ahead of *Glasgow's* original estimate. Both cruisers remained in the company of KJ3, acting under the orders of the Rear Admiral commanding 12th Cruiser Squadron, in *Effingham,* until Longitude 20° W was reached. At this point the French Squadron of *Dunkerque* class the destroyers *Georges Leygues* and *Montcalm,* accompanied by three others, met the convoy. HM Ships *Glasgow* and *Newcastle* were detached and they continued their patrol until, low in fuel, *Newcastle* was ordered to return to Plymouth and *Glasgow* to Portsmouth.

After re-fuelling and taking on provisions *Glasgow* left the Hampshire port and made passage up the east coast of England towards Rosyth, where she arrived on 7th November. Four days later the cruiser returned to the Home Fleet base at Immingham where she spent four days before steaming north to Scapa Flow. Here the crew was put through its paces, exercising with other British warships in the Home Fleet, as the *Glasgow* prepared for the rigours of war before being ordered to sail to try to intercept a German liner as she attempted to make her way back to Germany from northern Russia.

Surcouf : was a cruiser submarine armed with twin eight-inch guns, housed in a watertight turret forward of the bridge, and anti aircraft guns on top of an aircraft hanger abaft the conning tower. The submarine also carried a sixteen foot motor cruiser, which was used by boarding parties to seize surrendered enemy vessels as prizes, and had a compartment capable of holding up to forty prisoners of war. She had a complement of 118.

The following year, on June 18th 1940, in order to avoid capture *Surcouf* left Brest for Plymouth where the Royal Navy seized her on 3rd July. Three Britons and one Frenchman were killed and two injured in the action. After this the submarine sailed with a French crew under British operational control.

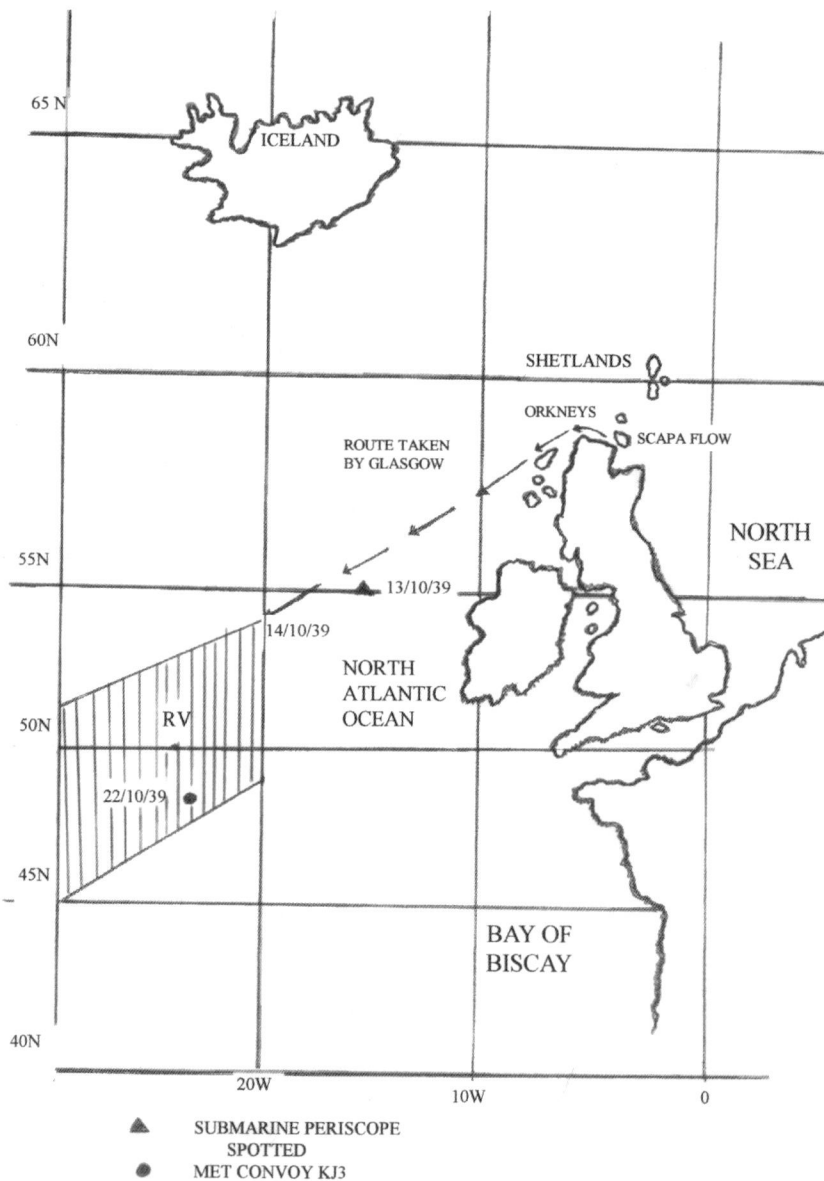

65 N
ICELAND
60N
SHETLANDS
ORKNEYS
ROUTE TAKEN
BY GLASGOW
SCAPA FLOW
NORTH
SEA
55N
13/10/39
14/10/39
NORTH
ATLANTIC
OCEAN
50N
RV
22/10/39
45N
BAY OF
BISCAY
40N
20W
10W
0

▲   SUBMARINE PERISCOPE
        SPOTTED
●   MET CONVOY KJ3

36

The Search for the S.S. "Bremen"

In mid-November 1939 HMS *Glasgow* in company with HM Ships *Maori* and *Zulu* tried to intercept the German liner, S.S. *Bremen* as she attempted to make her way back to Germany from Murmansk.

The designated search area was off the Norwegian coast to the northeast of the Shetland Islands. Although the information on the *Bremen* was scarce she was known to have refuelled at the North Russian port and had drastically altered her appearance by the removal of a funnel. Furthermore the liner was thought to be under a Soviet flag. HMS *Glasgow's* captain, Captain Pegram, had little information on the possible route the German ship might take and decided to patrol, during the hours of darkness, in the area around Stadtlandet. Experience gained in searching for the *City of Flint* suggested that few ships would have been found outside territorial waters south of here. The sweep was therefore extended to seaward, and northward, in anticipation that the cruiser would be in a good position to take advantage of available air reconnaissance relating to the enemy ship.

At the start of the patrol the weather was kind but during the night of 21st/22nd November the barometric pressure plummeted, the wind strength increased to strong gale force raising a steep sea, and visibility rapidly deteriorated to one mile. Conditions on board *Glasgow* were uncomfortable as she reared up like a wild horse and rolled from port to starboard, the slate grey waves racing along her sides. Spray broke from the bows as the ship bucked and tossed and, driven on the wind, sped like lances towards the bridge, into the eyes of the lookouts and onto the lenses of their binoculars, reducing their efficiency. *Glasgow* was now ploughing steadily through heavy seas at twenty knots. Mountainous seas were breaking over her deck and sweeping away to stern. Below in the heads water was washing backwards and forwards with the irregular motion of the ship. One or two of the men were feeling so sick that they clung onto anything they could find but hardly cared whether they lived or died. The seasick sailors didn't care; they were past it; they just clung on hopelessly waiting for their fate to fulfill itself. Aboard the destroyers the conditions were worse as they rose on the cresting waves to crash down again with a sickening jolt. Imperfectly fitted plates on the ships' sides moved almost imperceptibly to allow water to creep in, to further dampen the clothes and bedding of the crew. In consequence, the Allied ships were forced to reduce speed to 16 knots to prevent the bumping experienced by the destroyers.

Although the patrol was maintained for a time and a reported sighting of the enemy from *Rawalpindi* was picked up, *Glasgow* and the other searching ships failed in their quest.

Having been unsuccessful in the search for the *Bremen*, *Glasgow* returned to Rosyth where she took on fuel and supplies before heading back, on 6th December, to Scapa Flow from whence she patrolled off the Norwegian coastline. It was whilst on patrol that P.O A. E. Davey died, on 14th December, as the result of an accident and was buried at sea the following day. *Glasgow* continued to patrol the northern waters until 23rd when she returned to berth in Rosyth where the crew was able to celebrate Christmas and the New Year, before resuming her offensive duties.

Glasgow Tackles the U-boats

The beginning of 1940 saw HMS *Glasgow* involved in activities against enemy U-boats and on January 9th the cruiser picked up an Asdic contact, thought to have been an enemy submarine, in position 60° 45' N, 04° 25' E at a range of 1,400 yards. Through the Tannoy came the sound of a bugle call followed by "All hands to action stations" and throughout the ship men ran to their allotted positions.

On the stern of the cruiser where the depth charge trap was fixed there was great activity as men struggled to manoeuvre the heavy barrel shaped charges from their storage places to the trap. Orders came from the bridge "Set three charges at 250, 300 and 350." These instructions were relayed to the action team who inserted keys into the explosive canisters and turned them to set fuses which would detonate the weapons when they reached the prescribed depths. The ship closed on the target and the TI standing by the telephone, which connected with the bridge, shouted to the men by the rack "Stand by." He then heard the order "Fire one, two and three." and repeated it to the team who had awaited his instructions. At the touch of a lever a pattern of three depth charges filled with high explosive rolled off the rack into the water and sink in the depths below. Seconds later the ship shook violently and the sea threw up a black mushroom of water and smoke, which hung in the air before showering back down onto the surface. The contact was not confirmed by HMS *Edinburgh,* five cables away on the port beam, and thought to be non-submarine. As *Glasgow* turned away from the search the next order that came through the loudspeakers was "Starboard Watch to Defence Stations." The tension drained out of the men and those on the Port watch relaxed.

On 16th January *Glasgow* sailed from Rosyth for Scapa Flow where, at 10.44 am on 21st, she was in station six cables astern of HMS

Edinburgh when the latter hoisted "Investigating Contact Starboard Side", and both ships turned together onto the same course. Aboard *Glasgow* hands went to "action stations" and the cruiser obtained a firm contact on her starboard beam at 10.48 a.m. and surged forward towards it at 20 knots, keeping the "target" fine on the starboard bow, with the *Edinburgh* bearing away.

Down below the water line, in the engine and boiler rooms stokers and artificers sweated in their deafening, oil stinking ovens while sonar operators sat in their cubby hole, earphones clamped to head, intent on catching the echo rebounding from the hull of the U-boat submerged in ambush. Three highly trained men and an Asdic Control Officer (ACO), responsible for protecting the cruiser against the threat of attack from U-boats lurking below the waves, working in semi-darkness, applied themselves diligently to the task of searching out the underwater threat. One man, the first operator controlling the ACTU (Asdic Control Training Unit), sat hunched over his set as he directed the transmitter, which sent out sound waves underwater, seeking out the enemy below. When the sound waves struck an object a distinctive ping, or echo, was produced and he used his finely honed skills to determine whether the returning echoes were from a submerged U-boat or harmless shoals of fish. Quietly, the ACO monitored the developing search interjecting as necessary "You're losing the target", "Cut left" "Cut right." Suddenly, the echo becomes sharp and distinct. The operator stiffened slightly, he reached forward and pressed the tit in the centre of the control unit in front of him and reported " Classified Submarine." As his finger pressed the button an electric pulse marked the paper on the recorders and returned the stylus to the start position to initiate the next pulse of sound, forming a trace on the paper. To the left of the ACTU operator sat his "oppo" manning the range recorder while, to his right, a "Townie," operated the depth recorder. Each man, aware of the importance of carrying out his duty professionally, focused his eyes on the recorder in front of him. The impregnated paper, drawn downwards on its rollers, turned evenly as signals pulsed horizontally across it. The operator of the depth recorder turned the cursor wheel at the top right hand corner of the apparatus, and methodically tracked the pulses with a line of light. In response the cursor inched its way inexorably across the set and, on reaching the end of the trace on the far left of the screen, made an electrical contact which completed the electronic circuit and initiated the firing of the depth charges located at the stern of the ship.

Three depth charges, set to explode at 200 feet, 250 feet and 350 feet respectively, were dropped 100 yards after the last contact was lost in the ship's bow wave. Drums of explosive rolled off the stern rails. For a few seconds there was no sound, apart from the noise of the ship's engines, until the charges detonated. The surface of the sea shook and shimmered before huge columns of water boiled to the surface and fountained upwards, before settling down to leave large spreading whirlpools marking the position of the attack.

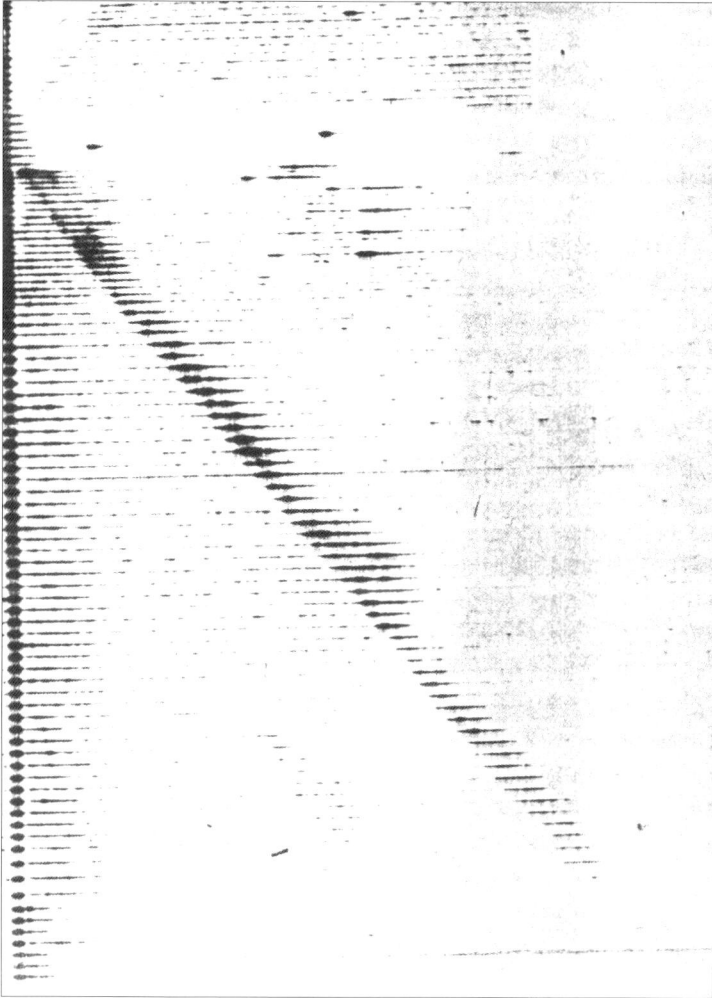

Asdic Trace – Depth

Six minutes later, at 10.52 am, *Glasgow* again made Asdic contact with an "enemy submarine" in position 58° 54.5' N, 01° 23'W at a range of 3,000 yards, and dropped three more depth charges set to detonate at the same depths as those dropped in the first attack. Three violent explosions followed and with them came the disappointment of failing to produce evidence of an enemy lurking below. It was subsequently thought to have been the same target picked up by the *Edinburgh* at 10.44 am. *Glasgow's* Captain expressed his concern as to the efficiency of the Asdic* set fitted to the ship and the number of depth charges carried on board at that time. He believed that the ship's fighting efficiency was compromised by the fact that an inadequate number were available to him, thereby limiting his ability to mount an attack on a target. Three days later the ship returned to Rosyth.

*ASDIC This was a device which enabled surface ships to detect submerged submarines by sending out sound waves underwater, producing a distinctive ping or echo if they struck a metal object. The Asdic dome stuck out from the bottom of the ship's hull, like a small blister, sending out pings, which echoed back when hitting underwater obstacles. It also produced echoes from shoals of fish, wrecks and confused whirlpools of water. Therefore, the operator had to be highly trained to distinguish the difference.

The Capture of the German Trawler "Herrlichkeit"

Sailing on the morning of 9th February 1940 from Rosyth, to relieve HMS *Southampton* off North Cape, *Glasgow* received information that two munitions ships had been sighted two days previously near Bergen. Captain Pegram decided not to attempt an interception of these vessels, preferring instead to establish a patrol out of the sight of shipping off the north coast of Norway. Two days after leaving harbour a Lancastrian registered ore carrier was spotted and challenged. Having confirmed the ship's identity, passage approval was given for it to continue.

The next day, in response to a signal from C-in-C Home Fleet, HMS *Glasgow* set a course for Svensgrunden Bank. Weather conditions deteriorated as the wind strength increased to roughen the sea and bring snow squalls. Because of the time likely to be taken to complete the operation, in the prevailing conditions, a sighted ship would not be boarded unless there was reasonable cause for suspicion as to its identity.

On 12th February just before the Forenoon Watch, a trawler *Ertnan of Harstaad,* was sighted and challenged. Convinced as to her identity she was permitted free passage to her port of registry nearby. Ten seine net vessels were also sighted as the *Glasgow* proceeded Northward. At 10.15 am a trawler was sighted, in position 69° 54' N, 16° 57' E and closed, her skipper making no attempt to disguise her name or port of registry. In fact, as *Glasgow* drew nearer and challenged the fishing vessel she was identified as the *Herrlichkeit.* The trawler surrendered and a prize crew, led by Lieutenant Iles, went aboard, at 10.30 am, taking 14 Germans prisoner. These were taken off and embarked in the cruiser, the operation having taken three hours under the prevailing weather conditions, and the captured "prize" ship was handed over to HMS *Southampton*. It was not possible to transfer the trawler's crew and *Glasgow* then proceeded to Scapa Flow with them on board. During the passage the skipper of the *Herrlichkeit,* who could speak a few words of English, was questioned. He was reticent in his responses and encouraged his crew to act likewise. He admitted leaving Cuxhaven the previous November to work the area around Harstaad and, having just finished filling his fish holds at the time of being apprehended, was about to return to his home port. When asked about the presence of other German trawlers in the area he replied "I must not speak".

Twenty four hours later, on 13th February, at dawn, *Glasgow* was off North Cape where she flew off her reconnaissance aircraft to search the waters to the westward. Nothing was sighted. However, the returning Walrus was able to report that the narrow part of Mageroy Sound was frozen, forcing shipping to round North Cape.

The weather deteriorated to prevent further flights that day. It was even worse on the 14th and the patrol was maintained without aircraft support. For the next two days the *Glasgow* followed the Norwegian coastline sighting nothing in the appalling conditions, until Saturday 17th February. By now the considerable sea state and accompanying swell would have made the boarding of enemy shipping impossible even had the boats, together with their falls and other gear on the upper deck, not been completely frozen and covered with ice.

In the days that followed, four trawlers were sighted fishing in the banks around the Norwegian coast but were verified as being Norwegian and Danish and allowed to proceed.

A course was now shaped for Scapa Flow and at dusk on Sunday 18th February the Norwegian tanker *Eli Knusden* was boarded as a precaution but her papers were found to be in order. HMS *Glasgow* returned to Scapa Flow where the German prisoners were put ashore before being taken into captivity.

During the patrol, Captain Pegram considered flying off his reconnaissance aircraft, whilst keeping the cruiser hidden, to prevent the enemy becoming aware of *Glasgow's* presence. Unfortunately the intensely cold weather conditions, where the wind blew strongly from the north, bringing with it frequent heavy snow showers, had prevented him from doing so. Captain Pegram later expressed some regret at not having made better use of the captured German trawler, to gather intelligence, by patrolling it inshore without arousing suspicion. He went on to recommend that should other such ships become available in future they be used for this valuable purpose.

Patrolling in the rough seas took its toll and on 21st February the ship's rudder developed a problem and a diver was sent down to investigate. Dressed in the clumsy and conventional heavy gear of the day he went over the side. Slowly he clambered down the light metal ladder that had been lowered for him and disappeared below the surface into the ice cold waters. Having completed his inspection the diver surfaced and made his report. On hearing the diver's report Captain Pegram decided that repairs were necessary to rectify the fault, and *Glasgow* sailed for Belfast Lough, where she arrived on 25th.February to undergo a refit. This was successfully completed towards the end of March and she departed for the Clyde on 22nd March 1940, to dock the following day in Greenock. Two days later *Glasgow* departed from the Clyde for Rosyth where, an expeditionary force destined for Stavanger and Bergen embarked on HM Ships *Glasgow, Berwick, York* and *Devonshire* on 7th April 1940. The troops were part of plan "R4" which had been prepared to deal with any German attempt to seize Norwegian ports. However, none of the ships were destined to sail until clear evidence was available that the enemy intended to violate Norwegian territory.

Norwegian Offensive

At 1.25pm on 7th April 1940 British aircraft spotted strong German naval forces crossing the Skagerak, towards the Norwegian coast, and the British Home Fleet sailed from Scapa Flow intent on engaging German battle-cruisers, while at the same time losing sight of the possibility that the enemy had intentions of effecting a landing in Norway. Consequently, an opportunity of intercepting the smaller troop carriers was lost.

On Saturday 6th April the 8th Battalion Sherwood Foresters set off from their camp at Shildon, County Durham, in two trains bound for an unknown destination. The trains stopped at Edinburgh where the Movement Control Officers either could not or would not divulge the intended destination of the troops to their officers. However, a Major went forward and asked the engine driver "where are we going to?" He immediately received the reply he needed "Rosyth!"

After a short stay in Edinburgh where the troops were given cups of tea the trains pulled into the dockyard station. The troops were met by a party of naval officers who quickly took charge and much to their amazement the soldiers were embarked in HMS *Glasgow*, where they were able to relax and enjoy some excellent naval rations.

A buzz went round the ship that she was due to sail, with the troops, at 8.00 am on 8th April but this was "scotched" when the orders were changed in the light of intelligence received. The Admiralty, on becoming aware that the German battle cruisers had been sighted, ordered the Cruiser Squadron at Rosyth to disembark those troops, which were to form the expeditionary force due to sail for Narvik, and join the Fleet at sea. The bemused troops were given a hot meal before being rapidly disembarked, along with their stores and equipment. They formed up on the jetty where they awaited further instructions.

At 12.45 pm the hawsers were slackened and *Glasgow* slipped from the quay. As the cruiser made her way out of Rosyth harbour bound for Norway the assembled troops cheered the ship's company. *Glasgow's* crew responded in the traditional manner. Similar orders had also been issued to other troop-laden ships in the Clyde, which were waiting to make passage.

On Tuesday 9th April the Germans landed 1,700 men in the town of Trondheim, the ancient capital of Norway, and the British Chiefs of Staff made hurried plans for landings to take place in the general area around it. That same day *Glasgow* and her sister ships *Manchester, Southampton* and *Sheffield* formed part of the battle fleet, as the Eighteenth Cruiser Squadron. British naval forces converged on Norway from a wide area and a number of units were detached, under the command of Vice-Admiral Layton, and ordered an attack on the Norwegian town of Bergen.

Whilst engaged in the offensive with the main force of the Home Fleet, on 9th April, *Glasgow* went into action against the *Scharnhorst* and *Gneisenau*. The enemy ships, however, were able to make good their escape in the mist and snow storms present at the time. Between 2.30 pm and 3.00 pm that day the Cruiser Squadron was subjected to dive bombing attacks and forced to turn away. At 2.45 pm an attack was launched against *Glasgow* from the starboard quarter. Two bombs of between 200lb–500 lb were released from a height of approximately 1,500 feet, while the aircraft was still diving, resulting in very near misses on the port side. One bomb burst on impact about fifteen feet from the ship's side and the other, under water, further forward. Although defensive gunfire was impeded, because of the fine angle of approach by the aircraft, close range weapons engaged it. Hands were at "Action Stations", manning the upper deck anti-aircraft armament while others, not required for this duty, were distributed throughout the ship as far as possible to reduce the possibility of casualties from shrapnel splinters. As the gunners engaged the enemy, shells slid into the chamber, the breech was closed, the gun fired and recoiled. Out came a shell case, in went the next shell and so it went on relentlessly. The movement of the men was rapid, accurate and automatic. The men had trained a long time for this. Between decks fire and damage control parties waited to go into action as required and in the sickbay the ship's surgeon and his SBAs waited.

A large proportion of the bomb, which burst on impact, entered the ship three feet above the lower deck level. This holed an area approximately six feet by three feet and the blast blew in four dead lights, one of which came inboard, to kill a rating. Further penetration of the ship's side occurred in about sixty places, caused by scattered splinters. Several mess decks were flooded to a depth of about a foot with water, which entered with the movement of the ship. Subsidiary flooding occurred and minor underwater damage resulted from the explosion of the second bomb. "A" turret was also temporarily put out of action as the result of power loss. Shoring of the damaged plating and frames commenced and was well on the way to being completed by 5.00 pm Coffer dams of wood and cement were built around the important lower deck hatches, including the lower steering position, to preserve access. While this repair work was being undertaken *Glasgow* received a signal from HMS *Aurora*, an Arethusa class cruiser, requesting assistance in picking up survivors from HMS *Gurkha*, which was sunk as a direct result of the air attacks. The cruiser responded and stopped to pick up men from the stricken vessel.

The work needed to effect emergency repairs, following the bomb attack, was completed by 11.00 pm and the ship was able to maintain a steaming speed at 26 knots.

Unfortunately two ratings, Acting Leading Signalman Eric William Sizer and Stoker Second Class Arthur Gudger, were killed in the attack. Five other ratings were wounded and transferred to HM Hospital Ship "*Amarapoora*" on arrival in harbour. These were Ordinary Seaman Robert Walter Burrows, Acting Leading Seaman Robert Nisbet Milligan P/JX 132376, Able Seaman Robert George Edwards P/JX 144393, Signalman Ivor Stuart Lockier P/JX 145592 and Ordinary Signalman David Cowper Pattie P/SSX 25072. Ordinary Seaman Burrows later died from his injuries.

Special mention was made relating to the exemplary behaviour of Chief ERA Second Class John Edward Milne P/M 24939, Chief Stoker Percy John Bower P/K 66148, Chief Shipwright Second Class Gilbert Henry Robinson P/M 15163 and Stoker first class Leslie Price P/KX 95358. Commander John Wilson Cuthbert RN was also credited with showing cool leadership and personality, putting into place the skilled organisation needed to deal with the required repairs, thus keeping the ship seaworthy and ready for action.

Glasgow was ordered to proceed with HMS *Sheffield* to patrol off Bergen in Norway, after re-fuelling in Scapa Flow, and left harbour late at night, on 11th April, under the command of Captain F. H. Pegram, RN, Senior Captain, bound for Standlandet. Captain Pegram ordered Captains (D) {Destroyers} D4 and D6 to sweep the coastline in the area of Aalensund and Kristiansund respectively, and rejoin him at dusk. Soon after the destroyers had proceeded to undertake their duties an aircraft report relating to the presence in the area of a battleship, cruiser and a destroyer was received. The destroyers were recalled in order to mount an attack on the enemy ships, but both Captains (D) considered that a torpedo attack would be impracticable, with which Captain Pegram concurred. Further information was received indicating that the large vessel was in fact a pocket battleship. The force closed to mount an attack after flying off *Glasgow's* "Shagbag" to determine the enemy's position before the ships entered the fjords. The Walrus returned unable to find the enemy, but it could not be recovered because of the lateness of the hour and the weather conditions prevailing at the time. It consequently flew off to fly in collaboration with the Norwegians in the vicinity of Molde, where it remained until 17th April. *Glasgow* retired from the coast, returning the following day when her captain sent the destroyers to enter and reconnoitre the Aalesund and Stor Fjords.

The destroyers searched their designated areas for the presence of enemy shipping without success, while German aircraft shadowed the cruisers. The aircraft found the destroyers and chose to engage them, rather than the cruisers, suffering badly in the conflict.

At 6.45 am on 13th April Captain Pegram received orders to make preparations for a troop landing to be effected at Namsos, a small port with wooden jetties and houses approximately 150 miles south of Trondheim, rather than the principal town itself.

Namsos in Norway

The operation was code-named "Henry" and its objectives were:

a) to secure Namson Fjord so that a force of two battalions could be landed on 17th April;

b) to disembark landing parties to secure:
   (1) the quay at Namsos
   (2) the quay at Bangsund
   (3) the road bridge over the river Nagsen south of Bangsund.

Having considered the information available, in conference with a Staff Officer, *Glasgow's* captain arranged for half the troops to be landed at Namsos with the remainder being sent to Bungsund. Captain (D) 6 (Captain R.S.G. Nicholson RN) aboard HMS *Somali* was ordered to conduct the landing, with Captain Pegram remaining with the cruisers off Kroken. The date of the proposed landing was to be Sunday 14th April at daybreak. However, for a number of reasons this could not be implemented and the operation was delayed until an hour after dusk. That same day *Glasgow's* Asdic equipment was causing a problem and the cruiser fell astern of *Sheffield*, with air-craft shadowing them.

The following day HM Ships *Manchester* and *Birmingham*, together with the *Empress of Australia* and a Polish liner were sighted in the area of Namsen fjord . *Glasgow* set off in company with *Sheffield* and the Fourth Destroyer Flotilla to patrol off Kya. Captain (D) 6 was ordered to remain on station because the Admiralty wished to main-tain radio contact with Major-General Carton de Wiart, VC, in charge of 146 brigade.

The Norwegian campaign had ebbed and flowed during the occupa-tion of Iceland and the Faroes giving the Royal Marines opportunities to fulfil many of their functions. The first marines to land in Norway following the country's invasion by the Germans were detachments from HM Ships Glasgow and *Sheffield* led by Captain W.F. Edds, RM, Senior Royal Marine Officer of 18th Cruiser Squadron.

On 14th April, seven days after German soldiers had entered Norway, the detachments landed at Namsos. The Allied invasion force of approximately 300 men, involving Royal Marines and seamen from the cruisers *Glasgow* and *Sheffield*, was transferred from the British cruisers to *Tribal* class destroyers, which came alongside 12 miles offshore and completed a landing at Namsos as dusk approached. The landing was unopposed but Captain Pegram was certain their presence had been spotted from the air: in point of fact the enemy had intercepted a naval signal on 12th April which men-tioned Namsos as suitable for a landing. A small advance party

51

reported the concealment of a considerable force either at Namsos or Bangsund ; that movement of a force larger than battalion strength southwards would be slow and conspicuous from the air. A total of eighteen officers and 541 men were landed, including boarding parties from the Sixth Destroyer Flotilla. Among the landing group were demolition parties, supplied with large quantities of explosives, who would blow up bridges and roads as and when it became necessary.

Soon after they had landed at Namsos a perimeter defence of the port was established. From this position "A" Company (Royal Marines) and a demolition party from *Sheffield* were tasked with reconnoitring the road and bridge 3 fi miles east of Namsos in preparation to demolish it, while "B" Company (Stokers and Seamen) from the same ship were tasked with providing support for "A" Company. "C" Company commanded by Lieutenant Commander Por, RN and "D" Company commanded by Captain D. G. Cornelius, RM from *Glasgow* were dispatched by lighter to take up a position about seven miles further south of the town of Bangsund. Here they were to establish a roadblock at the bridge of the road leading to Trondheim. Little was known about the local conditions and the marines, on arrival, finding the residents evacuating the town took up positions to cover the bridge and the road tunnel beyond it. Meanwhile the seamen set charges to enable the bridge to be blown should the need arise, with others given responsibility for providing covering fire-power over the quayside at Bangsund. The landing parties from both cruisers had to operate under difficult conditions to avoid detection from the air. The ground was covered by a depth of snow several feet deep and with no fresh snow falling it was virtually impossible to hide tracks and footprints made. All preparatory work had to be completed before daybreak and everyone had to remain hidden during the hours of daylight. Further instructions were given to the force that enemy aircraft were not to be engaged unless the position was under attack. No cooking facilities were available to the men, although eventually three electric cookers were installed at Battalion HQ and the officers and men received at least one hot meal a day and tea or coffee twice daily.

While the landings were being effected *Glasgow* and *Sheffield* "oiled" two destroyers from the Fourth Destroyer Flotilla. Soon after these had been completed a report was received from ashore that two enemy destroyers were on passage north off Trondheim. That same day Skuas from Naval Air Squadron 800 and 803 attacked and sank the German cruiser *Konigsberg* in Bergen harbour. HMS *Taku* was sighted during the night near the Kya light and her captain was advised as to the forthcoming landings and requested to maintain a watch south of Kya.

On his return Captain Edds commented "I consider that the officers and men of the Royal Naval and Royal Marine Battalion behaved splendidly under conditions which were difficult and trying in the extreme. Most of the personnel had been cooped up in ships for several months and as a result were "soft" and unfit. In spite of this they marched long distances along snow covered roads and then worked cheerfully through the night preparing their positions. To add to the difficulties Platoon Commanders in several cases had not seen their platoons as units until actually falling in on land. In the case of "A" and "B" companies the only shelters available were log huts which proved ineffective against the penetrating wind. By day they were forced to remain cramped under these same shelters to avoid observation from the air. Enemy aircraft were constantly active over the area, making strict concealment discipline essential. Those from "C" and "D" companies at Bangsund were more fortunate in that they had but a short distance to move from their landing position and warm comfortable accommodation was available. Furthermore, the closely-wooded country gave cover from air observation enabling men to move about more freely by day."

Two Petty Officers were singled out for particular mention in Captain Edds's report for their enthusiasm initiative and hard work:
1) Richard Fitzgerald, Battalion Chief Cook from HMS *Sheffield;*
2) John V. Lovell, Gunner's Mate HMS *Glasgow* — this was to be the first of a number of tributes to PO Lovell.

The element of surprise had been maintained and the troops were safely re-embarked without being attacked from the air. The harbour and two road bridges were secured to ensure an unopposed landing for a larger force which was to follow two days later. This landing, by "Mauriceforce," was to involve two battalions of the 148th brigade, two battalions of French Chasseur Alpins and other British units commanded by General de Wiart. The General flew across the North Sea by Sunderland flying boat on 15th April but was delayed by an air raid in the Namon Fjord, in which the only staff officer accompanying him was injured. Shortly after landing, General de Wiart and Captain Pegram held a short conference aboard *Glasgow* during which the General informed Captain Pegram that he would land with two battalions of troops on the night of 16th/17th April. After the conference had concluded Captain Nicholson, in *Somali*, was ordered to conduct the landing while the cruisers maintained a position off Kroken.

By this time the first flight of "Mauriceforce" was on its way, and Captain Pegram ordered all warships to keep clear of the coastal area to avoid being spotted by the enemy and have the landings compromised. According to the original plan, the Allied landing should have been undertaken by two battalions of 148th Brigade, which were already embarked in two British cruisers and a large transport ready to sail on the evening of 14th April. However, a Government decision diverted the 2,166 strong 146th Brigade, consisting of members of the Royal Lincolnshire Regiment, Hallamshire Battalion, Lancashire Regiment and King's Own Yorkshire Light Infantry to make the landings.

The troops of 146th Brigade, aboard the large transports *Chroby* and *Empress of Australia*, which had carried Their Majesties King George VI and Queen Elizabeth to Canada and America the previous year, were destined to reach Namsos on 15th April. Escort cover for the Allied invasion force was provided by two of *Glasgow's* sister ships, *Manchester* and *Birmingham*, HMS *Cairo*, plus three destroyers. The 148th brigade were relegated to the second flight, and after further delays were to find themselves in Åndalsnes instead.

On 16th April a 1,100 strong advance group from 146th Commando Brigade landed, and the platoons relieved *Glasgow's* company. Captain Pegram was advised that the destroyers had sailed with the two battalions and would re-embark the Naval boarding parties during that night from the destroyers. By remaining to seaward *Glasgow* had avoided being spotted by enemy aircraft. As the cruiser approached Namson Fjord, just after midnight on the morning of 17th April, *Glasgow's* commanding officer was advised by Captain (D) 4 (Captain P. L. Vian DSO, RN) in *Afridi* that HM Ships *Matabele* and *Sikh*, with the re-embarked landing parties aboard, had been delayed. *Afridi* remained in company with *Glasgow* to maintain an anti-submarine screen, having regard to the fact that earlier a suspicious craft had been sighted flashing a red light. At 3.11 am on 17th April *Matabele* and *Sikh* were sighted leaving Namson Fjord to re-embark the landing parties, and the operation was successfully completed. Having covered the landing of the expeditionary force under the command of General de Wiart the detachment, their task completed, returned to the cruisers in the destroyers. The landing parties were re-embarked in the approaches and *Glasgow's* Captain, believing it unwise to remain in the area, advised the Admiralty accordingly and, while awaiting further instructions, made passage towards Namsos.

HMS *York* reported the presence of enemy ships in the area and *Glasgow* steamed to a position some sixty miles off shore to avoid detection. In the mid-afternoon a report, relating the presence of five enemy destroyers near Standlandet, was received but *Glasgow* was much further away than *York's* force and Captain Pegram considered that little purpose would be served by returning to the area from where the report had originated. The Captain of *Sheffield* came to the same conclusion independently and both ships returned to Scapa Flow to refuel.

Five days later, on 21st April *Glasgow* left Scapa Flow for Rosyth, in company with *Sheffield*. Having embarked 650 men from the King's Own Yorkshire Light Infantry the ship sailed again on 22nd April bound for Åndalsnes, sailing in convoy with *Sheffield,* which had Rear Admiral Edward-Collins on board, and the following day the military personnel were transferred to destroyers to be landed ashore.

The next days were full of incidents; on 24th April, an accident involving *Glasgow's* starboard machine gun claimed the life of Ordinary Seaman Donald A. Pitt who was buried at sea later that same day and on 25th April *Glasgow* went to the assistance of the *Curaçao* which had been damaged by bombing, with 43 allegedly killed in the attack. When *Glasgow* found the *Curaçao* it was steaming along as though nothing had happened to her. Later *Glasgow* came under attack from German aircraft which dropped five bombs. The enemy's aim was not very good and the British warship escaped unscathed. One German plane which attacked under cover of a smoke cloud was engaged by the gunners on board *Glasgow* and brought down.

On 3rd May 1940 *Afridi* was sunk with the loss of 100 men including rescued troops and survivors from the French destroyer *Bison*, by enemy Ju.87 dive-bombers off Namsos, while covering the withdrawal of Allied troops from Namsos. Captain Vian, although originally reported missing, was rescued and continued to play a part in the war effort.

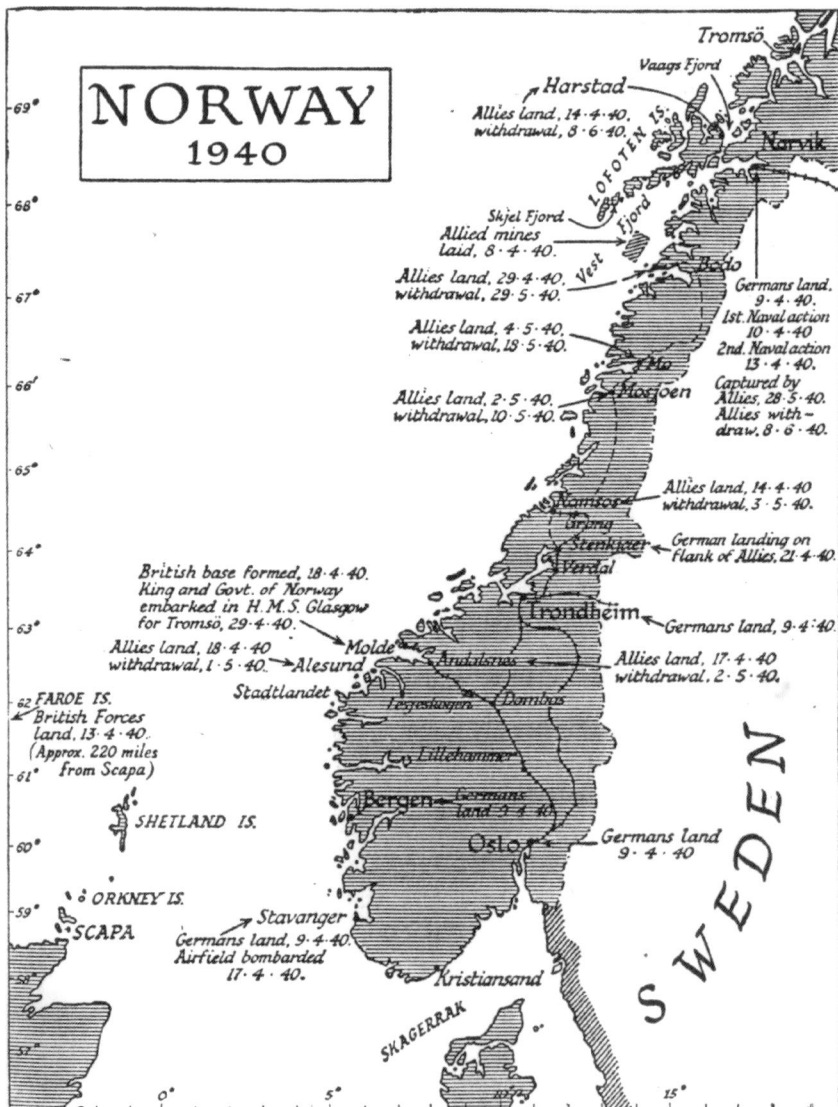

NORWAY
1940

Tromsö

Vaags Fjord

Harstad
Allies land, 14·4·40,
withdrawal, 8·6·40.

Narvik

Skjel Fjord
Allied mines
laid, 8·4·40.

Bodö

Germans land,
9·4·40.
1st. Naval action
10·4·40
2nd. Naval action
13·4·40.

Allies land, 29·4·40,
withdrawal, 29·5·40.

Allies land, 4·5·40,
withdrawal, 18·5·40.

Allies land, 2·5·40,
withdrawal, 10·5·40.

Mo

Mosjoen

Captured by
Allies, 28·5·40.
Allies with-
draw, 8·6·40.

Allies land, 14·4·40
withdrawal, 3·5·40.

Namsos

Grong

German landing on
flank of Allies, 21·4·40.

Steinkjaer

Verdal

British base formed, 18·4·40.
King and Govt. of Norway
embarked in H.M.S. Glasgow
for Tromsö, 29·4·40.

Trondheim

Germans land, 9·4·40.

Allies land, 18·4·40
withdrawal, 1·5·40.

Molde

Andalsnes

Allies land, 17·4·40
withdrawal, 2·5·40.

Alesund

Stadtlandet

Lesjeskogen

Dombas

FAROE IS.
British Forces
land, 13·4·40.
(Approx. 220 miles
from Scapa)

Lillehammer

SWEDEN

SHETLAND IS.

Bergen

Germans
land, 9·4·40.

Oslo

Germans land
9·4·40

ORKNEY IS.

SCAPA

Stavanger
Germans land, 9·4·40.
Airfield bombarded
17·4·40.

Kristiansand

SKAGERRAK

56

Evacuation of His Majesty
King Haakon of Norway

The Norwegian Government and people had expressed great disappointment over the Allied withdrawal, and many were of the opinion that it would be better for the Allied cause had they tried to take Trondheim and failed, rather than not to have tried at all. By 20th April, the majority of the Norwegian Government had established themselves at Molde which at the time seemed a safe haven, being close to the British base at Åndalsnes. A week later, Molde was bombed all day and shelter had to be sought in an improvised refuge a short distance from the harbour jetty. The bombing continued the following day, both at Molde and at Åndalsnes which was on fire and from which clouds of smoke could be seen rising over the mountain ridge. Occasionally, the rumble of anti-aircraft guns at work could be heard, but the German bombers were free to come and go as they liked for the two bases were virtually undefended. Molde was not only exposed from the air but also from the sea and land. The bombing was continuous, carried out with horrible ease and deliberation. For the Germans, the weather was perfect and for the bomber pilots there was no need to hurry. Flying over the Norwegian countryside from bases inside Germany, the pilots had orders to bomb, in addition to specified targets, clusters of small houses and to machine gun roads. They were able to perform both of these tasks as and when they pleased. That evening, orders were sent out to the British troops ordering their withdrawal from Romsdal. This gave the German forces in Trondheim the opportunity to link up with other units operating from Oslo. The whole of central and western Norway would thus fall under enemy occupation.

Molde had now become untenable as a base and His Majesty King Haakon and his Government were invited to leave the town in a

British cruiser that night and travel to any other Norwegian port, or England, as His Majesty might later decide.

Before the impending evacuation from Molde, Minister Nygaadsvold, the Prime Minister, had expressed to his colleagues an opinion that Norway should make peace with Germany on the best terms she could obtain. However, Minister Koht, Minister for Foreign Affairs, favoured continuing the resistance and the Cabinet were divided over the issue.

On board *Glasgow* Captain Pegram received orders, on 28th April 1940, from the Commander-in-Chief Home Fleet, to proceed to Norway in company with destroyers HM Ships *Jackal* and *Javelin*. The objective was to evacuate King Haakon (an Honorary Admiral of the Royal Navy) and his Government from Molde. The cruiser set out on her mission, sailing from Scapa Flow for Romsdal Fjord and keeping well to the westward. Twenty-four hours later the ship came under attack from two Heinkel 111s, which dropped six bombs from high level. Fortunately the bombs missed their target, although two fell approximately one hundred yards away.

In the late morning of 29th April a Heinkel dropped a bomb near enough to the makeshift shelter in which they were accommodated, to galvanise the Norwegian Government Ministers into action, reconciling them to the idea of departure. However, it was not until that afternoon that the British Embassy staff were informed that the King and his Ministers were willing to embark. By that time Molde was ablaze.

The Quayside at Molde ablaze after the German Air Attack   *(RNM)*

As *Glasgow* approached the Norwegian coast a heavy pall of smoke was observed in the vicinity of Almsund, Kristiansund and Molde. She proceeded up the fjord towards Molde while enemy aircraft were bombing the town, starting extensive fires. When the town Molde was sighted it was burning fiercely. Meanwhile, ashore, the Norwegian group had assembled at the entrance to the town, and as they did so a Heinkel flew overhead at 9.30 pm – an unusual hour for one to appear. As it did so the plane dropped a stick of incendiary bombs, which as bad luck would have it fell onto the quay from which the King and his companions were to embark.

The town was a vast furnace and an old church nearby caught fire. Wind fanned the flames, and the Embassy staff and members of the Norwegian Government watched its destruction helplessly while they awaited instructions on how to reach the *Glasgow*. The brilliance of the flames threw the shadows into darker relief, and it took some time to collect the group together. His Majesty and his son, The Crown Prince, had been seen arriving by car but several minutes were lost in trying to locate them. At 9.10 pm that day *Glasgow* went alongside the quay, the eastern end of which was already ablaze. Fortunately the light on-shore wind, which was blowing at the time, kept the flames away from the quay. Consequently, her fire parties were able to extinguish the flames in the vicinity of the ship. HMS *Glasgow* was lying alongside the burning quay, the ship's hoses turning the flames into smoke through which those wishing to embark had to pass. Ashore, a lamp stuttered to signal that the main Norwegian Royal and Government party was some distance north east of the quay, and that it was impossible for them to reach the jetty. HMS *Glasgow's* Captain requested that the Senior Naval Officer come aboard by 'puffer' and on his arrival Captain M.M. Denny, RN (later Admiral Sir Michael Denny) looked like the photograph from the "Text Book on Field Service", smart uniform, tin helmet, full webbing equipment, pistol, gas mask, black gaiters, boots, the lot. He informed Captain Pegram that he was under the impression that the cruiser had arrived to commence re- embarkation of troops. However, he made it clear that because of the lack of road communication to the town, with fires raging and the lack of available small craft, troops could not be re-embarked from Molde itself. He reported that the situation in the Molde area had deteriorated and was about to collapse, with four of his requisitioned trawlers sunk and the remainder almost certainly likely to be sunk by the next day. Captain Denny asked that the Admiralty be informed, with a recommendation that the evacuation of all British forces from Norway be immediate. Although physically exhausted as a result of operating under hazardous conditions for many days, Captain Denny insisted he remain ashore, to maintain a communication link, with Captain H.S.M. Harrison-Wallace, RN and assist such evacuation which might take place.

Eventually, at 9.30 pm King Haakon of Norway, Crown Prince Olav, members of the Norwegian Government and Ministers from the United Kingdom, France and Poland, who by then had all been accounted for, were transported in several cars, which sped through the town of Molde towards the port. The town was ablaze and under heavy attack from the air with German bombers dropping incendiary bombs. A bomb fell just behind the car conveying the King who wryly commented "Well intended, but the execution seems to be lagging behind." Eventually the cars reached the port where the *Glasgow* was waiting. His Majesty King Haakon and his companions picked their way through the flames and smoke along the quay, dodging the spurts of water issuing from the fire hoses, and at 10.35 pm His Majesty and Crown Prince Olav embarked in the *Glasgow* accompanied by members of the Norwegian Government, together with British, Polish, Danish and French Ministers and staff from the British and French Legations.

King Haakon and Crown Prince Olav of Norway
aboard HMS Glasgow May 1940

HMS *Glasgow*, in addition to the aforementioned, also took on board 117 survivors from six sunken trawlers, together with 17 officers and men of the Royal Artillery and most of the Base Staff at Molde, which included 18 injured.

Shipwright A. Smith, who kept a diary at the time, wrote that among those on board were a number of skippers from sunken Norwegian trawlers and army personnel who considered themselves lucky to be alive. The trawler-men stated that: " Each day during daylight hours German planes would bomb and machine gun the trawlers continuously, until they were compelled to shelter under the cliffs close to shore where they remained until nightfall when they would be able to resume fishing." The fishermen were glad to be aboard the *Glasgow* with her impressive armament. Apparently shaking your fist at an enemy plane from the deck of a trawler isn't very good! Not long after the passengers had embarked on the British cruiser lorries laden with gold bullion from the National Bank arrived. The precious cargo was to be taken to England and Captain Pegram, anxious to leave before dawn, ordered its loading. This was difficult and arduous and only 23 tons (65%) could be taken aboard by the time *Glasgow* left the Norwegian port. The remainder had to be left behind to be shipped at a later date by a national vessel or another of HM Ships when the evacuation had been completed.

In the midst of all this activity Molde was subjected to further bombing attacks, and as the *Glasgow* cleared the jetty at 1.00 am on 30th April with the town engulfed in a sea of flames, she became the object of attack with the fires ashore providing the enemy planes with all the illumination required to mount a night time-bombing raid. The raid was unsuccessful.

The town of Molde ablaze after the German Air Attack   (RNM)

Shrouded in smoke set against a background of flames and the products of combustion, *Glasgow* slipped her mooring springs and made her way slowly from the harbour. Suddenly, from the dense clouds that were rising heavenwards, an enemy bomber appeared intent on attacking the cruiser. British guns thundered into action and a hail of anti-aircraft shells were directed at the incoming plane. The German pilot took evasive action to escape the fearsome assault and turned away to disappear again from whence he came. Few of those on *Glasgow* who saw Molde being devoured by the flames will forget the tragic and dramatic sight it presented. Although the town was largely destroyed by enemy action no lives are thought to have been lost, most of the population of 3,000 having already fled.

When the Norwegian Government expressed a wish that His Majesty be landed at Mosjøen, Captain Pegram expressed his opinion that the ship would be subjected to a bomb attack before the King could be landed. King Haakon, believing that the Germans were aware of his departure stated that he wished to go to Tromsö. The Government Ministers concurred with this request and the *Glasgow* sailed for the Norwegian port. The Norwegian King was concerned that Tromsö would be bombed as soon as the Germans became aware of his presence in the town. Plans were subsequently made to ensure that the *Glasgow's* arrival in the Tromsö area should be as inconspicuous as possible. The use of a Norwegian boat which the local population was accustomed to seeing to convey King Haakon ashore made it easier for him to land without attracting unwelcome attention.

May 1st was a sunny peaceful day as *Glasgow* proceeded along the Norwegian coast towards Tromsö. Twenty miles from her destination Captain Pegram sent a destroyer ahead to make the necessary arrangements for a Norwegian guardship to disembark His Majesty, the Crown Prince, the Government, the staff of the British and French legations and the Danish Minister Oxholm. As she awaited the response *Glasgow* lay stopped in the water with beautiful though bleak and deserted snow covered rocks around her. The guardship, which arrived to take the King into Tromso, was the Norwegian armed vessel *Heimdal*, the same one that had taken him and Queen Maud (The youngest daughter of King Edward VII) to Trondheim for their coronation thirty five years earlier, and at 8.18 pm His Majesty, the Crown Prince and Government were disembarked from the British cruiser on to the *Heimdal* in Malangen Fjord. The King's intention was that he should find accommodation in a fisherman's hut in a secluded spot with his Ministers staying a few miles further away in scattered houses rather than in Tromsö.

The altered circumstances between the occasion of his coronation 35 years earlier, and May 1940 were foremost in the minds of those present as His Majesty was piped down the gangway. The scene was made all the more poignant by the desolate nature of the region in which he was about to seek shelter and the uncertainty of what lay in store for his country. As he left the cruiser, the King was as gracious and dignified as ever. For three weeks before embarkation in the British warship the King and his followers had effectively been 'refugees' and the atmosphere of strength, efficiency and quiet confidence prevalent on *Glasgow* as a direct result of the strong personality of her captain, Captain Pegram, gave them the tonic they needed to carry on. The hospitality and kindness shown by the officers and men was greatly appreciated and reflected in the personal letter which His Majesty sent to the officers and crew before leaving the ship.

At Sea
May 1st 1940

The Crown Prince and I wish to express our sincere gratitude to the Captain, officers and men of H. M. S. Glasgow for the extreamly kind hospitality shown us in so many ways during our stay onboard, a kindness never to be forgotten.

During these dificult times for Norway it has been a great help to us, and has also given us proof of the sympathy felt towards both us and our people by everyone in Great Britain and has given us confide. that our struggle for our freedom and indipend. will be supported by your great Nation.

We will follow your future activations with the greatest interest, and wish you all the best of luck.

Haakon.

Letter from HM King Haakon of Norway.

63

In recognition of the evacuation of King Haakon and the transfer of the Norwegian bullion the Prime Minister later presented silverware engraved "Molde to the Clyde" to the ship.

At Tromsö, on June 7th, that year HMS *Devonshire* embarked King Haakon, the Crown Prince Olav and their Equerries, the Norwegian Prime Minister, 56 Norwegian Government officers, 24 members of the Norwegian Air Force, 15 Political refugees, 3 members of the Diplomatic Corps, 11 members of His Majesty's King George VI's Mission to Norway, 10 members of the French Mission, and 342 British Army officers and men. Having them safely aboard the British cruiser headed for the UK where, after an uneventful passage, she disembarked them.

Icelandic Offensive

The Royal Marine's training for amphibious operations makes those who are ashore, awaiting drafting to a sea-going detachment, appropriate troops for an occupational force at short notice.

After the German invasion of Denmark and Norway had begun and the position of the Faroe Islands and Iceland appeared hazardous, units of the Corps were chosen to garrison the islands against enemy landings. Because of its strategic position, occupation by Allied troops of the Danish Faroes was considered to be of the greatest importance.

A force led by Lieutenant Colonel T.B.W. Sandall embarked in HMS *Suffolk* which made passage to Thorshaven, the capital. It was a perfectly planned and faultlessly executed operation which prevented a German invasion. Such an invasion, with the establishment of a hostile naval and seaplane base perilously close to the North of Scotland, would have been disastrous. Because it controlled the North Atlantic trade route the strategic position of Iceland, which is larger than Ireland, was very important to the Allies. Its occupation became necessary to prevent a German invasion.

Force "Sturges", a newly formed Royal Marine Commando Brigade commanded by Colonel R.G. Sturges, consisting of one infantry battalion, a battery of four-inch mobile guns and one of four two-pounders, together with a naval howitzer battery was given the task of landing a force in Iceland to prevent occupation by the enemy and they embarked on the cruisers *Glasgow* and *Berwick*. On 5th May 1940 the Second Battalion Royal Marines, under the command of Lieutenant Colonel A.N. Williams arrived at Greenock to join Colonel Sturges' unit. Two days later the liner *Queen Mary II* brought off 275 more Royal Marines and the next day their stores and ammunition required for the landing was embarked.

HM Ships *Berwick* and *Glasgow* set sail, on 8th May, in company with the destroyers *Fearless* and *Fortune*, making way at 22 knots for Iceland to secure Reykjavik and Hvalfjord. The weather during the passage was rough and many of the marines were very seasick. Force "Sturges" arrived safely in Icelandic waters at 2.30 am on 10th May, and when the cruisers were 30 miles off-shore from Reykjavik *Berwick* launched her "pussers spitfire" to reconnoitre the harbour, while *Fortune* conducted an anti-submarine sweep of the approaches before signalling to the cruisers that it was safe for them to proceed. *Glasgow* and *Berwick* approached the shore and as they closed, aboard *Glasgow* the men heard the order "Fo'c'sle men on the fo'c'sle. Stand by to anchor." A minute later there was a roar and a crashing just over the for'ard mess deck like a thousand tons of coal being emptied on the fo'c'sle as the anchor was released and the anchor cable rumbled up from the cable locker, along the deck and down the hawse pipe into the sea as the ships anchored half a mile from the harbour entrance to disembark the troops.

Aboard the cruisers they heard the piping of the call "Royal Marine landing party fall in on the Quarterdeck." Within ten minutes with equipment, ammunition and food the men were 'hanging on a split yarn', eagerly awaiting the order to move.

HMS *Fearless* secured alongside *Glasgow* to take the first flight of troops ashore as the weather deteriorated and fifteen minutes later the Royal Marine landing party embarked. The marines, dazed by lack of food and fatigued by the seasickness, were transferred ashore, in a violent snowstorm, to land at Reykjavik in the early hours of 10th May 1940. The snowstorm, which provided cover for the first troops to land , enabled *Berwick* to steam into the inner harbour and secure alongside the main jetty, virtually invisible from those on shore. The berth was clear and there was no opposition. As one of the officers observed, the landing was "like getting out of a train on to a platform" The time was 4.00 am. Once ashore two platoons, under Major S.G. Cutler, RM set about achieving their objective, namely the occupation of the German Consulate to impound any secret documents found.

Soon after their unopposed arrival at the Consulate the marines found the Consul's wife and daughter, in their nightclothes, trying to dispose of all the confidential books and secret papers in a bath which contained blazing paraffin. The fire was extinguished and most of the papers were saved. The Consul-General, Herr Gerlach, was then escorted round the house while a search was made for possible booby traps. After the search had been completed, the Consulate staff were given time to pack some personal possessions, but were warned that if they secreted away any books or papers then they would be allowed to take nothing. Herr Gerlach asked to be allowed to fetch his overcoat from the cloakroom. Escorted by Major Cutler and a sergeant the German reached for his coat and, as he did so, slipped his left hand into the pocket. Major Cutler quickly seized Herr Gerlach's arm and took a loaded revolver from the pocket. The German was then put under an armed guard. Cars were commandeered and the Consul-General, his family and staff were embarked on board HMS *Fearless*. Also on the island were other Nazis besides the Consul-General and within forty-five minutes of the "Force" landing the majority had been arrested. This group included a number of Germans who had come from a so-called shipwrecked merchant vessel (An officer from a U-boat who had been landed to 'look after them' was arrested later and returned to England).

By 9.30 am that morning Colonel Sturges was able to report "All quiet, inhabitants friendly." The occupation had been bloodless without a single shot being fired, even by accident. One hour later the *Fearless* returned to secure alongside HMS *Glasgow* and twenty German prisoners of war were transferred from the destroyer to the cruiser. Just before 11.00 am nine more prisoners were embarked, and at midday the destroyer HMS *Fortune* brought three more.

The Icelandic people, who are an independent race, accepted the situation philosophically without welcoming it. One group of inhabitants was strongly pro-British while another, which had been subjected to a programme of carefully cultivated relations by the Germans pre-war were equally pro-German. The remainder adopted an attitude of "Iceland for Icelanders" but recognised that the Germans might have "invaded" had the British not done so. This group of people regarded the British as the lesser of the two evils.

On 11th May *Glasgow* left the Icelandic capital bound for Liverpool, in company with the destroyers *Fearless*, *Fortune* and the cruiser *Berwick*. The next day she arrived on Merseyside to discharge the prisoners, including the German Consular Staff, at the Princes Landing Stage, Birkenhead, and for necessary repairs to be undertaken.

The Bizarre Capture of the S.S. "Gabbiano"

Captain H. Hickling, an officer who had served on board the cruiser's predecessor in 1914, assumed command of HMS *Glasgow* from Captain Frank Pegram, on a wet and windy day in Liverpool on 6th June 1940.

Four days later he was to be instrumental in the capture of an enemy ship in a British dry dock, an event which must rank among the most unusual events of the Second World War.

With France still reeling from Hitler's onslaught Benito Mussolini, the fascist Italian leader, having formed an alliance with Germany, decided that he could safely engage in the hostilities with little risk to his armed forces.

Aware of Mussolini's intentions the Admiralty issued orders, on 10th June 1940, that all Italian shipping in home waters was to be seized. At the time this order was issued the *Glasgow* was berthed in the Merseyside port of Liverpool undergoing repairs and her captain, aware that an Italian vessel, the 6584-ton S.S. *Gabbiano* from Naples was berthed in a neighbouring dock, sent an armed boarding party to seize it.

When the boarding party, led by Lieutenant Commander Hugonin, seized the Italian ship her captain, totally unprepared for the event and having no idea that his country was at war with Britain, nearly died of fright. No resistance was offered and after the ship's papers had been handed over a somewhat puzzled crew, having packed up their belongings, was marched ashore and taken into captivity. War with Italy was formally declared at one minute past midnight on the night of 10th/11th June 1940 and the S.S. *Gabbiano* was turned over to the authorities, as a prize of war on the following day, 11th June.

Glasgow remained on Merseyside until repairs had been completed. On 7th July she sailed for Scapa Flow, where on arrival the cruiser found herself to be in the company of HM Ships *Rodney, Nelson, Renown, Repulse, Barham, Norfolk* and *Southampton.*

Collision with HMS "Imogen"

On 16th July 1940 the *Southampton*, Flagship of the 18th Cruiser Squadron, and the cruisers *Sussex*, *Shropshire* and *Glasgow* ventured out from Scapa Flow, accompanied by destroyers from the 7th and 8th Divisions. In the 7th destroyer Division were HM Ships *Cossack*, commanded by Captain P.L.Vian, DSO, RN {Captain (D) 4}, *Sikh*, *Fortune* and *Fury*, and those in the 8th Division were the destroyers *Inglefield*, commanded by Captain P. Todd, DSO, RN, {Capt (D) 3}, *Imogen*, *Zulu* and *Maori*.

The ships were on a mission, into the North Sea, to intercept and engage a German squadron understood to have been out there. It was a beautiful summer's day with a slight sea swell when the ships left Hoxa Gate and made passage southeastwards at speed. Very soon the cruisers and destroyers found themselves enveloped in a thick fog, while overhead the roar of enemy bombers could be heard. Having learned that the enemy squadron had turned back Admiral Sir Charles Morton, KCB, DSO. C-in-C Home Fleet issued orders for the hunters to return to base. Although the time was 9.00 pm it was still daylight as the cruisers led the way northwards with a division of destroyers keeping station on each quarter to form, as they went, an arrowhead formation. The ships steamed along at 20 knots, off Duncansby Head in northeast Scotland, towards a fog shrouded Scapa Flow. The blanketing canopy had settled down, to the wave top level, reducing visibility to such an extent that those on the *Glasgow's* bridge could barely make out her foc'sle. Only the fog buoy towed by the ship in front showed that company was being kept.

Rear Admiral M.L. Clarke, DSC, aboard the *Southampton* decided to abort the approach into harbour and signalled the squadron accordingly. The ships turned back southwards, out of the clinging impenetrable fog, into clear weather before being ordered, for a second time, to enter the fog bank which by now had thickened even further. Again came the order to turn, which was instantly obeyed, and once more the squadron emerged into the clear.

Darkness was falling fast, as midnight approached, when the cruisers altered course towards Scapa Flow for a third time. The *Glasgow*, the rear ship in the line, had to turn away on each of the three occasions in fog. The speed of the ships varied from 22 knots in clear weather to 15 knots in the fog.

Although the cruisers' captains had received signals relating to the manoeuvres, the whereabouts of the destroyers was uncertain at all times. It was 11.35 pm when the cruisers as "Force C" approached Scapa Flow at a speed of 15 knots, with the destroyers stationed two miles astern, one on each quarter. Making their way in the gloom Rear Admiral Clarke issued the order "Cruisers alter course in succession to 130 degrees" and they turned, shrouded in fog. As the helms were put over, single short siren bursts were heard from two of the cruisers. These were thought to have been the *Shropshire* and the *Sussex*. *Glasgow* turned in the wake of the *Shropshire* and then steadied on her new course, sounding one long blast as she did so. *Glasgow*'s captain, Captain Harold Hickling, didn't like these "follow my leader" manoeuvres at all and, as a precautionary measure, instructed the engine room to ensure that all watertight doors be properly closed. He also warned those on the bridge to be especially vigilant because the visibility had further diminished, preventing even the jack staff from being visible. His concern proved to be prophetic!

At 11.53 pm HMS *Inglefield* was observed, through the gloom, broad on *Glasgow*'s port bow, steering on an opposite course. Sounding one long blast the cruiser reduced speed to slow ahead. Approximately 20 seconds later a second destroyer loomed out of the fog dead ahead of the *Glasgow* and, in spite of putting the helm hard over to starboard and the engines to full astern, the cruiser struck HMS *Imogen*, under the command of Commander C.L.Firth, MVO, forward of the bridge, abaft "A" gun. At an angle of 20 degrees the cruiser embedded herself in the frail body of the destroyer, penetrating as far as the engine rooms, to lock the two ships together in a deadly embrace. The force of the impact heeled the destroyer over on to her starboard side until the upper deck was almost awash.

Down in *Glasgow*'s engine room the telegraphs rang urgently in turn "Stop both". "Full speed astern". The engine room responded immediately but this made not the slightest difference to the situation and the warships remained locked together like malformed Siamese twins. The cruiser's engine room telegraphs clattered to signal: "Stop both". Again the response was swift, the order being immediately obeyed, and *Glasgow's* engines stopped.

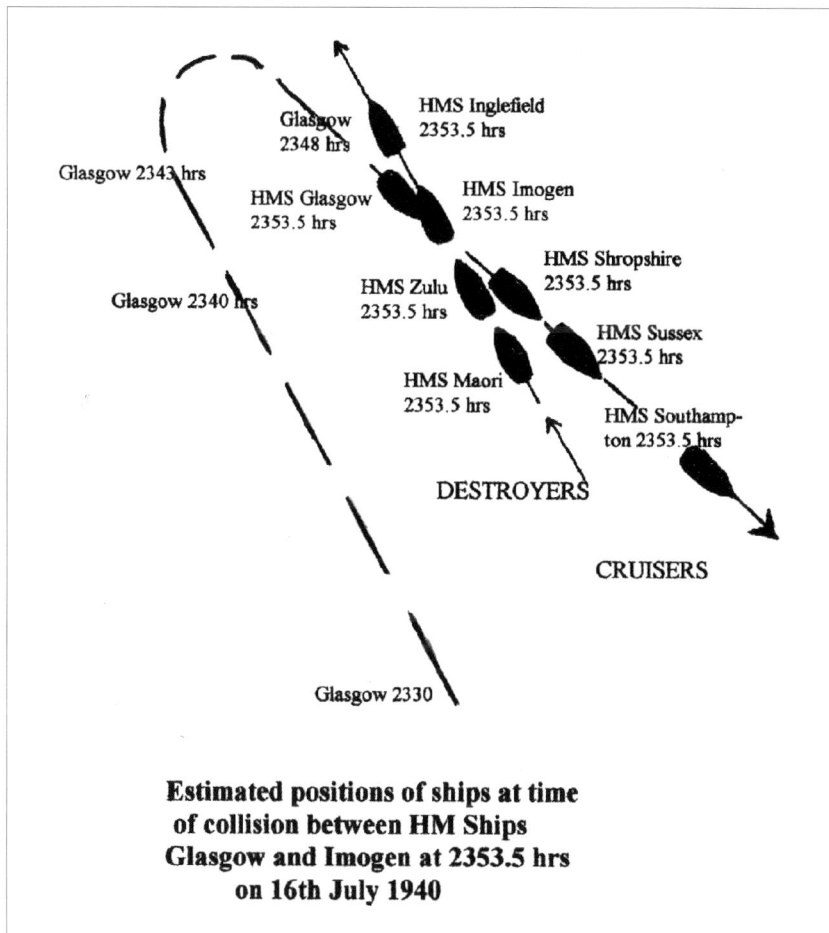

Glasgow 2343 hrs

Glasgow 2340 hrs

Glasgow 2330

Glasgow
2348 hrs

HMS Inglefield
2353.5 hrs

HMS Glasgow
2353.5 hrs

HMS Imogen
2353.5 hrs

HMS Shropshire
2353.5 hrs

HMS Zulu
2353.5 hrs

HMS Sussex
2353.5 hrs

HMS Maori
2353.5 hrs

HMS Southamp-
ton 2353.5 hrs

DESTROYERS

CRUISERS

**Estimated positions of ships at time
of collision between HM Ships
Glasgow and Imogen at 2353.5 hrs
on 16th July 1940**

Aboard the cruiser the ship's company tumbled out of their hammocks in an orderly fashion, believing that the ship had been torpedoed. When they realised this was not the case they did what they could to rescue shipmates from the stricken destroyer.

As the two ships collided a sheet of flame shot up, fuelled by a shower of fuel oil released from the destroyer's ruptured furnaces, the heat from which was felt on *Glasgow's* bridge. The source of the fire was thought to have been the ready-use petrol stored under *Imogen's* bridge structure. Soon the two ships were ablaze as the flames licked and danced between them, bringing the added danger that the *Imogen's* forward magazine might explode and destroy them both. Captain Hickling, aware of the imminent danger and knowing *Glasgow's* fuel storage compartment, located in the cruiser's bows, held two thousand gallons of aviation fuel gave the order both for it and the forward magazine to be flooded.

The *Glasgow's* Commander J.W. Cuthbert, gave the order "Abandon Ship" to those on the *Imogen's* upper deck and they made their way, via lower boom and emergency escape ladders, across to the cruiser's bow. As a further precaution, in case the destroyer sank, fourteen Carley floats were dropped into the water from the cruiser and her port whaler was also lowered. Petty Officer George Derrick of *Glasgow* climbed into the stricken destroyer to assist with the evacuation of wounded men and found *Imogen's* Yeoman and Coxswain badly injured. With no thought to his own safety Petty Officer Derrick lowered himself over the destroyer's side, with the Yeoman on his back, to allow those in a Carley float below to attend to the wounded man. When almost all of the men had been evacuated from the *Imogen* he entered the fo'csle and, with the aid of a torch thrown to him from one of the cruiser's seamen, carried out a further search for survivors but found none. He then went into the Petty Officer's mess where again he found no one.

The collision had severed *Imogen's* fire main which prevented its use to contain the spreading fire threat, and *Glasgow's* fire control party played as many hoses as were available, from the foc'sle and lower deck scuttles, onto the flames. For a time they seemed to be winning the fight but as the ready–use ammunition, which had been scattered everywhere by the force of the collision, ignited the flames flared up afresh and the fire quickly became uncontrollable.

Captain Hickling now had a very difficult decision to make. Aware that the invasion of Britain was imminent and with only a handful of cruisers available to oppose it, he knew that the loss of his ship would seriously compromise the strength of the naval force, more so than the loss of a destroyer. Armed with this knowledge he told his second in command Commander Cuthbert that he had no alternative but to extricate the entangled *Glasgow* and leave the *Imogen* to her fate.

Although *Imogen's* Captain had been reported missing, he came aboard *Glasgow* after all his men had abandoned ship. At the time of the collision he had been thrown from the compass platform onto the five-inch gun deck!

In danger of blowing up, *Glasgow* manoeuvred astern attempting to break free from *Imogen's* side but the destroyer clung on tenaciously refusing to give up her grip. Captain Hickling informed the engine room that he required all possible available power to free the cruiser and rang: "Full astern both". The engine room responded and, as the helm was put over first to starboard then to port, *Glasgow* gathered sternway to slowly prise her way from the limpet like hold of tangled and distressed steel. As the cruiser went astern the Carley floats, in the V formed between the two warships, were caught in the wash from *Glasgow's* propellers.

Aboard the cruiser the engine room telegraph sounded: "Stop both" and there was an immediate response. One of the Carley floats with Petty Officer Derrick aboard turned turtle throwing him into the water. Sucked down by the disturbed water he struggled to keep air in his lungs, before again rising towards the surface to emerge beneath the other floats. When he was able to extricate himself he emerged near a ladder to find Midshipman E. J. M. Lucas, standing in the whaler. With one hand on the ladder the Midshipman called out to the Petty Officer in the water " Come on, pull yourself up; you want to see Pompey again; you can manage it." Petty Officer Derrick climbed halfway up the ladder before he was helped aboard by other crew members.

Once free of the trap the cruiser circled slowly round the stricken destroyer amid exploding ammunition to make a search for the Carley floats and boats. This was unsuccessful because the fog was now so thick that even *Glasgow's* own whaler was picked up by the destroyer HMS *Zulu*.

The *Imogen* was last seen at 00.45 a.m. on 17th July burning fiercely, surrounded by a sea of blazing fuel oil at 58° 34' N, 02° 54' W.

Glasgow managed to rescue ten officers and 135 ratings from the stricken destroyer. Ten of these were wounded and transferred to HM Hospital Ship *Isle of Jersey* where one, a Petty Officer, died later from his wounds.

Seventeen of the destroyer's ratings were posted missing presumed dead, dying in their mess decks or on watch. One officer, Midshipman Lucas, and one rating, Able Seaman Keilty, were posted missing from the *Glasgow*. Midshipman Lucas, who had been lowered in the lifeboat to take charge of the men on the Carley floats and render assistance where needed, had started to climb the jumping ladder at the time when *Glasgow* had gone astern. Due to the oil covered state of the ladder and his own exhaustion he slipped off and was not seen again. Able Seaman Keilty, one of the ratings manning the Carley floats to assist survivors, transferred from a float with men aboard to an empty one and was last seen near the bows of the *Imogen*. When the search and rescue mission , following the collision had been concluded Captain Hickling ordered *Glasgow* to turn eastwards, away from ships, away from the rocky Scottish coastline, and away from the fog to steam towards Norway. Later that morning he returned to Scapa Flow where the damage could be assessed. A gash had been cut about six feet above the waterline, some sixty feet long, giving the bows the appearance of some prehistoric crocodile.

The Board of Inquiry held to investigate the collision between the two warships found that Rear Admiral M. L. Clarke, DSC, commanding the 18th Cruiser Squadron, had failed to exercise adequate control over the various units, compounded by the fact that he had ordered a dangerous manoeuvre. In consequence of this he was relieved of his command and ordered ashore. Captain P.L.Vian, DSO, RN was also censured for failing to form the destroyers in close order astern of the cruisers when entering the fog banks.

Captain Hickling and Commander Firth were absolved of any blame.

The *Glasgow* returned to Liverpool where she entered the Canada Dry Dock, on 21st July1940, to enable vital repairs to be carried out.

On the 9th August Engine Room Artificer Mansfield fell into the dock from the quayside and although he was quickly sent to hospital he later died. His funeral was held three days later on 12th August 1940. The following month, on 4th September, with her repairs completed, *Glasgow* departed from Merseyside for gunnery practice at Scapa Flow. She remained at the naval base until the end of the month when she sailed for Immingham, where she arrived on 1st October.

Three weeks later *Glasgow* sailed for Rosyth to enable an ASV type 286 to be fitted and for the MF/DF aerials to be removed from the foretruck and relocated near the bridge. The work was completed by the 29th October when she made passage to Greenock on the Clyde. In November the cruiser left the Clyde bound for Gibraltar where, on her arrival, 385 men of the 191st/200th Anti-Aircraft Battery, Royal Artillery were embarked for transportation to Malta.

Two days after her arrival in Valetta harbour *Glasgow* was sent out again, this time to provide a defensive screen for the aircraft carrier

HMS Glasgow in Dry Dock at Liverpool   *(NMM)*
following the collision with HMS Imogen.

HMS *Illustrious* en route to Alexandria, in company with the cruisers *York*, *Berwick* and *Gloucester* and four destroyers. The escorting ships were to protect the carrier as she made her way, in darkness, to within striking distance of the Italian fleet at Taranto. Seldom can a ship have been more closely escorted with a cruiser stationed ahead, astern and on each beam of the *Illustrious* and destroyers on her port and starboard bow and quarters, all one mile distant from the carrier, all ships darkened and steaming at thirty knots. A high standard of station keeping and vigilance was called for as the carrier made numerous changes without being able to signal her intentions to the escort vessels. Against the dark horizon, with her double ended shape and overhanging flight deck, *Illustrious* proved difficult to see as she twisted and turned to "find the wind" necessary to fly off her aircraft. In the gloom those on *Glasgow's* bridge strained their eyesight, keeping watch for any change of direction made by the carrier and ready to react at a moments notice. Had *Illustrious* and an escort turned inwards they would have been approaching each other at a closing speed of more than sixty knots and likely to be in collision within as many seconds. On the other hand had they turned outwards, travelling at the combined speed of an express train, they could have lost contact with each other never, in the pitch darkness, to be regained.

Planes flying off from *Illustrious* attacked the Italian fleet in Taranto harbour, catching them by surprise, and inflicting considerable damage on Mussolini's warships.

Glasgow Helps Destroy the Italian Navy

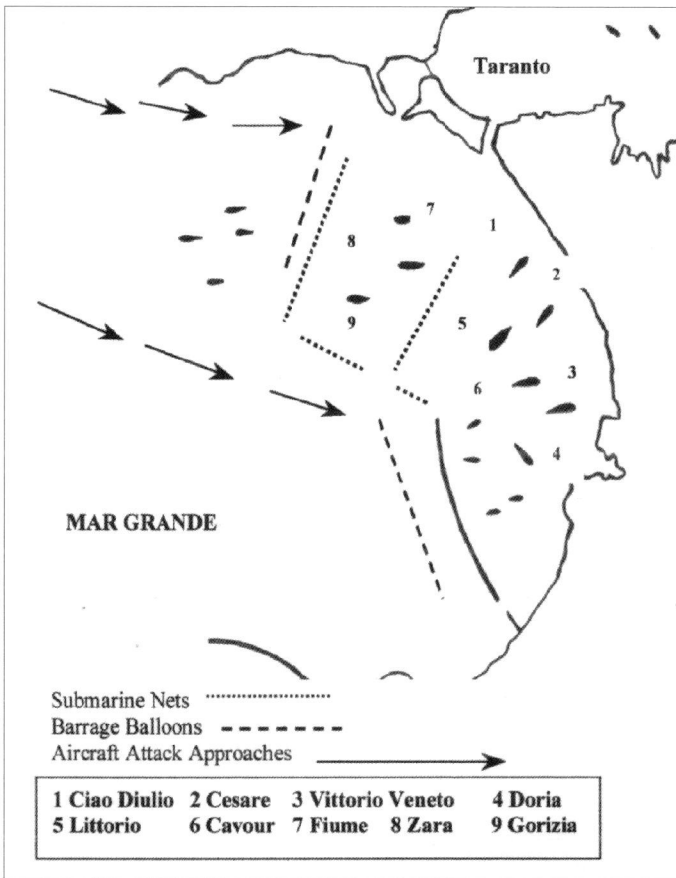

Air Attack on Italian Fleet Taranto 11th November 1940

79

Photo-reconnaissance carried out by the RAF provided Admiral Sir Andrew B. Cunningham, and his planners aboard HMS *Illustrious*, with details of the layout of Taranto harbour where the Italian Fleet were known to be at anchor. Included were details of the anti-torpedo nets and barrage balloon defences provided within it.

The resulting photographs were flown to the *Illustrious* in the afternoon of 11th November 1940. These showed that five battleships were at anchor in the outer harbour, while an RAF Sunderland flying boat reported that a single heavy ship was joining them. Among the battleships at their moorings were two brand new vessels which were fast and armed with fifteen-inch guns. Cruisers, destroyers and submarines made up the rest of the fleet, and no aircraft carriers were present.

Admiral Cunningham detached *Illustrious* and her escorting cruisers and destroyers to steam to a position, 170 miles south east of the Italian port, from which an attack on the enemy ships could be launched.

On the night of 11th November Swordfish aircraft were flown off from the British carrier under cover of darkness and headed towards their targets in Taranto harbour. The plan was to bomb the Italian Fleet using torpedoes with newly developed magnetic warheads. These were designed to detonate under a ship to inflict more damage than those which relied on the weapon striking the side of a ship to cause detonation. The aircraft, flying at 30 feet, homed in on their targets, a cluster of warships lit up by the ghostly light from parachute flares, catching the Italians completely by surprise. Weaving their way between the barrage balloon defences the planes released their torpedoes from ranges which varied from 400 yds to 1500 yds. The deadly cylinders containing approximately 400 lbs. of high explosive hit the water and made their way, unerringly, 35 feet below the surface at 25 knots, towards the ships. Released of the weight of bombs or torpedoes the British planes' pilots saw the weapons strike home and, flying at mast height, manoeuvred their outdated aircraft back on to a reciprocal course for base, evading as they did so an umbrella of multi-coloured flak.

A photo reconnaissance mission flown the following day revealed that the battleship *Conte di Cavour* lay beached with almost all her decks awash, the *Littorio* was down at her head and the *Cavour* had been badly damaged by a torpedo which had exploded beneath her, effectively breaking her back. The *Caio Duilo* also suffered a similar fate to the *Cavour*, causing substantial damage. Three torpedoes had also struck the *Italia*. In addition to the success achieved against the battleships, bombs also hit the cruiser *Trento* and a number of destroyers.

The assault on Taranto effectively marked the demise of the battle-ship as the mainstay of sea power, after 400 years, and swung the balance of power in the Mediterranean very much in the favour of the Royal Navy. Totally demoralised by the action the Italian navy's future actions were characterised by excessive caution.

The 3rd Cruiser Squadron was then detached to escort a convoy passing through the Sicilian channel, on 27th November, towards Pantellaria.

Silhouetted against the light of the moon the four cruisers *York*, *Berwick*, *Gloucester* and *Glasgow* presented a "heaven sent" target to the commanders of the Italian submarines that lay in wait. With eyes firmly pressed against their periscopes each of the captains calculat-ed the range of the British warships, issued orders to loose off the torpedoes and patiently counted off the seconds to impact. Aboard *Glasgow* a heavy thud was heard. Three more quickly followed, sounding as though someone had carelessly dropped an armoured hatch, as torpedoes found their mark against the hull. Fortunately, the electric torpedoes had all fired prematurely, causing no damage. Had they run their full course the 3rd Cruiser Squadron might well have ceased to exist!

The following day a flotilla of corvettes, outbound from England, was not proceeding at a speed to satisfy the C-in-C, Admiral Cunningham, and *Glasgow* was ordered to round them up. Out of a clear blue sky six German Ju. 87's swooped down to attack the cruis-er, releasing large bombs as they did so, to bracket the ship with high explosives. An "Air Attack" alarm was sounded and the cruiser's crew raced to action stations. While the guns' crews closed up orders were given to the helmsman to alter course. Down in the engine room the telegraphs in the engine room clattered to signal "Full speed ahead."

When the order "Open Fire" was given the gunners responded immediately to send a fusillade of shells up towards the attackers. It was not long before the Corvette Commander signalled that one of the bombers had been hit and brought down. Credit for this was given to *Glasgow's* starboard multiple pom-pom's crew whose shooting had been so effective. During the attack one of the bombs exploded close by and the sea heaved up, lifting the cruiser out of the water and shaking the rigging of the foremast like a whip as it did so. At the time it seemed certain that *Glasgow* had been hit on the starboard side. However, when a thorough search of the ship had been made, after the enemy dive-bombers had been repelled, such damage as had been caused proved to be of little significance.

Luck had been on the side of HMS *Glasgow*. The carrier and escorts arrived safely in Alexandria on 15th November, where, that same day, 426 RAF and Cypriot RASC personnel boarded the *Glasgow*. Having completed the embarkation of the troops and their equipment the cruiser set sail for Piraeus, where she delivered the troops, before returning to the port of Alexandria two days later.

Change of Luck – Suda Bay, Crete

On Tuesday 3rd December HMS *Glasgow's* luck changed. As she lay at anchor in Suda Bay on the Island of Crete, inside a line of buoys believed to be supporting an anti-submarine net, she came under attack from Italian torpedo bombers. That day, at 3.38 pm, an air raid warning was sounded and the cruiser's crew went to "Action Stations." Three minutes later two Italian SM (Savoia Marchetti) 79 planes were sighted bearing green 90° making their approach at a height of approximately 50 feet. The enemy aircraft were engaged by the crews of the multiple pom-poms as they headed towards the ship.

Torpedo Damage to Bow

From a range of 3,000 yards each aircraft launched its deadly load and, having released it, swept over the ship so low that their propellers could be plainly seen. Either because there was no anti-torpedo net or that it was simply ineffective, a torpedo struck the *Glasgow* forward of the cable locker, at 3.44 pm, just below the water line, sending up a column of flame and smoke about 60 feet high as it detonated. The explosion blew a hole about 22 feet square out of both sides of the ship.

A minute and a half later a second torpedo struck the ship aft. This time in the spirits and wine store!

As it exploded, the second torpedo blew a hole approximately 22 feet by 16 feet out of the starboard side of the ship with a second one approximately 22 feet by 7 feet on the port side, together with part of the keel.

Damage to Stern caused by Second Torpedo

When the second torpedo exploded well under the ship aft it altered the cruiser's shape trapping as it did so, high concentrations of carbon monoxide gas in the hull. This resulted in several of the ship's company being temporarily overcome by the effects of the poisonous gas as they attempted to carry out essential repair work in this area. Fortunately they all quickly recovered.

The resulting fires were quickly put out and at 4.00 pm the Royal Artillery personnel disembarked. In spite of the damage the ship remained seaworthy, but the steering gear was put out of action. Had the ship been underway at the time of the attack the effect might have been more severe. Although the main and secondary armament remained intact and operative, "Y" turret was stood down because of the structural weakness of the ship in the vicinity of the turret. At 4.15 pm orders were received to "Raise Steam for Full Speed if possible", but because of problems associated with the performance of the starboard inner engine and propeller the ship was unable to get under way at this time. Later it became apparent that the safety of the ship depended on it getting away and clearing Kaso Strait,as quickly as possible, and the ship sailed for Alexandria at 9.42 pm.

During the action Surgeon Lieutenant G. R. E. Maxted, RNVR, and Royal Marine A. Bragg were killed and seven ratings were injured. The day after the attack at 4.30 pm the funerals of Surgeon Lieutenant Maxted and Royal Marine Bragg were held, after which *Glasgow* rendezvoused with the cruisers *Gloucester* and *York*.

The following day, on 5th December at 12.28 am, during the passage to Alexandria the starboard inner propeller and shaft fell off. This affected the warship's performance, but in spite of the handicap she was able to proceed and still maintain a creditable speed of 18 knots.

Soon after her arrival in Alexandria, repairs were put in hand to permit the ship to fulfill its role as a warship.

The Italian torpedo planes, which had attacked the ship, failed to reach their base, and a reconnaissance aircraft sent out by the enemy reported that the *Glasgow* had been sunk. The loss was reported over the Italian wireless and gave rise for the ship's company to make ribald comments.

At 11.05 pm on 20th December 1940 Chief Stoker Bowers, who had been commended for exemplary behaviour during the Norwegian Offensive, fell overboard from the Dock's steam launch. Although a search for him was immediately made unfortunately no trace of him could be found and this was called off at five past midnight. His body was found six days later at 7.36 am on 26th December.

By mid-February 1941 essential repairs had been effected and she emerged from the dockyard with a new bow section, once again ready for active sea service, and she left the Egyptian port bound for Aden, via Port Said, escorting HMS *Illustrious* through the Suez Canal, as she did so. The carrier was en route to a shipyard in America.

Magnetic mines, sown by the Germans, had caused the narrow waterway of the Suez Canal to be effectively blocked by a number of severely damaged merchant vessels. With its vast resources the Suez Canal company had quickly dredged a temporary channel to bypass each wreck to permit the passage of big ships with care. In fact, it was a hazardous operation that faced the crews of *Glasgow* and *Illustrious*, making use of the services of local canal pilots to navigate the treacherous waters, as they travelled southwards. The two ships proceeded with care, their captains realising that a few feet too far to starboard would result in fouling a wreck; too far to port would run their ship aground.

Safely through the Canal the warships parted company and *Glasgow*, making passage for the South African port of Durban, headed into the Indian Ocean where the German pocket battleship *Admiral Scheer* was preying on unarmed merchant vessels. On 24th February *Glasgow* anchored in Mauritius to take on board stores and to refuel. As the 'Oiler' came towards the cruiser bows on, in a strong wind, it miscalculated its approach and despite going full astern collided with *Glasgow* and pushed in a plate. The required repairs were carried out during the night and the following day she was ready for sea. This was just as well because news was received that a German Raider was operating in the area and the cruiser set off at maximum speed in search of the enemy, putting paid to a planned "Crossing the Line" ceremony.

The Hunt for the Pocket Battleship Admiral Scheer

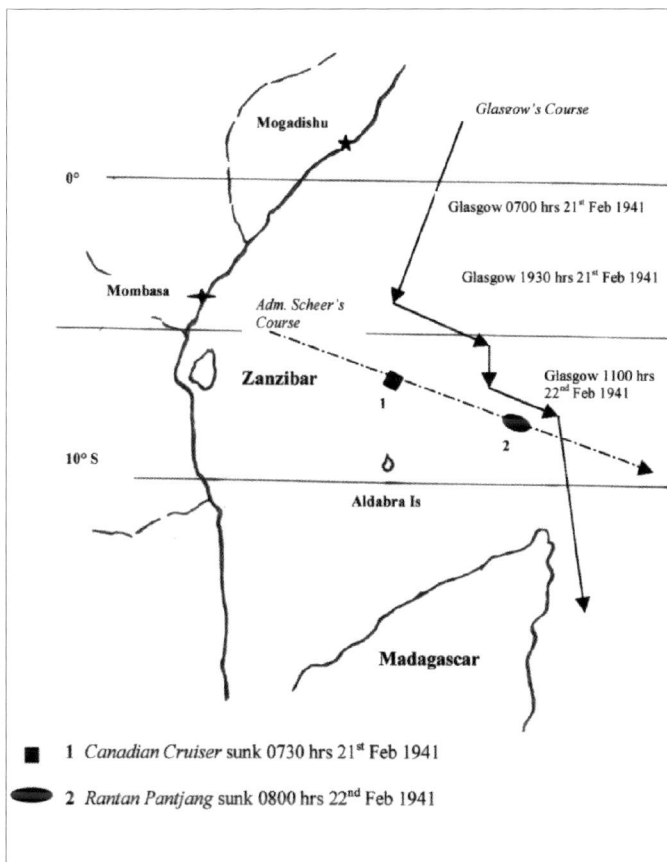

Glasgow's Course

Mogadishu

0°

Glasgow 0700 hrs 21st Feb 1941

Glasgow 1930 hrs 21st Feb 1941

Mombasa

Adm. Scheer's Course

Zanzibar

Glasgow 1100 hrs 22nd Feb 1941

1

2

10° S

Aldabra Is

Madagascar

■ 1 *Canadian Cruiser* sunk 0730 hrs 21st Feb 1941

● 2 *Rantan Pantjang* sunk 0800 hrs 22nd Feb 1941

In its operational zone north of Madagascar the commerce raider, *Admiral Scheer*, sought out vulnerable merchant ships like a predatory shark, periodically launching its reconnaissance aircraft, an Arado, to search the sea ahead. During one such flight, on 17th February 1941, its pilot spotted a freighter heading northwards, approximately sixty miles off the British Aldabra Islands, and the German warship set a course in pursuit. The Admiral *Scheer* failed to catch up with the freighter but encountered instead the tanker *British Advocate*, which was carrying a cargo of 4,000 tons of unrefined oil and 4,000 tons of petrol to Cape Town. The tanker's captain was persuaded to stop with no loss of life to his crew, and the vessel was seized as a prize of war.

Four days later the *Admiral Scheer's* captain, Captain Theodor Krancke, ordered that another reconnaissance mission be flown. Upon the aircraft's return to the ship the German pilot, Lieutenant Pietch, reported to Captain Krancke that he had spotted a merchant ship, due east of Zanzibar. The commerce raider altered course and headed, at speed to intercept the freighter. Shortly after sighting it Captain Krancke, suspecting that the ship could be a neutral, demanded a recognition signal which would identify its name and home port of registry. The freighter's captain responded with the reply "You have no right to stop a neutral ship on the high seas. This is an American ship." Captain Krancke's suspicions were aroused, the latest British merchant codes were consulted and the ship was identified as the S.S. *Canadian Cruiser*. The insolent reply from the freighter invited Captain Krancke to try a bluff and he ordered his Yeoman to signal "Name your master and ship immediately." It worked. Back came the reply "Captain Smith, *Canadian Cruiser*." The German captain gave the order for the freighter to stop. The merchant vessel momentarily obeyed the instruction before increasing speed in an attempt to escape. Under her stern water boiled furiously and the freighter's bow wave rose before, in the failing light, two large searchlights on the *Admiral Scheer* illuminated her from stem to stern. Captain Krancke, standing on the bridge, deep in thought, observing the manoeuvres of the *Canadian Cruiser*, was handed a message from the W/T cabin which read: "Enemy wirelessing "RRR" followed by her name, position and message "Being chased by battlecruiser." The German captain ordered the crews manning the anti-aircraft guns to open fire and they responded immediately. The first salvo whistled harmlessly over the freighter; the second hit the bridge and deck structure and the stark light of the searchlight showed up smoke and flying debris. Tracer shells arced across the evening sky in a constant stream, like mating fireflies, as the salvoes got lower.

Aboard the *Canadian Cruiser* the wireless operator continued to send out signals into the ether. Captain Krancke was handed a second message from the *Scheer's* W/T cabin "Mauritius acknowledges reception of RRR signals." "Zanzibar, Mombasa and Aden acknowledge reception of signals."

The German ship continued to bombard the freighter and eventually the *Canadian Cruiser* stopped in the water. A boarding party was put aboard her as she wallowed in the swell and Captain Krancke issued orders to prepare the freighter for sinking. Five explosive charges were primed and set. These detonated and the violent explosions which followed quickly sent the 7,178 ton freighter to the bottom of the Indian Ocean.

Down in his sea cabin aboard *Glasgow*, with only a thin partition separating him from the plot and remote control wireless office alongside, Captain Hickling heard a Morse key begin to chatter.

On hearing three R's repeated twice he quickly reached for the voice pipe on the bulkhead by his bunk and asked that the bearing and distance of the raider be worked out and reported back to him as soon as possible. Half a minute later Captain Hickling received the answer he needed, together with the information contained in the RRR message " I am being chased by a battle cruiser in position 6 ° 36' S, 47° 13'E and ordered that *Glasgow* proceed at maximum speed to intercept the raider. He then went to the plot to confer with Commander Cuthbert and the warship's Navigator Instructor Lieutenant Wright. Clearly marked on the plot was *Glasgow's* position, approximately 400 miles due east of Mombasa, with those of the *Canadian Cruiser* and enemy warship further south.

Captain Hickling was aware that the important convoy WS.5B, consisting of twenty large ships and guarded by the cruisers *Australia* and *Hawkins*, was steaming north between *Glasgow* and the Kenyan port. He also knew that eight other British cruisers were no more than 1,000 miles distant, five of which were within the vicinity of the convoy. Armed with this knowledge he concluded that the pocket battleship [The Germans had no battle cruisers] would make a run, at speed, for the wide-open space to the east. HMS *Glasgow's* Commanding Officer considered his options and decided that he could exploit a strategic advantage by steering east-south- east, should the raider retire from her killing zone on a course set between east-north-east and east-south-east. He decided to act on his hunch and set forth on the new course at twenty-four knots.

That same evening C-in-C East Indies Admiral Ralph Leatham sent a signal "Glasgow from C-in-C East Indies. With reference to *Canadian Cruiser*'s distress message – investigate and report."

Taking a lead from another naval tactician, Lord Nelson, more than one hundred years earlier at the Battle of Copenhagen *Glasgow's* captain asked the Chief Yeoman to delay reporting receipt of the signal until the following morning. Steaming through the night the cruiser's radar searched the sea ahead, to port and to starboard, but the longed for "blip" was missing.

Aboard the *Admiral Scheer* Captain Krancke received orders from the German Naval Operations Command to return to Germany unobtrusively before the end of March without further contact with the Allies. Realising that the British were endeavouring to counter the activities of the commerce raider, he decided to remove his ship from his operational area as expeditiously as possible.

Heading south-southeast *Admiral Scheer* ran into a tropical storm during which rain was beginning to thrash down, reducing visibility on the horizon. Emerging from behind a rainbow, which formed in the early morning sunlight, a freighter suddenly appeared right ahead.

Those aboard the freighter saw the German ship approach and, having been aware of the presence of an enemy surface raider in the vicinity, sent out a RRR signal (Raider, Raider, Raider. The SOS of merchant shipping attacked by German Commerce Raiders) giving: name, position and course to assist the British naval authorities to deduce the general direction in which the *Admiral Scheer* might take to escape the net closing in on her. That same morning, as dawn broke, Captain Hickling ordered the *Glasgow's* Walrus to be catapulted to reconnoitre ahead of the warship and, with some trepidation on the part of Captain Hickling, the C-in-C East Indies was informed of the British cruiser's position, course and speed.

The reconnaissance "Shagbag" was already on its perch, that is resting on its catapult rails. All the pilot and observer had to do was to climb into the seats and close the Perspex dome. However, before taking off, firstly the engine had to be tested and a last minute examination made of the aircraft's floats, while the Torpedo Officer responsible for the catapult checked the compressed air tanks; out of which the air hissed out satisfactorily. The engine started up with a sudden roar; rose to a high pitched whine, and then sank a tone or two to a steady rhythm. In the cockpit the pilot lifted his thumb. The TO set the works in motion and there was a sharp report, followed by a swift snorting blast, and the "Walrus" shot into the air.

Somewhat despondent at the lack of information as to the whereabouts of the enemy raider Captain Hickling took breakfast on the bridge, where the thought of tackling a stale egg from Aden, washed down with a cup of Kye, did little to improve his diminished appetite. Suddenly through the voice pipe, from the plot, came "Captain, sir! Another distress message. Dutch ship *Rantan Pantjang*." "She bears south east from us, one hundred and thirty miles."

Discarding his meal, Captain Hickling quickly went below to look at the plot and noted, with suppressed excitement, that the course made good, since receipt of the *Canadian Cruiser's* report was heading for the position where the raider had engaged her second known victim. The captain had no sooner returned to his seat than the Walrus returned to the ship and was recovered. While the aircraft was being checked over and refuelled ready to continue with its reconnaissance the pilot and observer reported to the cruiser's commanding officer on the bridge that nothing had been sighted. Orders were given that they continue to seek out the raider without breaking radio silence and, if possible, without being spotted by the enemy. A few minutes later the little single-engine plane soared again into a sky laden with rain clouds.

Captain Krancke, having no alternative but to engage and destroy the freighter, ordered the German warship to open up with her main armament, sending out salvo after salvo towards it, before the steamer disappeared again behind the rainbow. The *Admiral Scheer* raced after the little ship, like a terrier after a rat, ploughing through the torrential tropical cloudburst which quickly reduced visibility to a mere twenty yards or so. Despite the respite afforded by this lack of visibility time was running out for the little ship and destruction rapidly closed on her. Running before the storm the freighter bought a little time but suddenly the wall of rain ceased, the clouds parted, and the two ships found themselves barely 3,000 yards apart. Urged on by a sense of self-preservation the steamer tried to escape, using the sideways movement of the rainbow, but before it could do so shells from the German ship hit it amidships and she hove to.

The gallant little ship was the Dutch registered *Rantan Pantjang* bound for Singapore with a cargo of coal. A boarding party from the *Admiral Scheer* went aboard her, placed explosive charges and detonated them. It was not long before the brave little ship, which had led the German warship such a dance and betrayed its position to the

Royal Navy, slid under the surface of the Indian Ocean, which closed over her.

Hardly had the prisoners from the Dutch freighter been safely put away in their quarters when an aircraft warning sounded. A tiny speck some twelve miles away was moving slowly against the rain clouds. It had seen the German ship and was coming closer; soon it was barely ten miles away. *The plane, which the German warship had spotted, was the Walrus from Glasgow.*

Aboard the commerce raider the pilot of her reconnaissance aircraft, Lieutenant Pietch, sought permission from Captain Krancke to take off and launch an attack against the intruder but his request was turned down. By changing course from south-east to east by north-east when the British plane had first been sighted, but before it had seen the pocket battleship, her captain hoped to deceive the British pilot of his intended route. Although the plane departed the area twenty minutes later the German ship remained at action stations.

On board *Glasgow*, as the forenoon and afternoon watch-keepers changed over, the plane returned, the pilot giving the thumbs up sign as it circled prior to landing. Within ninety seconds of touching down the aircraft was stowed back on its catapult, a new record, and the two crew members reported to Captain Hickling on the bridge where the observer Sub Lieutenant H.G. Harris, stated that a pocket battleship had been sighted some eighty miles ahead of *Glasgow* in a position 8° 30' S, 51° 35' E at 12.32 p.m. Sub Lieutenant Harris further reported that no merchant vessel had been seen and although they had shadowed the enemy ship for more than twenty minutes, until low on fuel, they had been forced to return to the cruiser, the German ship had given no indication that it had sighted the plane. Captain Hickling dismissed the two aircrew with orders for them to resume shadowing the enemy warship.

When the Walrus was well into its third mission *Glasgow's* captain advised his C-in-C that the cruiser was hot on the heels of the German vessel and then addressed the ship's company, over the Tannoy, as to the situation and his intentions.

Visibility in the search area decreased as the afternoon wore on and the Walrus returned at the end of the Afternoon Watch. The helmsman manoeuvred the ship to create the 'duckpond' and the Walrus flew round in a circle, before coming down to settle in small area of calmer water. Its floats touched down, sending up a silver cascade and the Walrus hopped into the air like a rabbit surprised in a furrow, bouncing once or twice but finally ending up safely in a gentle glide over the surface. The engine revved up again and the pilot guided the plane towards the protection of the port side and came to a halt directly under the deck crane of *Glasgow*.

The pilot climbed out of the cockpit and tried to catch hold of the swaying crane hook above him but the Walrus was pitching first one way then the other like a drunk, and it was no easy job. Before long he caught the hook, snapping it expertly into the Walrus's lifting ring.

Walrus being hoisted aboard HMS Glasgow after completing her mission.

The pilot signalled and the crane driver set his machinery in motion, raising the plane from the surface of the sea with ease and neatly deposited it on the catapult rails. The Shagbag was neatly back on its perch. Sub Lieutenant Harris reported that no further sighting of the German pocket battleship had been made. Often, he reported, the plane had flown blindly in rainsqualls under a cloud base of 1,100 feet and visibility had been less than three miles. Despite the efforts of the pilot and observer the search was in vain and the opportunity to engage the *Admiral Scheer* had been missed.

Meanwhile the C-in-C had established Force "V", consisting of the cruisers *Glasgow*, *Emerald*, *Capetown* and *Shropshire* and the aircraft carrier *Hermes,* and put into operation a concerted and co-ordinated plan to seek out and destroy the raider. The efforts were in vain and the German warship was able to make good her escape.

Aboard the *Admiral Scheer* wireless operators in the second W/T cabin, which had been set up in the former Midshipmen's mess to monitor foreign broadcasts, reported that the wireless signals picked up in their earphones were painful to listen to. Judged by the touch, speed and strength of signals, these were deemed to have been from a naval source, meaning that there had to be a British warship near-by. In all probability it was the wireless signals from *Glasgow,* less than 100 miles away to the north at the time, which had burst into the receivers of the German cruiser with such deafening volume.

In the twenty-four hours that followed the British cruiser, with her top speed of 32.5 knots, closed in on the German ship, whose position was now somewhere to the east.

The C-in-C South Atlantic detached the heavy cruiser *Australia* and the light cruiser *Hawkins* from convoy escort duties to join in the hunt for the enemy ship. From Mombasa the aircraft carrier *Hermes* and the cruiser *Capetown* were sent out into the Indian Ocean, while HM Ships *Canberra* and *Shropshire* were ordered to proceed north from their more southerly positions to join the hunt to close the con-centric circles around the enemy ship.

Possibly deceived by the change in course *Glasgow* passed her quarry in the night and reported the failure to find the German to the C-in-C. Captain Hickling received a signal from Admiral Leatham after the operation: "Your Engine room department and flying per-sonnel have done very well. Stop. Just not enough luck". Captain Hickling responded "Scheer bad luck."

Recapture of Berbera – British Somaliland

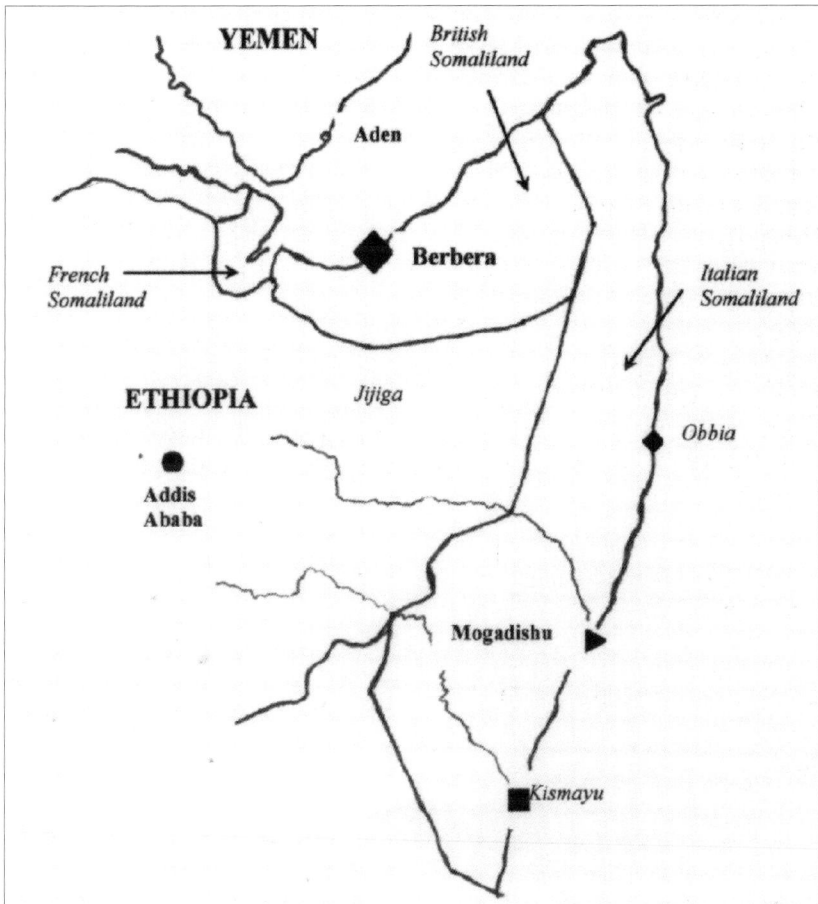

In August the previous year, 1940, the Italian forces had launched a serious offensive against British Somaliland, the coastal strip on the African shore of the Gulf of Aden. The resident British Garrison was based at Berbera the seaport capital, and consisted of four battalions of Indian and African troops, against which the Italians pitted twenty six battalions of troops equipped with artillery and tanks. The Italian advance was delayed for four days by the Garrison, assisted by the Somaliland Camel Corps, inflicting over 2,000 enemy casualties at a cost to itself of approximately 200. This action enabled the British force to be evacuated by sea, prior to redeployment in Kenya.

In February 1941 allied forces, under the command of Lieutenant General Sir Alan Cunningham, advanced from Kenya into Italian Somaliland, first capturing the port of Kismayu before reaching the capital Mogadishu a week later. Having taken the capital Cunningham's forces then turned inland where, after a four hundred-mile advance, they came close to the British Somaliland border at Jijiga.

A plan was formulated, its principal objective being to recapture Berbera, before establishing a bridgehead and an Army supply base for more than 15,000 troops. To achieve this objective a 3,000 strong military strike force, with equipment and transport, was embarked into eight of His Majesty's Ships, supplemented with tugs and lighters and one Motor Transport Vessel at Aden. From the Yemen port they were then to be conveyed to the coast of British Somaliland and landed at Berbera on open beaches, inside the reefs, which lay to the east and west of the port.

Several potential difficulties were envisaged; these included those of locating the town of Berbera and the required breaks in the reefs in poor visibility, the possibility of tows breaking to cause havoc for the strike force during the approach, and the uncertainty of finding suitable landing facilities ashore for motor transport. In spite of these the project was considered to be practicable.

The expedition consisted of two parts with HMS *Kandahar*, with a Senior Officer aboard, and HM Ships *Chantala, Chakdina, Netravati, Parvati* and the S.S. *Beaconsfield* and *Tuna* together with tugs and lighters forming the first part. Part two was made up of HMS *Glasgow*, with Senior Officer Force (D) aboard, and HM Ships *Caledon* and *Kingston* with *ML 109*. *Kandahar*, accompanied by the other ships, in-group one, all carrying troops, departed from Aden, at night, on 14th March 1941. The group was soon in trouble with tows breaking and propellers being fouled, all within ten miles off Aden. At this juncture the *Beaconsfield* and the *Tuna*, assisted by the *Shoreham*, were delegated to take command of the tugs and lighters. This released HM Ships in the group to proceed and reach their rendezvous position ten miles north off the Berbera light as planned.

The second part of the expedition left Aden a day later, overhauling the *Kandahar* with its troop convoy just before midnight, to reach the rendezvous as intended at 1.00 am on 16th March. The *Shoreham*, with the transport convoy had been set by the tide seven miles to westward and had been unseen during the passage.

Glasgow with Officer Commanding troops, Colonel Pollock, aboard, in company with the troop convoy in HM ships *Caledon, Kingston, Kandahar, Chantala, Chakdina, Netravati, Parvati* and *ML109* were set to land the invasion force, principally Punjabis, at the main beach two miles west of the port of Berbera. The landings to be accomplished under cover of the *Glasgow's* bombardment. Kingston Force (R) had on board a commando unit of 200 Somalis under the command of Major Musgrove. These were to land on a subsidiary beach to the east of Berbera under cover of the *Kandahar's* bombardment.

The transport convoy, consisting of the *Shoreham, Tuna* and *Beaconsfield*, each with a tug and two lighters in tow, were lagging behind halfway across the Gulf of Aden at the time the troop convoy rendezvoused. Immediately after reaching the rendezvous *Glasgow, Kandahar, Kingston* and the *ML 109* increased speed from twelve to twenty knots making for Berbera light. Their task, to locate the breaks in the coral reef on the approaches to the invasion beaches. The *Caledon, Chantala, Chakdina, Netravati,* and *Parvati* were instructed to arrive at 2.30 am off the west beach. As the ships approached the shoreline the lights of the traffic using the Hargeisha to Berbera road were plainly visible.

In the early hours of the morning, at 2.00 am on 16th March, *Glasgow, Kandahar* and *Kingston* sighted the Berbera light three miles to the south. The *Kandahar* and the *Kingston* turned and proceeded towards the beach on the eastern side of the town, leaving *Glasgow* to launch, after stopping, its motor boat and skiff. Caution was the watchword, because the one hundred fathom line was very close to the reef, as the motor boat and skiff under the command of Commander Vernon went ahead to locate the gap in the reef off the west beach. Finding the gap proved to be more difficult than at first thought and, because of these difficulties, the landing of the first tows was delayed by over an hour. The *Kandahar* and *Kingston* found their gaps however, off the eastern beach at exactly 3.00 am The enforced delay caused concern for *Glasgow's* Captain and Colonel Pollock, neither of whom was looking forward to effecting a daylight landing.

Just before the landing, timed to take place on the eastern beach, a Somali fisherman came alongside the *Glasgow* in a canoe. He reported that Italians were still in the town and in the vicinity of the lighthouse but that others had left in lorries during the night. The fisherman was then sent to assist Commander Vernon find the gaps in the reef. These were found just before four in the morning and the Somali fisherman was suitably rewarded.

At 4.13 am the signal "Land. Follow *Glasgow's* boats" was made and four minutes later the cruiser commenced the bombardment of the main beach, to the west of the town, with its four-inch armament and pom-poms. The bombardment employed the identical strategy used against an E-boat attack. Fifty percent of the shells were set to explode on impact with the others set to detonate fifty feet above the target. This bombardment was intense, effective and accurate, lasting barely three minutes. Seven minutes after *Glasgow* made her "Land " signal *Kingston* received the order to invade and *Kandahar* put down a sustained effective bombardment, which lasted for ten minutes.

The tows then proceeded in towards the beaches, making success signals from the west beach at 4.48 am and the east beach at 5. 26 am. While the allied troops were being disembarked the Italians retaliated by firing shells, which fell amongst the tows and ships lying offshore, from about half a dozen guns. The flashes from the Italian guns were spotted and plotted by *Glasgow's* Gunnery Officer and the cruiser put down a concerted bombardment using her six- inch, four-inch and pom-pom armament, effectively silencing the enemy's retaliation. HMS *Glasgow* then concentrated her firepower, directing it onto the trenches in the vicinity of the lighthouse and to the west of the airfield. HMS *Kandahar*, meanwhile, directed her guns at the trenches to the east of the native quarter. The firepower of both *Glasgow* and *Kandahar* proved to be extremely effective and accurate, enabling the invasion troops to be landed, before daybreak, to advance on Berbera. The town was re-captured at about half past nine in the morning. When enemy aircraft were heard a blind barrage was put up and further air movement ceased.

Following the recapture of Berbera the RAF provided fighter protection over the town and reconnaissance of the road approaches to the port and the surrounding countryside. This provided confirmation that they were deserted, removing the likelihood of a counter attack. Just before ten that morning the following signal was sent to C-in-C East Indies " The British flag flies again over Berbera". This was not strictly correct because, in the course of preparation for the assault on the seaport, provision of a Union Jack had been overlooked and one was borrowed from the Somalis!

The transport convoy entered the harbour, in the wake of the town's recapture, and by early afternoon all ships, tugs and lighters had been secured and unloading commenced. A special prefabricated Motor Transport pier, devised by Commander Vernon, was put in place and a slatted track put along the sand spit enabled the vehicles to be offloaded from the *Beaconsfield* by early evening. Two days later, following the seizure of the town as a direct result of the action, which involved the co-operation of all three services, the required bridgehead was established, and the battle for Berbera was over. Berbera had been recaptured eight months, to the day, after being evacuated the previous August, with over one hundred prisoners of war being taken during the offensive and no Allied casualties being reported. Satisfied that the Allied military presence in Berbera was secure and well-provisioned HM ships withdrew. HMS *Glasgow* headed the withdrawal, departing on 21st March 1941 for Aden where it arrived three days later.

Glasgow's Captain Harold Hickling, the ship's acting Gunnery Officer Cdr. Maurice L. Vernon, Lt. Roger Blake, Leading Seaman John Emms, P/JX 145051 and Able Seaman Michael T. Crennell, P/JX 157044 were all recommended for awards.

The cruiser sailed nine days later from Aden for Mombasa to escort a convoy, whose total tonnage was in excess of 250,000 tons.

Glasgow returned to the Seychelles five days afterwards to patrol in the Indian Ocean between Mauritius and Colombo. It was during one of these patrols that Boy Seaman Cheverton tragically died during the Middle Watch on 18th June, and in keeping with naval tradition he was buried at sea during the forenoon that day.

On 29th June *Glasgow* entered harbour in Singapore where more repair work arising from the torpedo attack in Suda Bay was carried out. From mid-September that year until early December HMS *Glasgow* patrolled the Indian Ocean, Arabian Sea and Bay of Bengal, providing escort for troop convoys, docking as and when necessary in Trincomalee, Bombay, Madras and Colombo.

Early in December, on 3rd, Albert Smith, Shipwright 1st Class, recorded in his diary that *Glasgow* was making a name for herself as the result of her efforts to entertain crews of the ships she escorted. "After tea each evening the cruiser would take up station alongside a ship in convoy and broadcast, via loudspeakers, music played by the band. Each broadcast lasted an hour and these were particularly appreciated both by the troops that were being transported and those on the *Glasgow*. This entertainment gave birth to facetious names, such as "Hickling's Circus" "Better and Brighter convoys by Harold Hickling" "Band Wagon" etc. as we steamed close by to rousing cheers. It was great to hear a spontaneous 'Oi' echo over the waves at the end of our 'Lambeth Walk'. The efforts of the lads to signal, either with arms or flags, their appreciation is quite amusing and we get as much a kick out of this "Hickling Circus" or "Better and Brighter Convoys", as the troops do."

Troops cheer HMS Glasgow as she passes troopship　　　(IWM)

This was the month when 'buzzes' about Japan were rife, and *Glasgow* was ordered to leave Trincomalee quickly and head for Colombo.

On 8th December 1941 War was declared against Japan.

A Tragic Accident –
The Sinking of HMI Ship "Prabhavati"

During the early evening, at 5.00 pm, on 6th December 1941 the tug HMIS *Prabhavati* departed from the port of Cochin, in southwest India, bound for Basra in Iraq, via Karachi, with two lighters the *Hingoli* and the *Hetampur* in tow. Three quarters of an hour later that same day, HMS *Glasgow* sailed from Colombo, in Ceylon (Sri Lanka) after receiving the latest intelligence reports for the area and embarking an interpreter. Captain Hickling had orders to search the Laccadive Islands, assisted by HMIS *Lawrence*, where according to intelligence reports a Japanese submarine and/or a parent ship might be operating.

Another submarine was suspected of being present off the port of Marmagoa, in Goa, where three German and one Italian merchant ships lay. The activities of these ships had aroused suspicion and *Glasgow* received further orders to patrol the area and intercept any ship attempting to escape.

In the afternoon of the following day Kalpeni, the first island to be visited in the Laccadive Islands, was approached and a landing party, including the interpreter, was put ashore. Here the group was received in a friendly manner and the local Headman declared that neither he nor any of the fishermen had noted anything untoward. In possession of this information the landing party re-embarked on to the cruiser and she proceeded, that evening, towards the island of Kavaratti, another island in the Laccadive group.

On 8th December 1941 war was declared against Japan and a signal received from the East Indies Station, in the early hours of that day, required *Glasgow* to commence hostilities against the new enemy. Further signals, received three hours later, provided information that submarines, other than those already reported, might be

101

operating in the Indian Ocean. The original orders issued before the ship left Colombo were amended. These required *Glasgow* to undertake a sea and air search of the Laccadive Islands during daylight before proceeding to carry out reconnaissance of Marmagoa harbour at dawn the next day. By 6.30 pm that day HMS *Glasgow* had completed these tasks and, zigzagging at 15 knots, proceeded northwards through the calm waters of the Indian Ocean.

HMIS *Dipavati* patrolling off Goa on the West Coast of India, reported the presence of a submarine 9.5 miles west off Aguada Point. Further signals were received aboard *Glasgow* confirming that the Indian warship had made anti-submarine contacts and that she had also sighted a submarine.

Things were not going well for the British captain, Lieutenant Stafford, of the Indian naval tug HMIS *Prabhavati*, which was towing two lighters when, in the early afternoon of that same day, a link in the chain bridle at the tug's stern parted. This released two twelve-inch coir hawsers, being used in the tow, into the sea. *Prabhavati* stopped and was turned to enable the hawsers to be recovered. The ship's Executive Officer supervised the work on the lighters, while the tug's captain gave orders that he be advised of anything sighted. The work was difficult and arduous and it was not until 11.55 pm that the operation was completed.

In the meantime HMS *Glasgow* was proceeding northwards to investigate the *Dipavati's* submarine report, her captain unaware that the tug was in his operational area in spite of receiving regular intelligence updates. At 11.40 pm at a distance of approximately 10 miles, a white light was sighted off the British cruiser's port bow. In good visibility, on a calm moonlit sea the cruiser closed to investigate, increasing speed as she did so to 20 knots. *Glasgow's* Captain issued orders to establish identification of the vessel by signal lamp. No acknowledgement was received and, as *Glasgow* approached, the configuration of the lights changed, appearing low down towards the water line. Being suspicious of the unusual appearance of the lights Captain Hickling ordered the signalling to cease and the ship was manoeuvred into a position which afforded a moonlit view of the "target." Although not silhouetted by the moon, the object ahead presented itself as a submarine on the surface, with its "conning tower" amidships and low hull forwards and aft easily discernible. *Glasgow's* captain, aware that lighters had been towed to the Persian Gulf in the recent past, ordered that all intelligence reports and received signals be scrutinised. No information relevant to the scenario that presented itself was available. The officers on the cruiser's bridge considered the possibility of coastal tows but this was ruled out having regard to the fact that the warship was so far out to sea. HMS *Glasgow* went to First Degree of Readiness and just before midnight the vessel ahead was seen at a range of 7,000 yards silhouetted against the moonlit background, presenting itself to the Officers on the cruisers bridge as a large ocean going submarine.

Unaware of the approaching danger preparations were being made on board *Prabhavati* to get the tug and her lighters underway.

Captain Hickling still undecided about the "target", altered course to ensure that the "submarine" was not in a direct line with the moon and as he did so moving lights on the upper deck indicated that repair work might be underway. Captain Hickling gave the order "Searchlight ready." "Searchlight ready Sir." came back the answer. The second order was given "Guns ready to open fire as soon as the searchlight lights up the target ." "Very good, Sir." came the response and, on the stroke of midnight, a searchlight was switched on.

A powerful beam of white light shot out into the darkness, like an accusing finger, and then focussed to illuminate the "target", still showing dark against the moonlight at a range of 6,000 yards. Still a doubt remained in the Captain's mind and, after much deliberation, he took the unusual step of seeking the views of his senior fellow officers on the bridge who confirmed that they too were of the opinion that the illuminated vessel was a large ocean going submarine. The silhouette of the "submarine" as seen by officers on the bridge of the *Glasgow* was formed by the two lighters *Hingoli* and *Hetampur* in line astern behind the tug *Prabhavati* alongside bridging the gap between them.

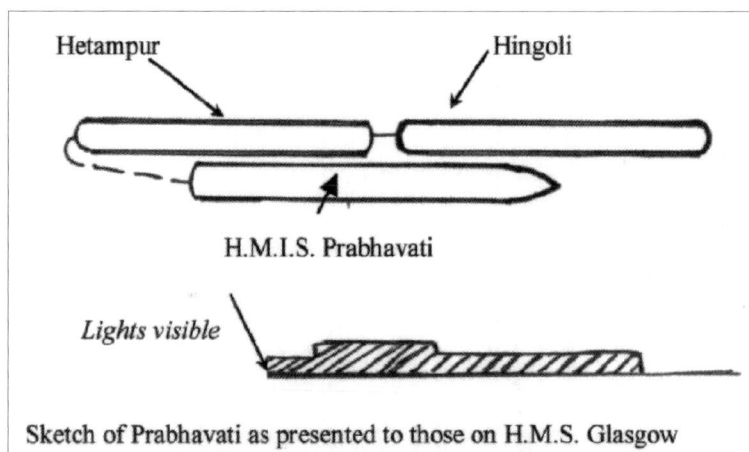

Sketch of Prabhavati as presented to those on H.M.S. Glasgow

It was the tug's upperworks, which simulated a "submarine's conning tower" with the lighters forming the hull before and aft of the "tower".

Deck lights on the "enemy vessel" were extinguished as soon as the beam of the searchlight lit up the "target" and a "crash dive" was anticipated by *Glasgow's* skipper, who issued the order "Open Fire." and a total of eight salvoes were fired.

Aboard *Prabhavati* her Commanding Officer, Lieutenant D.M. Stafford, RINR (Royal Indian Naval Reserve) heard an explosion rend the air forward on the tug as the first shell from the cruiser scored a hit. He immediately issued the order "Action Stations" and rushed forward to the bridge. A second shell exploded amidships and, on gaining the bridge, Lieutenant Stafford found the Signalman dead among the bizarre metal and wood sculptures that had been created as the port wing had been blown away. There was no sign of Lieutenant G. Jackson, or the gun's crew; just a gaping hole in the deck from which yellow acrid smoke rose into the moonlit sky. At that range it was hardly possible to miss, and the guns of *Glasgow* now hurled shell after shell into the target. A few seconds later the explosion of direct hits could be seen. Debris began to fly through the air, steel plates were peeled back, and dark yawning holes appeared like freshly dug graves as the tug's flank was ripped open. Other shells continued to fall in various places on the vessel and the lighters alongside, sending shards of hot metal scything through the air to kill or maim those unfortunate to be in their path.

Ten minutes after the "attack" the tug was still afloat and on an even keel, with clouds of steam issuing from the engine room hatches and all companionways. Five minutes later the tug heeled over on to its port side. In doing so it thwarted the crew's efforts to launch the tug's starboard boat and effect the rescue of those who were either on the *Hetampur* or in the water trying to clamber on to it. Further forward the *Hingoli* had been badly damaged by gunfire from the British warship before the order "Cease Fire" was given. *Prabhavati's* skipper ran aft and ordered the lighter *Hetampur* to be hove to alongside the sinking tug to permit the transfer of injured Indian seamen from it. Her Commanding Officer, now aboard the lighter and aware of the impending danger, ordered that it be slipped from the towing vessel. Moments after the vessels had parted the *Prabhavati* sank beneath the glassy surface of the ocean with survivors scrambling up from the water, on to the lighter, as it did so.

Lieutenant Stafford was immediately faced with yet another problem as the other lighter *Hingoli* began to sink by the head and he ordered the towing chain be released to avoid being dragged down to the seabed by it.

Glasgow closed to pick up survivors, and as it approached those on the cruiser's bridge saw that the stricken vessel was in fact the tug HMIS *Prabhavati,* wearing a white ensign, alongside a lighter and not a "Japanese submarine." Boats were immediately lowered from the cruiser, which proceeded to pick up survivors from the water. By 2.00 am on 9th December all thirty nine survivors of the tragedy had been rescued and put aboard the *Glasgow.* Out of the Tug's complement of fifty-nine twenty-one men died, one rating dying after being rescued. The lighter *Hetampur,* which was thought to have remained seaworthy at the time of the time of the incident, sank six hours later, at 8.00 am.

Albert Smith, Shipwright 1st Class, recalled after the incident "Identification at sea, at night, is very difficult and this undoubtedly resulted in the appalling tragedy of the sinking of the *Prabhavati.* No one was more sorry than *Glasgow's* captain and crew. To think how jubilant we could have been had our marksmanship accounted for a sub."

On *Glasgow's* return to Bombay a fleet of ambulances awaited to deal with the injured.

The Board of Inquiry held after the accident took into account that:

a) HMS *Glasgow* had been looking for an enemy submarine reported in the search area several days earlier, further supported by a report from HMIS *Dipavati,* six hours earlier that night 8th December, that one was active within seventy miles of the position where the incident occurred.

b) Intelligence reports and signals received by the *Glasgow* had failed to indicate the possible presence of the *Prabhavati* in the search area. Equally *Prabhavati* had not been aware of the presence of the *Glasgow* in or near the position where she had encountered the tow problems.

c) The range at which the *Prabhavati* was illuminated by searchlight did not permit positive recognition.

d) No one on the *Prabhavati* had spotted the *Glasgow's* approach, thereby failing to maintain a proper watch.

Glasgow's Captain was exonerated of blame for the action taken.

The cruiser set course and speed for Colombo and at 8.00 a.m. on Thursday 11th December she sighted a merchant ship ahead of her.

Two and half-hours later *Glasgow*, travelling at a modest 20 knots, was still only able to see a smudge on the horizon belching out black smoke. The warship's Walrus was launched to investigate the merchantman's need for such hurry. When the pilot returned he reported that the captain of the fleeing vessel, which was British, had been scared into thinking that the *Glasgow* had been a commerce raider. On arrival in Colombo the news of the loss of HM Ships *Repulse* and *Prince of Wales* added to the gloom present in the ship.

Glasgow Returns Home

HMS Glasgow in "War Colours" 1942

Between January and March 1942 HMS *Glasgow* was engaged in convoy escort duties between Colombo and Mombasa and it was at this time that Captain Hickling was granted sick leave, delegating command of the cruiser to his Executive Officer, Commander J.W. Cuthbert, who had been promoted to Captain. Thus, for a short period of time HMS *Glasgow* had two Captains. Captain Hickling had become a sick man, not helped by the fact that he had lost his son, a Midshipman, in the service, nor by the incident involving the loss of the *Prabhavati* the previous year. Although he returned to the ship he was unable to continue as her Commanding Officer, and just before he left the ship to return to hospital Captains Hickling and Cuthbert were joined by a past Captain, now promoted to Rear-Admiral, P. F. Pegram, and a photograph was taken to record the occasion.

Captain Hickling Rear-Admiral Pegram Captain Cuthbert   *(RNM)*

On 30th March the 5,853 ton vessel HMT *Muncaster Castle*, carrying 3,000 tons of Government stores, a crew of 71, 14 gunners and 265 passengers was en route from Freetown via Table Bay, Capetown, to Colombo. South of Liberia she was torpedoed, and 4 crew members, 1 gunner and 19 passengers died, one of whom was Royal Marine A. Johnson who was making passage to meet up with *Glasgow* in Colombo.

When G*lasgow*'s tour of duty ended she made her way, under the command of the newly promoted Captain J.W. Cuthbert, via Durban, Simon' s Town, and Freetown, for a major refit in New York, arriving there on 6th May 1942.

According to Shipwright A. Smith HMS *Glasgow* had sailed 99,770 miles since leaving England, having completed 89,884 with only two screws, and crossed the Equator no fewer than 34 times. Shortly after her arrival in Brooklyn Navy Yard, and while anchored there, the USS *Lansdowne* collided abreast *Glasgow*'s No 140 bulkhead but the cruiser sustained no damage.

On 22nd May Captain Cuthbert, left the ship to take up another command, but before doing so addressed the ship's company. His farewell speech surprisingly short, comprised three words only: "Goodbye you buggers." The crew responded in the traditional manner giving three cheers. A crew member recorded that 'It was the best and most sincere accorded any captain'. Commander G. Otway-Ruthven, referred to as "Utterly Ruthless" by those in the Gunroom, assumed command. (It was a title not deserved, for a man who was good at his job and promoted to Captain later in his career)

On 4th July a detachment of sailors from HM Ships *Glasgow* and *Penelope*, led by the Royal Marine Band, took part in the American celebrations. Marching along, all in step and with heads held high, down Fifth Avenue with bayonets fixed on a very hot day they created quite an impression with the local population.

In Brooklyn the crew received "royal" treatment ashore and were feted wherever they went, often not being required to spend money. A number of *Glasgow's* crew stocked up with thick American china and cutlery, (which included knives which had handles longer than the blade and forks with cutting edges). It was amazing how many went down the Gash Chute to the ditty "Tinkle, tinkle little spoon. Knife and fork will follow soon." American cigarettes were also hoarded and sold to the dockyard maties, when the ship returned to the UK, and the money raised was used to buy British ones.

While undergoing her refit *Glasgow* was equipped with a full set of aircraft warning (type 281), surface warning (type 273) and gunnery radars (type 282, 284, 285). This not only took up quite a lot of space but also required that additional radar operating personnel be accommodated in the already overcrowded ship. Initially, there was a degree of resentment against the radar contingent but later this evaporated when the routine dusk and dawn "Action Stations" were abandoned, because the 273 set was able to detect approaching enemy aircraft eighty miles away.

On 5th August HMS *Glasgow's* new Commanding Officer, Captain Edward M. Evans-Lombe, (later to become a Vice-Admiral) assumed command and addressed a depleted crew assembled on the Quarterdeck.

The major refit was completed on 14th August 1942 after which *Glasgow* went to Norfolk, Virginia, for seagoing trials to test the newly fitted propellers and undergo gunnery exercises. Here the gunnery officer was surprised when the radar team was able to offer him fall of shot information in addition to target ranges. He was even more surprised when told that the team could also watch the shells on their outward journey, albeit only for a few thousand yards.

Shipping losses along the U.S. coast, due to U-boat attacks, had caused food shortages and the cruiser's "Walruses" were off-loaded to enable the ship's hangers to be used to store food destined for Bermuda. The ship was made ready and she left the Norfolk Navy dockyard, on 28th August, bound for Bermuda to deliver much needed food supplies, including ten tons of potatoes in the starboard hanger, before returning to Pitch House Jetty, Portsmouth on 3rd September.

During the week prior to 16th October the crew worked hard to load stores and re-ammunition the ship before she sailed for Scapa Flow, to join the 10th Cruiser Squadron. The crew was kept at "Action Stations" during daylight hours, but was allowed to stand down reduced to keep normal watches at night. The passage was cold and miserable and Hugo Huntington-Whiteley, a Midshipman, recalls how cold he was at his station at the oerliken gun on top of "B" turret. He was served a cup of thick pea soup for lunch on the first day out which scalded his tongue at the first taste but was stone cold by the time he had reached the bottom of the mug!

Most of the ship's company were new to the ship and the remainder of the year was spent completing an intensive work programme designed to make them part and parcel of a homogenous crew. As many of them had never felt a ship's deck beneath their feet before, this was no easy task. Training went on day after day and often into the night as well. Bombardment, anti-aircraft and torpedo firing practice took place under circumstances which were often as realistic as possible. Simulated control and other breakdowns, direct hits, etc. were incorporated to train the crew to meet the wartime emergencies likely to be encountered.

In harbour the midshipmen kept watch on the quarterdeck during daylight hours and took turns, on a rota basis, taking charge of the ship's boats. These were attached to a boom which led out from the starboard side of the ship, from which the duty midshipmen descended by rope ladder to the water line, taking the same route on return if the boat was not hoisted on board. Any return journey from ship to shore at Scapa took about three hours depending on the weather conditions that prevailed at the time, and woe betide the young man who made a mess of coming alongside and incurring the Commander's wrath!

On 5th December HMS *Glasgow* returned to the Clyde to enter John Brown's Shipyard, Dalmuit where steam pipes were fitted around all the turrets, the director towers and through the mess decks. The crew deduced they were not going to the Med!

Tram journeys into the city of Glasgow, at that time, cost one penny regardless of the distance travelled. After a run ashore, Hugo Huntington-Whiteley returned from the city centre (and the line ran for 15 miles) but could not remember the name of the shipyard. The masts of the ship suddenly and unexpectedly came into sight and an appearance before the Commander was averted when he was able to pull the communication cord, get off the tram and be back to the ship in time.

On Christmas Eve the ship sailed from the Clyde to arrive in Loch Ewe on the north-west coast of Scotland, en route to Scapa Flow on Christmas Day.

Loch Ewe, which is not unlike a deep fjord is, in winter, one of the bleakest parts of the British Isles even though the Island of Lewis, in the Outer Hebrides, affords it some shelter from the worst weather of the North Atlantic. The snow-covered hills are frequently purged by a biting bitter wind; while on the loch itself the cold black water is whipped up to form angry white horses, which scurry along the surface. Beneath a leaden cover of low laying stratus clouds scraps of scud scamper past, at mast height, to herald a coming storm or act as reminders of one past.

When the Captain visited the mess decks, which were decorated with a few inflated condoms, to wish the crew a Happy Christmas he got little response to his greeting!

It is customary in the Royal Navy for the youngest person on board ship to be invited to ring in the New Year and, on New Year's Eve 1942, this honour fell to David Dixon. Accompanied by the Chief Buffer, who kept count, David rang the ship's bell sixteen times; eight times for the old year and eight for the new.

Russia – Journey to Hell

Upon the invasion by Germany of the USSR, a nation that had, at best, been a dubious neutral became one of the Allies, however dissimilar the political views of Britain and the USSR might have been. The situation is best summed up by a remark attributed to Winston Churchill that "If Hitler invaded Hell, I would at least make a favourable reference to the Devil."

Supplies to Russia came initially solely from British sources, with a greatly increasing quantity from America from January 1942 onwards. Cargo inward was entirely war material, or directly connected with the war effort, transported in convoys of ships, entering Russia via the North Russian ports of Archangel and Murmansk. The cargoes outbound consisted of explosives, motor vehicles, tanks and aircraft, in addition to general cargo and fuel oil.

Returning from Russia the ships were often in ballast but, where circumstances permitted, the Russians loaded cargo to obtain desperately needed currency. Such cargo included large quantities of sawn timber, some ores, cotton, and tobacco. Sometimes unusual items appeared on a ship's manifest, including badger hair or caviar.

At all times the German threat, based in northern Norway, remained to these convoys either from the sea or from the air and the constant presence, in British waters, of warships was required at all times. Furthermore, ships from the Home Fleet had to be constantly available in support of the Russian convoys lest a sortie be made.

The German surface ships, including the battlecruiser *Scharnhorst*, the *Admiral Scheer* and the cruisers *Admiral Hipper* and *Prinz Eugen* enjoyed the advantage that they could sortie at will, whereas the escorts had to be on the alert all the time. These surface ships were supported by U-boats, which were able to exploit the deplorable conditions which existed most of the time to prevent effective Asdic surveillance from being maintained, while the air threat to the convoys was posed by German bombers and dive bombers.

Early in 1943 on 17th January 1943 Convoy JW52, consisting of 15 ships formed up in Loch Ewe. By mid-afternoon the winter's day had turned to night, when the convoy cleared the entrance to the loch and headed, in company with their escorts the destroyers *Blankney, Ledbury, Middleton, Bretomart, Lotus, Starwort, St. Elstan and Northern Pride,* into the North Minch at a speed of 7 fi knots on its way to Murmansk.

Leaving the sight of land behind their crews realised this would be no pleasure trip. As the ships made passage the wind strength increased as the barometric pressure fell and the temperature rapidly dropped below freezing aboard *Glasgow,* as she went north. The path of these convoys lay along the so-called northern route by Greenland, Iceland, and Spitzbergen and around the cape of Murmansk, the Russian port on the Murman coast of Lapland. The number of freighters in a convoy might be anything from a dozen to thirty, sometimes even more, and the war materials that they carried were of incalculable value.

The Royal Navy supplied the covering forces for a 250-mile gap between Iceland and the Faroes. These are inhospitable waters which lie within six degrees of the Arctic Circle, in the direct path of the worst of the Atlantic Depressions. Even in summer, short though it is, it is a cold and dreary place often blanketed in fog. In winter it is a place of the damned, a sea to match the Wagnerian legend where the wind often blows at a steady force ten, moaning and whining, raising the green sea into angry mountains. Anyone on deck in these conditions is lashed with rain, sleet and snow, with spray freezing in the rigging.

In the convoy itself were usually destroyers, frigates, corvettes and patrol ships as a U-boat screen, all of them small ships; in addition a line of light cruisers ran parallel to the convoy on its exposed flank, i.e. to the southward of the route, from which direction any possible German attack could be expected to come.

The cruisers served as a covering force against surface attack and they remained detached from the convoy itself ready to intervene in an emergency.

Cruisers: HM Ships *Kent, Glasgow* and *Bermuda* left Scapa on 13th January heading first for Seidesfjord before going on to Akureyri on the north coast. From here they were to proceed to reach longitude

30° E where they were due to pick up convoy RA 52, 24 hours after it had sailed and provide cover as far as longitude 5° E, before returning to the Icelandic port where British forces were not very popular and the Icelandic people only spoke to the crews when purchases were made. Aboard *Glasgow* Captain Evans-Lombe informed his officers "the principal danger-zone lies to the south of Bear Island and our intention is to advance at a speed of fifteen knots to meet up with the convoy in the vicinity of Bear Island."

Meanwhile, HMS *Onslaught* made her own way to Seidesfjord, while HM Ships *Musketeer, Matchless, Offa, Beagle, Bulldog* and *Piorun* were to rendezvous in Iceland the day following the departure of convoy JW52 from Loch Ewe. Here they were to meet up with a returning convoy RA52 which was due to leave Kola Inlet on 29th January.

Cruisers from 10th Cruiser Squadron: HM Ships *Sheffield, Berwick* and *Jamaica* had also sailed from Scapa Flow, on 18th January, for Seidesfjord to fuel before providing cover for JW52 from longitude 10° E into Kola Inlet. The convoy enjoyed particularly good weather and made a fast passage, and apart from one merchantman that had to be sent back the convoy safely reached Russia on 27th January 1943.

Enemy attacks had been on a small scale, with the escorts driving off the U-boats by energetic counter-action based largely on direction finding wireless reception. The cruiser covering force of HM Ships *Kent, Glasgow* and *Bermuda* had gone right through the convoy, while Admiral Fraser (Second-in-Command, Home Fleet) in HMS *Anson* had provided distant cover from a position south-west of Bear Island. The escorts, including HM Ships *Blankney, Ledbury* and *Middleton*, only had two days rest before they were ready to relieve the destroyers escorting the homeward-bound convoy RA52.

While German naval forces were being charged with the task of cutting the British lifeline to and from Russia, the Home Fleet was being called upon to protect and defend the convoys which formed this lifeline. The vital importance of the convoy escorts can best be appreciated in relation to the enormous quantities of war material — the output of mines and factories all over the world-which each convoy carried. The number of freighters sailing in an Arctic convoy might be anything from twenty–five to thirty or more, averaging from 6,000 to 8,000 b.r.t, and the war material that they carried, mainly armour and heavy weapons including ammunition, amounted to an average of half a million gross register tons. One gross register ton (b.r.t) is a cubic measure corresponding to 40 cubic feet, and the interior space of a ship is expressed in b.r.t. Roughly a third of the available space was taken up by the ship's machinery (boilers, engines, propeller shafts and tiller gear), and the remaining two-thirds represented the net tonnage available for cargo. Therefore, a single freighter of 6,000 b.r.t carried, apart from lighter war materials such as ammunition, guns and other weapons, 18 twin-engine bombers (partly dismantled), 155 14-ton tanks and 51 28-30 ton tanks. Hence one Arctic convoy of twenty freighters carried in terms of aircraft and armour alone: 360 twin-engine bombers, 3,100 14-ton tanks and 1,020 28-30 ton tanks.

The Arctic convoys sailed round the most northerly point of Norway to Murmansk. The farther north they kept the safer they were from attack, but their voyage took proportionately longer and this was a time when hours could be decisive. Furthermore, the sea to the north became increasingly rougher. The wind, which blew in directly from the Pole, churned up mountainous seas, while visibility was obliterated in flurries of snow. The dark sky precluded light and it was literally impossible to see one's own hand. Occasionally, the Northern Lights would cast an unsteady erratic green-yellow or red-violet gleam, while at noon, the day would turn a pale grey for about two hours although the sun never rose above the horizon. The cold was almost unbearable and watch-keepers on warships and freighters alike shivered in spite of sheepskin clothing and many layers of woollens. Depth charges froze fast to the decks, gun sights and breeches became encrusted with ice, and the lubricants on the munition-hoists froze hard. A warship which failed to take special precautions to safeguard the lives of her crew and keep her armament free of ice could not hope to survive an action in these waters.

Aboard *Glasgow* Captain Evans-Lombe, who had been studying a wireless weather report, handed the form to his Navigating Officer "The sou'wester is freshening and it looks as if we're going to have a rough sea tomorrow. What do you think, Pilot?" The Navigating Officer nodded " Yes, Sir. I reckon it'll blow like this for days. There'll be snow squalls too. Seems as if we're in for some genuine Arctic weather. No place for a married man, Sir". He pulled the hood of his duffel coat over his head and thrust his hands deep into the pockets.

Glasgow gathered speed and with a foaming bow wave steamed north, where the daylight hours are short and the silhouette of her high bridge structures, her two funnels and the two triple turrets fore and aft were only faintly discernible in the gloom. The sea broke in over her bows, hissed along the tops of the turrets and sent lashings of spray up to the bridge. The wind blew hard from the north and the slender ship running before the sea began to roll heavily. Snow squalls impeded visibility, the sky was as dark as the sea, and the escorting destroyers were hardly discernible. From time to time a breaker reared up before the cruiser, stood for seconds in a column of pale foam, then collapsed over the bows and ebbed away before the breakwater in gurgling eddies. Smaller breakers churned up to port and starboard by the cruiser's bows, disintegrated in white pennants. The night was very cold. Cold too were the lashes of salty spray which flung themselves across the armour of the forward turrets and whipped up to the bridge. The dense snow and quickly-forming ice obscured the lenses of the range finders and directors rendering them practically useless and the vigilance of the bridge, the look-outs on deck, and the searchlight platforms were therefore of vital importance. From the bridge little could be seen through the driving snow. When the snow flurries abated for a while as though gathering strength for their next onslaught, huge dark waves loomed in sight rolling alongside, blue-black, white crested, thundering down the cruiser's sides. The breakers, coming at long intervals rushed across the fo'c'sle with a deafening roar, shrouded the bows in a veil of swirling foam, swept across the anchor chains and, as the bow rose, drained away through the scuppers. Little could be heard above the roar of the sea and the intermittent howling of the gale. Occasionally there would be the sound of one of the watch-keepers trying to keep his feet warm by stamping his boots on the deck.

For the next six days the convoy and its escort clawed their way north-westwards, battered by a raging sea and malevolent winds of hurricane force. The convoy was now just about inside the Arctic Circle, about 160 miles east of Iceland. When the convoy approached the Polar Ice region the temperature fell remorselessly and steadily with daylight limited to barely two hours of twilight around midday. During the night the barometric pressure continued to fall steeply and a westerly gale erupted. It did not take long for a short rough sea to build up in the shallow waters. The merchant ships, deep laden and with high deck cargoes, were top heavy and as they took the waves beam on they began to roll precariously, often heeling over so far that their gunwales were going under.

Those who served on board the *Glasgow* during these convoys remember being generally overcome with what has been described as utter weariness, and being subjected to the biting cold and bouts of seasickness. The weather was bitterly cold with the wind chill driving the temperatures down much further than normal. This severe cold, combined with the spray from mountainous waves, caused ice to form on the superstructure and deck fittings, bringing fear that the ship might turn turtle due to the weight of it. Aboard *Glasgow* the flying spray froze on all exposed surfaces, the deck, guard rails, guns and rigging and soon the ice which formed was more than six inches thick. The Captain and crew were aware of the dangers of icing up and men were set to work to remove the accumulated ice weight to reduce the risk of capsize.

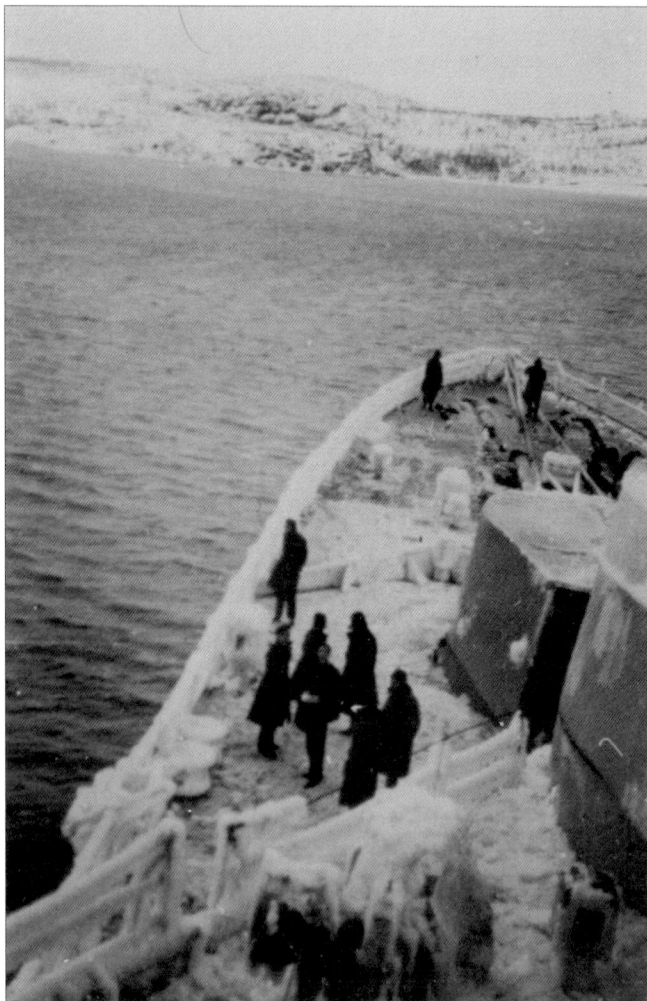

Ice on the Fo'c'sle of HMS Glasgow as she enters the Kola Inlet

The mast, rigging, guns, and guard-rails were pretty well iced up, but the ship's company chipped away at it using axes and steam hoses, weather permitting, and relieved the situation. The crew was continually employed in chipping off ice to safeguard the safety of the cruiser and during the passage the gun directors etc., had to be swung every 15 minutes to prevent icing up.

John Goodyear, who was twenty at the time, recalled that the weather was atrocious during the passage to Kola Inlet, but this was preferred because it was too rough for the U-boats to surface. Within the convoy itself were usually destroyers, frigates, corvettes and patrol ships as a U-boat screen, all of them small ships; in addition a line of heavy and light cruisers ran parallel to the convoy on its exposed flank, i.e. to the southward of the route, from which direction any possible German attack could be expected to come. These cruisers served as protection against surface attack and remained detached from the convoy itself standing by ready to intervene in an emergency.

Ron Condy, then nineteen, remembers that for most of the young crew their main concern was that of survival, in particular being aware that *Glasgow* was among a number of ships which were charged with the responsibility of protecting the convoys from attacks launched by the German battle cruisers *Scharnhorst* and *Gneisenau*. The latter two ships were operating from the Norwegian fjords at that time, and the *Glasgow's* crew always thanked their lucky stars that they failed to venture forth because, had they done so, a cruiser would have stood little chance of surviving an attack made against them.

Four days later, on 21st January, HM Ships *Bermuda, Kent* and *Glasgow* provided cruiser cover for the convoy which was located and shadowed by the enemy two days later, but U-boats making contact were driven under by the escorting cruisers and destroyers while the convoy took evasive action. The next day, during an attack by four torpedo bombers, two of the convoy were lost but the remainder finally arrived in Kola Inlet on 27th January.

Here the Inlet runs roughly north and south, with Polyarnoe on the western shore and on the opposite shore lies Vaenga, where there was an auxiliary hospital with beds for 74 patients and a Russian operational aerodrome. The town was also the northern terminus of the railroad link to Murmansk, which lay sixteen miles away by road. Here, during many months of the year, for perhaps three days at a stretch, snow and ice rendered the road impassable with gales and fog in the Inlet making it equally difficult for boat traffic. Although the convoy was headed for Murmansk, HMS *Glasgow* was too big to enter the harbour there and consequently entered into Vaenga Bay where she berthed alongside the town jetty.

In Vaenga, those members of each watch who were allowed ashore were prohibited from venturing far from the ship. Several remember passing the edge of a large forest, as they walked in an area where there was little to see apart from snow and ice, where dozens of planes could be seen concealed by the trees.

Hugo Huntington-Whiteley, Midshipman RN, recalls "It was a desolate place and the frozen ground was covered with snow as far as the eye could see, and the Russians were muffled up to the eyes in warm clothing. *Glasgow's* crew lived in balaclavas and duffel coats on deck at that latitude, and wore leather rather than rubber sea boots because it was found that rubber did not allow the feet to breathe and ice formed inside the boot. Some wore kapok suits for extra warmth. Those Russians we saw were not very communicative when they warily swapped chocolate for red star badges."

E. Young, who was a gun sweeper recalls "it took quite a long time to get to Murmansk with the convoys only able to travel at six knots. This caused *Glasgow* to roll uncomfortably from side to side, often more than 30 degrees. When off duty the guns' crews were issued with chipping hammers to rid the ship of ice, up to five inches in diameter, from the guard-rails. The deck was all iced up and we were all chipping away like woodpeckers to get off as much as we could. The flight deck was iced up with the spray continually coming over the side. Outside, the cold was so intense that crew had to put Vaseline onto their faces to prevent the skin from cracking open and you didn't venture up on deck unless it was absolutely necessary."

John Goodyear recalls "I was part of the W/T department where the watch routine was four hours on followed by four hours off, during which you got your head down wherever you could find a soft spot. Every so often between watches we would don oilskins and huddle round the funnel in an attempt to keep warm, but even then our oilskins froze solid. Conditions in our mess were pretty cramped to say the least, with hammock billets being originally provided for ten bodies. In this space twenty men crowded together each vying for a spot. My first billet was under the mess table and the second was on the table under the mess shelf, where on occasions when rough weather was encountered the milk, utensils etc., fell on me! Later on I was able to get a proper billet, but this was next to the ship's side, where when the ship rolled I was bounced against the steel plates. Those in our mess were subjected to further discomfort when anyone went to the third W/T office below, because they had to get to it via a hatch in our mess before descending a ladder, disturbing us as they went."

Harry Winward who, as an LTO, was in his early twenties recalls a mate of his who was a three badge AB, who had been recalled at the outbreak of war. "This AB, who was about forty five years of age and thought by us twenty year olds to be ancient, had his duty position on the searchlight platform.

Anyone required to be on duty in an exposed position was issued with a massive sheepskin coat with a huge collar which when turned up almost completely covered one's head. These coats seemed to weigh a ton even when dry. After four hours on watch, having been drenched with freezing spray at regular intervals, this AB would eventually appear coming down our ladder with his coat frozen on him. Two or three of us, who had come off watch at the same time, used to literally pull his coat off him while he hung onto the ladder. He was utterly unable to get out of it himself. We always got a lovely smile when he saw us waiting for him. What a genius the bloke in the Regulating Office must have been to give such a job to a seemingly white haired old man! One afternoon, during the couple of hours or so of murky twilight that was our day it was necessary for me to do some sort of maintenance on one of the pom-poms or oerlikons. I had to take the cover off a metal housing which contained some moving parts. Removing the cover exposed an oil bath contained some of the moving parts and like an idiot I dropped one of the screws from my frozen fingers into this oil. I then had to fish about for the object I had dropped in the oil, which was barely still liquid because of the intense cold.

Fred Yates on left

Fred Yates, recalls "The sight-setters and gun-layers for the "A" and "B" six-inch turrets, who were in a cabin forward of the bridge and trained to 15 degrees port and starboard, were exposed to freezing spray driving through the sighting ports when the ship was closed up for action stations." These ports were required to be open at all times but when the crew were called to "Defence Stations" a little cheating went on and they were closed down to prevent the occupants from freezing.

However, when closed up routinely at dawn and dusk for "Action Stations" the ports were left open because when the turrets were trained to its maximum all was visible to the bridge! The temperature was often so low that the mucus in your nose would freeze solid."

In an attempt to reduce the discomfort of those engaged in escort duties to and from Russia Lord Nuffield donated leather helmets, leather knee-length boots and thick waterproof coats to the crews. Unfortunately, these proved to be too cumbersome to be worn within the confines of a turret. However, the gift of some thick knitted woollen "long johns" which had been found uncomfortable to wear and thought to be unhygienic were quickly put to another good use. The long johns were quickly altered by detaching the legs from the waist, un-picking their seams and flattening them out to form sleeves, before re-sewing the garment to make up a thick warm roll neck sweater! When the crew was allowed ashore in Russia, Lord Nuffield's donated clothes came into their own because the Russians proved to be particularly inhospitable.

Food was eaten in the turrets when the crew was closed up at "Action Stations" and would often consist of peadoo, kai, and corn-dog wads. The sight-setters and gun-layers in their cabin forward of the guns used to supplement their evening meal with tins of cold baked beans and Nestle's cream, which were opened with use of a "Pussers Dirk"! However, when the crew was stood down from "Action Stations" Ron Condy recalls that the food aboard was considered to be good, with meals being cooked in a central galley and then brought down to the mess decks where the crew ate. He also remembered that there was always a supply of fresh bread available with meat and cheese also being readily available. Any food that was not considered palatable was ditched, particularly on a Sunday when at suppertime a great lump of cheese arrived down on the mess deck. This was immediately thrown out through the nearest porthole!

There were lighter moments when, at appropriate times during darkness, a message would be piped from the bridge " Northern Lights are now showing off the port/starboard side". Harry Winyard recalls that "those interested hurried into our duffel coats and went up on top to see and marvel at what must be one of the most beautiful sights in the natural world. I also remember thinking at the time I shall probably never see this sight again if I get through this war."

Although the ship was operating in atrocious weather conditions, Captain's Rounds were still conducted and the crew were required to emery paper the knives, and "bluebell" most other things including spoons, forks, mess fannies, mess kettles and spit-kids to keep them tiddly.

Harry recalls "With the peace time complement increased to nearly 900 Captain's lower deck rounds were chaotic to say the least.

There were no proper storage facilities for all the extra gear we were issued with, such as sea boots, sheepskin coats, duffel coats etc. which had to be either taken up top or stored in separate heaps on the upper deck. Fortunately this didn't happen very often. I seem to recall that for rounds to take place the ship had to be in harbour on a Saturday forenoon and on most Saturdays of course we were not."

Aboard the merchant vessels modifications were made to protect the holds against damage caused by the carriage of tanks and other tracked vehicles. To combat the severe cold extra heating was provided and the men were provided with the appropriate clothing, issued by the Ministry, to wear on watch. This consisted of — starting from the inside-two pairs of heavy woollen ribbed long johns, then a flannel shirt topped by a roll neck jersey. A sheepskin lined leather jerkin on top of which a duffel coat was worn completed the outer layers. Heavy lined mitts covered the hands, and two pairs of woollen stockings reaching to the knee protected the feet. The last things on were a pair of sea boots, which were two sizes too large to enable them to be pulled on.

One captain recalls that when his ship approached the Kola Inlet he decided to take a bearing on a headland. To do this he had to go up to the "Monkey Island" where the standard compass was placed, this was the ship's main compass and totally unprotected from the weather. To take the bearing it was necessary to remove the brass binnacle top covering the compass. He tried to do this but with the heavy mitts on found it quite impossible. He removed his mitts and foolishly grasped the two brass handles of the binnacle top to receive what he described as an 'electric shock' which caused him to immediately release his hold, thereby saving him from a serious injury to his hands. As it was he received burns which took over two weeks to heal!

After the Convoy Conference the ships made their way towards Murmansk, keeping well off the Norwegian coast to avoid the torpedo bombers that were operating from there. Many of the skippers had not previously sailed in those northern latitudes and it made a lasting impression on them. Entering the Kola Inlet was eerie; a blanket of snow covered the whole of the landscape and the ships had to push their way through ice to reach their berths. It was quiet and still and very cold. The ships had arrived safely after a hazardous voyage with their valuable cargo of much-needed tanks, vehicles and ammunition and there was a great sense of relief amongst the crews. The ships had to wait in turn to discharge their cargoes, before laying off to anchor out in the Inlet to await the assembly for the return journey to the UK. Those who made these trips were impressed by the total dedication to the war effort shown by the Russians, many of whom were women. For those on the merchant ships there were no pubs or dance halls to visit — no time off in fact, just work for at least twelve hours a day. Relations with the local inhabitants were cordial but not overwhelmingly friendly. They were, no doubt, pleased with the efforts made to assist them in the continued resolve to defeat the enemy but there was a prevailing feeling that they, the locals, were not free to say or do what they wished. There was, as might be expected in periods of hardship, a small black market which was illegal and warranted severe punishment on discovery.

Having little to barter with, apart from cigarettes, those from the merchant ships who succumbed to the temptation to make a quick profit found to their cost that the rouble was worthless outside the USSR. It could, however, be used to purchase cheap beer and vodka in a solitary building ashore which consisted of a large room in which drinks were served by a waitress, strictly on a rationed basis.

Trying to maintain station in the winter months in severe gales in ballast condition was extremely difficult and at times impossible. Many convoys became scattered, making it difficult for the escorting warships to maintain contact with their charges. Often the vessel would pitch and roll violently in the mountainous seas, the stern would rise out of the water to leave the propeller to thrash madly about and the ship making no progress at all. When daylight broke the merchantmen would find themselves quite alone. When the storms abated the escorts, if there were sufficient numbers of them, would attempt to round up the missing flock and bring them back into the fold. It was not always possible to reform into one convoy and sections would band together and proceed.

In these severe conditions there was some consolation that the enemy would be having a bad time also, keeping him well below the wave height and therefore restricting his capability.

Convoy RA52, which comprised eleven ships in four columns, conveying goods from Russia left Kola Inlet on 29th January 1943,with cruiser cover provided by HM Ships *Bermuda*, *Glasgow* and *Kent*.

Screening Diagram for RA 52 at Night

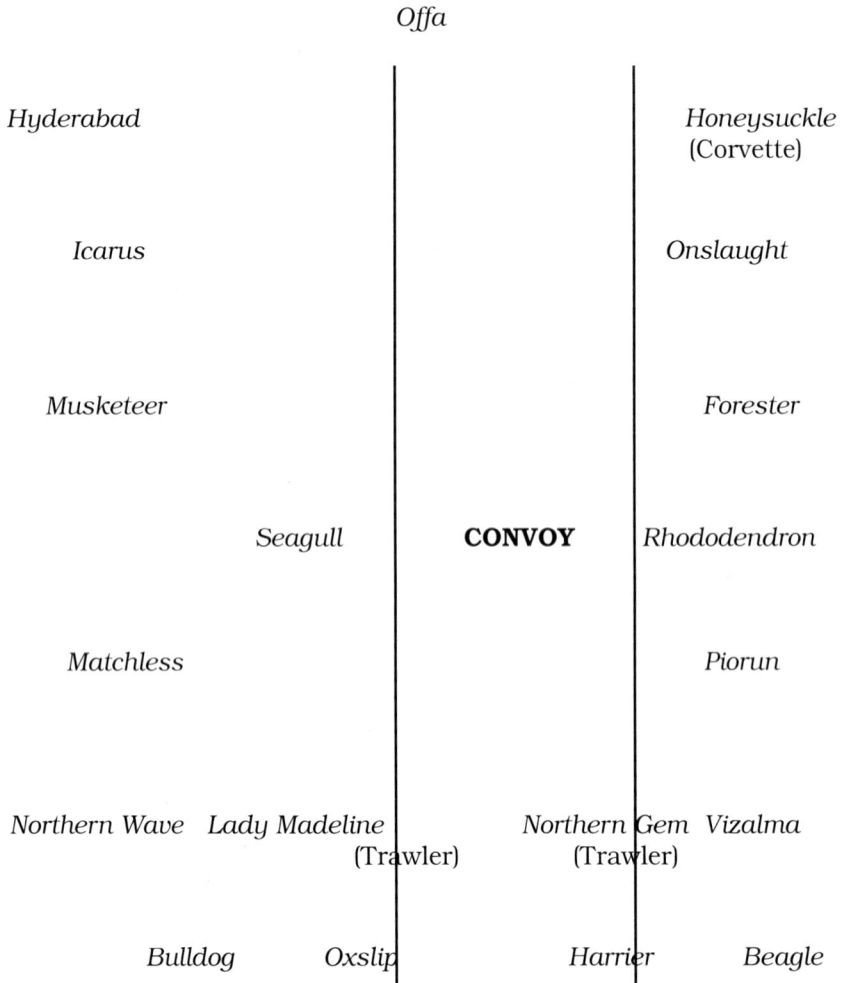

Offa

Hyderabad			Honeysuckle (Corvette)
Icarus			Onslaught
Musketeer			Forester
	Seagull	**CONVOY**	Rhododendron
Matchless			Piorun
Northern Wave	Lady Madeline (Trawler)	Northern Gem (Trawler)	Vizalma
Bulldog	Oxslip	Harrier	Beagle

The officer commanding the destroyer escort received information that two enemy submarines had overtaken the convoy, one on either beam, at about 10.00 am that morning to close and meet in a position approximately fifteen miles on the port bow of the merchantmen. At about 11.30 am HMS *Beagle*, protecting the rear starboard quarter, passed a message that she considered that the convoy had been sighted and that the U-boats were planning to attack. Shortly after

126

this she signalled again to say that she thought it possible that the convoy had not in fact been spotted and the enemy submarines were due to make a routine rendezvous. The order was given for the convoy to alter course to starboard and at 1.00 pm a new course was set to steer 260°.

Due to the cold air and comparatively warm sea, a low lying mist formed around the ships' wakes and thus provided excellent cover for a U-boat carrying out an unseen attack whilst submerged. At 2.12 pm a submarine attack was mounted against the convoy and, as far as is known, only one U-boat took part. The earlier alteration of course had probably prevented others from joining in.

A torpedo was fired from the port beam which hit the second ship in the port wing column, amidships on the port side. This was the American merchantman *Greylock* carrying a supply of 'fertiliser' (Appetite) to the USA. HM Ships *Harrier, Oxslip, Northern Wave* and *Lady Madeline* went to her rescue. Fortunately there were no casualties nor was there loss of life. It is believed that the torpedo had been fired from outside the outer screen while the U-boat was submerged, because those on the *Harrier* had seen the torpedo running near the surface, apparently at the end of its run.

Although the *Seagull*, the outer port wing ship was stationed 5,000 yards from the convoy operating its Asdics and 271 Radar set it failed to detect any echoes despite the fact that operating conditions were good at the time. An anti U-boat operation was quickly put into action and a search for the enemy, involving six destroyers led by *Musketeer*, began. Because RDF silence had been ordered, the destroyer's 286 and 285 sets had been turned off and as a result no RDF contacts were obtained. The search for the enemy was in vain and the convoy continued maintaining course and speed, and the remainder of the convoy arrived safely in Loch Ewe on 8th February 1943.

Viewed with the benefit of hindsight it was almost miraculous that any of the Allied convoys managed to get through to Russia. Operating from bases situated in the Norwegian fjords the powerful German surface fleet — the battle cruisers *Scharnhorst, Gneisenau,* the pocket battleships *Admiral Scheer,* and *Lützow,* the heavy cruisers *Admiral Hipper, Prinz Eugen* and *Nürnberg* together with the light cruiser *Köln* were strategically placed to wreak havoc among the merchant shipping. Had these ships chosen to put to sea in force and made a concerted effort the Allied supply line of goods and materials to North Russia would have been severed and remained so.

127

In spite of the prevalent atrocious weather and potential dangers posed by the threat of enemy warships these convoys continued right through to the end of hostilities, although at the frightful cost of men and shipping lost. All to what avail?

Field Marshal Lord Allanbrooke concluded:

"We kept on supplying tanks and aero-planes that could be ill spared and in doing so suffered the heaviest of losses in shipping conveying the equipment to Arctic Russia. We received nothing in return except abuse for handling the convoys inefficiently. We had absolutely no information as to what the Russian situation was as regards equipment. Russia even refused to keep us informed as to the distribution of her forces."

Towards the end of her escort duties the food supplies aboard *Glasgow* ran low and the crew was sustained by a diet of ships' biscuits and corned beef until she called in at Reykjavik, where the ship was re-stored with good food and oil. Ron Condy recalls "although the Icelandic people were not particularly friendly towards the crew, their countryside was beautiful."

Reykjavik was not, by all accounts, a good "run ashore" and visits to the city were forbidden. For seamen, on ships calling into the port, there was only a wet canteen available, in a 'nissen' hut, where they served bottled beer. Most of the crew was young, mainly aged eighteen years of age, whose lives had been turned upside down by the war. A lot of them were away from home for the first time, and they were often naïve as to what to expect when drink affected the older members of the crew. Fred Yates recalls "one young man was just about to finish his cigarette and swing into his 'mick' for the night when an older mess mate "Wiggy" Bennett came back aboard 'tanked up' and became affectionate towards the younger man. Fearful of losing his "ring" the young seaman stubbed his 'Senior Service' cigarette out on the back of the "Wiggy's" wrist thereby putting an end to the affection and preventing further interest!"

In Iceland the weather was liable to close down quickly, and Fred recalls the mail boat, after delivering mail ashore was about to return to the *Glasgow* when the fog came down so thickly that passage back to the ship was impossible. Overnight, the boat's crew was hosted by the Americans at their local army base, where they were able to enjoy superb food. The following day the weather improved and mail boat was able to return. As it approached *Glasgow* the Bowman, in giving an impressive display with his boat hook, knocked his hat off. This fell into the sea, bobbing its way along towards the stern. The Bowman thinking quickly, as the boat came alongside, secured the mail boat with a line to the 'lizard' and shinned up the rope ladder. He then went along the boom to bound on to the Quarterdeck and sped down the companionway just in time to rescue his hat, much to the amazement of the Officer of the Watch, the Quartermaster and the side party.

Fred also recalls, "at this time C.W. candidates were aboard, who often lacked good personal hygiene, frequently failing to wash properly. This problem was usually sorted out by the killicks who had the offenders taken off to the bathroom, where they were physically scrubbed down with mess scrubbers! "

After shore leave the cruiser was ordered to patrol the Denmark Straits, using the various harbours in Iceland (Akureyri, Reykjavik and Seidesfjord) as a base. Visibility in winter in those latitudes was bad, the nights in that latitude were long, and more often than not the sea was extremely rough. One night in Seidesfjord *Glasgow* dragged her anchor and ended up on a rocky underwater ledge with a list of 20 degrees. As a consequence of this, once the ship was floated upright the ship had to sail to the large port of Akureyri to have the hull examined by divers.

During the summer and autumn the Denmark Straits is ice free and it is nearly 200 miles wide, but when a storm beats up from the north, and still more when a hurricane from the north-east blows it is not wide enough to let the vast front of great waves storming in from the Greenland Sea pass unhindered. The result is that the Straits become a wild sea tunnel in which enormous volumes of rolling water pile over each other through the narrow channel. As the water can escape neither to the east nor west, because Greenland is on one side and Iceland on the other, it piles into the sky, and breakers fifty feet high are not uncommon. In addition, the seas, which beat vainly against rocks on either side, roll back into the Strait, and a boiling seething chaos is created in which the heavy seas seem to roll in all directions. The irregular motion of the ship took its toll and one unfortunate young seaman who could not overcome his seasickness was given the nickname 'Gashbucket Geordie' by his messmates because he was obliged to lie on the mess bench very close to the gash-bucket, for obvious reasons. Eventually he had to sleep on cordage abaft number one funnel with his messmates taking turns to take his scran up to him. At the end of the tour of duty he was taken off the ship.

JW* J.W. convoys were those that ran north-east to Russia;
RA* R. A. convoys those returning empty from Russia

The Kola Run

If you've been based at Scapa Flow,
That healthy resort as you well know,
For Jolly Jack all said and done,
We're destined for the Kola Run.

The Kola Run what can that be?
Sounds like a cushy run to me,
Thus quoted a green horned HO. Sprog,
Whose brains were fashioned in a bog.

An easy run, Oh! No my son,
Experiencing the Kola Run,
Would alter youthful smiles and joys,
By sorting out men from the boys.

For those who ever made this trip,
On merchant or naval ship,
Well know the bitter cold and fear,
Of "U" boats stalking convoy's rear.

The heavy seas and nights so bleak,
And with no troubles yet to seek,
The escorts solid as a rock,
Like shepherds guarding o'er their flock.

Some "U" boats pierced the convoy screen,
And sometimes Junkers joined the scene,
Unfortunately some mates died,
But we were lucky – we survived.

Let's raise our glasses, readers all,
To men of courage standing tall,
To those who perished in the Barents Sea,
Who did their duty – and made you FREE.

Those who served on HM Ships escorting merchant vessels to and from Russia eventually received medals from the Russian government in acknowledgement of the part played in the struggle against a common enemy.

„СОРОК ЛЕТ ПОБЕДЫ В ВЕЛИКОЙ ОТЕЧЕСТВЕННОЙ ВОЙНЕ 1941—1945 гг."

УЧАСТНИКУ ВОЙНЫ

Initially these were not considered to be legitimate campaign medals but eventually common sense prevailed and those who endured the terrible conditions associated with the Russian convoys are now permitted to wear these medals so deservedly earned. The back of the medal is inscribed in Russian - "To the participant of war on the occasion of the 40th anniversary of the Victory in the Great Patriotic War 1941-1945."

Blockade Runners – The Regensburg

In mid-January 1943 *Glasgow* sailed from Scapa Flow to patrol the Norwegian coastline between Seidisfjord, Akureyri, Skaalfjord and Hvalfjord. While anchored in Hvalfjord on the East Coast of Iceland, with HMS *Belfast*, part of both ships' companies were allowed to visit the American canteen, which had been built ashore there. A battle between the lads from *Glasgow* and *Belfast* developed and went on for hours. As the "wounded" were brought back aboard, Bob Burnett, Rear Admiral 10th Cruiser Squadron, signalled his disapproval and decreed that *Glasgow* and *Belfast* were never to be given shore leave together at the same time again! The two cruisers were supposed to be "Chummy Ships"!

After her tour of patrol duties *Glasgow* returned to Scapa Flow on 7th March where Captain Evans-Lombe received notice that His Majesty King George VI was to inspect ships of the Home Fleet. After her patrols *Glasgow* was not looking her best and, with little time available to clean the ship up before the impending inspection, her Captain decided that unorthodox measures should be taken in order to afford the best possible image to the Royal visitor. He asked the Navigating officer to work out the effects of the tides on the ship, in order to calculate which side would be presented to the King on his approach to the cruiser and, having determined this, gave orders for that side of the ship to be painted. His Majesty arrived on board on 19th March and was impressed by the state of the ship and the turn-out of the crew!

It was on this same occasion that one of the off-duty crew members, assembled on the Quarterdeck in No. 1's "Rig of the Day," awaiting the inspection, received a direct hit from an over flying seagull. He was instantly accorded the nickname "Seagull" by which he has been known from that moment on, right up to the present day.

HM King George VI aboard HMS Glasgow 19/3/1943 (WM)

At this time in the war Axis blockade-runners were transporting contraband goods, and Admiral Leatham, C-in-C Plymouth was given overall control of operations to prevent them plying their trade. Intelligence reports received from agents, together with the interception of U-boat signals, provided him with information as to the enemy's movements and he set about his duties. Three enemy blockade-runners, the *Regensburg*, the *Karin* and the *Irene*, were being routed through the Denmark Straits where U-boats U191, U635 and U469 were stationed, around Iceland and eventually into Norwegian waters in an attempt to escape the attention of the Allies. It was important that the blockade-runners met up with the U-boats, at some stage, in order that the surface vessels received modified Metox German radar warning equipment. This equipment enabled the enemy ships to detect Allied radar transmissions. The *Regensburg* had in fact received its new set from U 161, in the Azores, on 23rd March. Although the blockade-runner might not be able to escape detection, the new equipment would give its crew sufficient time to man its armament guns before a nocturnal or mist shrouded attack was mounted against her.

In waters close to the English south coast the cruiser *Newfoundland* and two destroyers kept watch. Further north, Coastal Command was alerted, while aircraft based in Iceland and Home Fleet ships took the appropriate action.

On 29th March 1943 the cruisers *Glasgow* and *Belfast*, with their accompanying destroyers *Intrepid* and *Echo*, were stationed on patrol in the Denmark Straits. Early into the Middle Watch, at 2.05 am on 30th March, *Glasgow's* radar picked up an unidentified blip on the screen. The ship went to "Action Stations" with guns and searchlights trained on the appropriate bearing. HMS *Glasgow* closed on to its target and her captain, Captain Edward M. Evans-Lombe, gave the order for star shells to be fired from the four-inch guns. On reaching their set altitude the shells burst and drifted down, on parachutes, from the darkened sky to light up the inky black water below. Aboard the cruiser its searchlight shutters were opened to reveal, illuminated in the stark light, a single funnelled merchantman. It was the German blockade-runner *Regensburg*, homeward bound from Rangoon, with a cargo of rubber, as it entered the Denmark Straits in a raging blizzard.

HMS *Glasgow's* Commanding Officer ordered the captain of the *Regensburg* to alter course and follow the cruiser. This request was disobeyed and the command to open fire on the enemy ship was given. After the first salvo the captain of the *Regensburg* signalled that he would stop. However, he ordered the ship to be scuttled and a series of explosions were heard. After the sea-cocks had been opened the crew abandoned ship, some lowered boats while others leapt overboard, to brave the icy waters of the sea, which had a temperature of 46° F, and the heavy swell carried the Germans away from their sinking ship. Aware that U-boats were operating in the area the warship's captain ordered the Gunnery Officer to exercise the six- and four-inch armament on the deserted enemy vessel, taking care to avoid hitting the life boats.

Glasgow's crew made a vain attempt to rescue the survivors of the enemy ship who had been exposed to the bitterly cold conditions, in very rough seas, for more than twenty minutes. A force six wind increased the turbulence of the sea, driving heavy snow showers across its surface, adding to the misery of those in the boats, on floats and in the water. Tragically after this length of time, exposed to the elements, they could not handle the ropes which were thrown down to them.

HMS Glasgow attempting to assist survivors in the icy waters of the Denmark Straits 30th March 1943

Out of 118 on board the *Regensberg* only six were saved, one officer and five men, and these were on tiny rafts. The survivors had survived by paddling vigorously to keep their blood circulating.

Unable to expose his ship to the risk of attack from U-boats known to be operating in the area, *Glasgow's* Captain had no option but to leave those survivors who were still alive to fend for themselves. It was not an easy decision for him to make!

Captain Evans-Lombe later blamed the stupidity of the German skipper for the loss of so many of the crew saying "If he had not lost his head, I could have brought him to the sheltered position I indicated, and there was still nothing I could have done to stop him scuttling his ship. His men would have been saved. "He went on to say that rescue was nigh on impossible because the men from the *Regensburg* were frozen to death, on rafts, in their sodden clothes as they were buffeted about by the waves in the icy water.

Hugo Huntington-Whiteley recalls that the Warrant Officers and Petty Officers on board *Glasgow* had been recruited before the War and were of a very high quality. He singled out for a particular mention, on this occasion, a seasoned campaigner, the chief gunner's mate Chief Petty Officer Lovell. CPO Lovell had started his working life as a north country miner and was a man who knew no fear and did his duty in the best of Naval traditions. In action he would cheer the gun crews manning his four-inch battery with cries of " Come on lads! Lets give it to them: one for Coventry, one for Portsmouth" as he chose all the badly bombed towns and cities as encouragement to better shooting.

Glasgow had to use torpedoes to give the sinking abandoned vessel its coup de grace and these were prepared for firing. "Torpedo tubes 2,4,6 and 8 ready" was relayed to the bridge "Torpedo tubes numbers 6 and 8 Fire" came back the order. There was a slight jolt as the torpedoes left the tubes and those on deck saw the dark oily canisters plunge into the water like swimmers starting a race, and shoot away towards their mark. A great fountain of water leapt up out of the sea, shining in the cold glaring white light of the starshells. Then came the roar of the explosions, each accompanied by a blinding flash, sending up a great volume of water which fell back into the sea. The torpedoes hit the ship and lifted it in the water. Water rushed into the gaping holes and an hour and a half later, at 6.25 am, the enemy ship sank in position 66° 40' N, 25° 31' W.

Although *Glasgow* continued to search the area for survivors and a number of bodies were spotted in the water, encrusted in ice the effort was, unfortunately, in vain.

On 5th April *Glasgow* returned to Hvalfjord, where the prisoners were handed over into captivity.

A number of Glasgow's crew have made mention of the fact that they saw women and children in the water dead, and covered with a coating of ice. One recalls that one of those rescued was a woman. Unfortunately it has not been possible to confirm these recollections. However, having regard to the fact that

112 were left behind, this would suggest that the stricken ship was conveying personnel other than the normal complement of crew at the time of her interception. If this was the case then it is quite possible that women and children were amongst the dead.

The enemy's blockade-running campaign came to an end the following year and can be summarised as follows: in all it cost Germany twenty ships, of which fifteen were sunk or captured by the Allies, or scuttled themselves when intercepted. The RAF sank two, one exploded and was destroyed in harbour and a further two were sunk by U-boats! The success enjoyed by the Allies was due to surface ships and aircraft working closely to achieve a common goal.

Glasgow returned to patrol in the Scapa Flow area until 30th April when she was relieved. It was during one of these breaks from patrol, from 5th – 8th May, that the cruiser acted as escort to the liner *Queen Mary* which was carrying Winston Churchill across the Atlantic to a conference in America. The *Queen Mary* was the fastest liner in the world at the time, being the holder of the "Blue Riband" for the fastest Atlantic crossing and *Glasgow*, with a top speed of 32 knots, was able to keep up with the liner for two days, until it ran into the inevitable Atlantic gale. When she did the cruiser sustained damage to fittings on the foc's'le which forced her to reduce speed. The *Queen Mary* carried on at 30 knots and disappeared into the squally gloom, unperturbed by the weather, after signalling "Thank you. We will go it alone now".

HMS *Glasgow* continued to patrol the waters to the north of Scapa, occasionally returning to Plymouth for replenishment of supplies. In mid-July she was recalled to patrol the south coast of England, using Devonport as her base, on anti-submarine patrols as part of B5 Escort group with its Senior Officer, Captain H.T. Bayliss RN, aboard the escort carrier *Archer*.

On 14th August *Glasgow* sailed from Guz to join the 2nd Support Group, operating in the Bay of Biscay, and rendezvoused with HMCS *Athabaskan* and HMS *Grenville* before proceeding northward to meet up with the 40th Escort Group in area "Musketry North." While on their way, they sighted a group of seven Ju. 88's which turned away when *Glasgow* opened fire. On reaching the Escort Group *Athabaskan* and *Grenville* were detached to return to Plymouth. *Glasgow* was then joined by HM Ships *Landguard* (S.O.) *Waveney* and *Bideford* and the warships patrolled off the coast of Spain between Cape Ortegal and Cape Vilaño.

The general plan of the patrol was to sweep to the eastward by day as far as Cape Ortegal, and to the westward by night. The ships were spread two miles apart by day, as it was considered that U-boats were attempting to make the passage through the area submerged. By night these Allied warships ships were stationed at five miles apart, carrying out a Radar sweep for U-boats on the surface. These searches were unfortunately hindered by the large number of Radar contacts obtained from small fishing boats in the area.

At 10.00 am on the 21st, relieved by *Bermuda*, *Glasgow* departed from the area to return to Plymouth, As she made her way homeward the cruiser altered course to investigate a Very light distress signal and found a dinghy containing survivors of a Halifax aircraft , which had been shot down while on anti-submarine patrol. With the aircrew safely aboard, *Glasgow* returned to Guz where they were disembarked.

Two days later the cruiser entered dry dock for general maintenance work and the installation of the latest air and surface ranging radar. Unfortunately, while servicing a port four-inch gun a dockyard worker fell off the mounting to the bottom of the dock sustaining injuries from which he died.

On 6th October 1943 work was completed, dock was flooded and HMS *Glasgow* moved out to engage in sea trials, to calibrate the newly fitted Asdics and radar equipment, before proceeding to Portsmouth where she secured port side to at the South Railway Jetty.

Crew members reminiscing about experiences on board *Glasgow* often refer to how uncomfortable things were in wartime. Because visibility suddenly increases at dawn and the ship would go to "Action Stations", as a matter of routine, they had to take gas masks and anti flash gear with them wherever they went on the ship. The signal to go to "Action Stations" would frequently be made half an hour before dawn in readiness for any surprise attack launched by the enemy. Depending on the time when dawn occurred the ship's crew would have to rise at any time from 4.30 am onwards.

While the crew was at "Action Stations" they had to wear the anti-flash gear and have the gas masks available for use until they were stood down. Often this would be an hour after the original signal had been given.

Another problem they encountered was that the food was very basic and often badly cooked. The daily tot of rum was welcome in that it acted as an appetiser, which enabled the crew to eat food, which would otherwise have appeared unpalatable. One had to learn to get by on unsatisfactory food.

Frequently conditions aboard were cramped with the crew sleeping in hammocks — these were not uncomfortable to sleep in but putting them up and taking them down again involved quite a lot of physical effort. When these were not being used by their owner the hammocks were stored in a hammock rack, which was basically square in shape, however, when "Action Stations" were sounded the hammock was left "in situ" and, in an emergency situation the hammocks would have been made available for damage control repairs. The crowded conditions also made leisure pursuits difficult. These were mainly sedentary such as reading writing, and playing cards. However, when the opportunity presented itself the crew would go ashore to get a decent meal, have a few beers and a sing song in one of the local bars, although time spent in port was short because of the demands for shipping at that time. Having a beer was something they looked forward to because apart from the tot they were not allowed to drink any alcohol.

Separation from one's loved ones and the uncertainty relating to what was happening at home because of lack of news put a strain on crew members and their families alike.

Pack Drill

Early in April 1943 the use of Pack Drill as a form of punishment for defaulters was debated in the House of Commons. A question was raised by a Labour MP asking whether pack drill was currently in use as a form of punishment in the Royal Navy and if not when had it been abolished. Mr A. V. Alexander First Lord of the Admiralty replied amid cheers from his fellow MP's " Pack drill is not and never has been used as a form of punishment in the Royal Navy." This evoked a response from another Labour MP "Tell that to the Army."

A report of the proceedings appeared in the evening edition of the Liverpool Daily Post and Echo on the 7th April which was read by a fireman, working in the Merseyside Docks, who then wrote to his local MP, the First Lord of the Admiralty, Admiral Hawood and the Prime Minister Winston Churchill challenging the validity of the statement made in the House, alleging that he had witnessed, on the Liverpool North Dock, two seamen who had been subjected to "bestial and barbaric punishment" until they were on the point of collapse.

The matter was fully investigated and in reply it was stated that the drill, witnessed by the fireman, had been part of a No. 11 punishment carried out by defaulters from one of the ships under repair at Liverpool. The prescribed punishment described in Article 570 K.R & A.I. permitted the inclusion of one hour's drill during the Dog Watches. Captain (D) Liverpool stated that the drill had been carried out in accordance with King's Regulations. The men had had rifles and were dressed in Drill Order, i.e., web belt, bayonet and gaiters, whereas 'Pack Drill' in the army meant drill in full marching order: rifle, pack, haversack, water bottle, etc; he went on to report further that, having regard to the facts that Naval ratings do not wear

141

anything like military equipment, the allegation, on the occasion reported, was unfounded. Nothing like this had happened nor, so far as was known, was it likely ever to occur in the Royal Navy.

Captain (D) further stated that the drill did not exceed one hour and there was no question of any of the men being on the point of collapse. In fact, it was unusual for defaulters to be drilled in the evening at Liverpool, but on the occasion in question there was no extra work on which the men could be usefully employed at the time.

Following the investigation into the allegation it was proposed that a C.A.F.O. be issued directing that extra work be substituted for drill when the latter could not be carried out other than in sight of civilians.

The good name of HMS *Glasgow* was in danger of being tarnished when a sailor serving aboard her wrote a letter to R.J.Taylor, MP for Morpeth, albeit after the Fleet Order had been issued, stating that Pack Drill had been carried out on the cruiser. Having regard to the fact that a specific order had been issued prohibiting the use of Pack Drill as a form of punishment no further action was taken.

Sir Dudley Pound

At the end of 1929 Rear Admiral Sir Dudley Pound, flying his flag in the *Renown*, commanded the battlecruiser squadron within the Atlantic Fleet comprised of four battleships ; HM Ships *Nelson, Rodney, Barham* and *Malaysia*, the battlecruisers *Renown, Repulse*, and *Tiger* and the aircraft carriers *Furious* and *Argus*. The cruisers *Vindictive, Frobisher, Canterbury* and *Comus* with two destroyer flotillas completed the force. By March 1936 he had been appointed as C-in-C Mediterranean and three years later, in May 1939, First Sea Lord. It was in the latter position that he was instrumental in ensuring that the island of Malta received a significant anti-aircraft defence system incorporating 112 guns.

Early into the Second World War the First Sea Lord expressed doubts not only as to the ability of battleships to withstand attacks from the air but very perceptively realised that the Italian leader Benito Mussolini would defer entry into the war until May 1940. He also tried to keep France in the war so that the French Fleet operated in the Western Mediterranean using ports in North Africa. Control of the French Fleet was necessary and instructions were given that if France tried to settle for peace their Fleet would be sunk rather than let it fall into the hands of the enemy. Realising the importance of keeping the Atlantic Trade routes open, by securing the western exit to the Mediterranean (Straits of Gibraltar) he had the British Fleet relocated from the Eastern Mediterranean to Gibraltar.

At a time when the Battle of Britain had been won by the RAF boosting the morale of the British public, there remained the threat posed by the Battle of the Atlantic. U-boats were ranging further afield to wreak havoc amongst shipping. Furthermore destroyers and escort vessels were in short supply and Coastal Command was

143

woefully short of long range aircraft. In the South Atlantic, the Indian Ocean and the Pacific enemy surface raiders were operating against British traders. The general public could not be told everything; but the Navy was stretched to the limit and Sir Dudley Pound was subjected to attacks both in Parliament and by the Press. By July 1943 Lady Pound had died and the health of Sir Dudley was failing fast, with his workload taking its toll.

In September that year the First Sea Lord and executive head of the Royal Navy became gravely ill and died on 21st October, the anniversary of the Battle of Trafalgar.

On Tuesday 26th October, his funeral procession was routed from the Admiralty to Westminster Abbey where a Memorial Service was held. It was a grey misty day, in keeping with the occasion, as the Duke of Gloucester, representing His Majesty the King, the Prime Minister, members of the Government and numerous dignitaries representing the armed services and allied associations, made their way to the Abbey. There, in the dim half-light of the ancient building, the service was both fast moving and impressive.

Once the service was over the caskets containing the ashes of Lady Pound and those of the late First Sea Lord were taken to Portsmouth, to be lodged overnight aboard HMS *Victory*. The following day, 27th October, the caskets were conveyed in a procession from Nelson's old flagship, on a gun carriage pulled by sailors, to HMS *Glasgow*, which was berthed alongside the South Railway Jetty.

Guard of Honour aboard HMS Glasgow for Funeral of Sir Dudley Pound

144

When the funeral party had embarked *Glasgow* slipped and left harbour. The ship proceeded slowly on a calm, foggy, still and silent day to Spithead, about 30 miles off shore near the Nab Tower, where the burial service was conducted at 1.15 pm With the ship's company fell in on the upper deck the White Ensign was removed to reveal a small casket of ashes. The caskets of Sir Dudley and Lady Pound were then committed to the deep with due reverence and ceremony.

Following the committal senior naval officers cast wreaths onto the water where they remained floating as *Glasgow* turned slowly and returned to port.

Sir Dudley Pound, an officer of untiring energy and forcefulness, had been an effective commander who had stood up for the Royal Navy against Winston Churchill and died in post, aged sixty-six, worn out in the service of his country. While accepting the role played by the First Sea Lord in his service to his country and the Royal Navy one of *Glasgow*'s crew commented that the ceremony seemed to represent a lot of effort, in wartime, for little purpose.

Destruction of the Brest and Bordeaux Flotillas

Early in November 1943 *Glasgow* was engaged in protecting convoys bound for Gibraltar. Having safely delivered her charges the cruiser set sail, on 12th November, bound for the UK. While on passage she was attacked, on the 18th, by a Liberator from Coastal Command and the crew went to "Action Stations." Midshipman David Dixon recalled that the aircraft, seeking out enemy destroyers, approached the *Glasgow* and carried out a text book attack, during which flares were dropped before the plane flew round to silhouette the warship against the backdrop of light. Having failed to raise the pilot by signal, orders were given for *Glasgow's* starboard pom-poms to engage the incoming aircraft. The gun crew responded immediately, sending a stream of shells into the sky to register a hit and the target rapidly took evasive action before disappearing. *Glasgow* continued on her way homeward to dock in Plymouth on 20th November.

At sea, canvas covers are used to prevent water from getting into the gun muzzles so the first round of a quick-firing gun was always a dummy to break the cover when the gun crew opened fire. When the Liberator returned to its base a dummy pom-pom shell was found embedded in one of its fuel tanks! After several gins the matter was all smoothed over.

Five days later Captain Evans-Lombe handed over command of the warship to Captain C.P. Clarke, DSO,RN. before it resumed convoy escort duties in the Azores. Before assuming command of HMS *Glasgow* Captain Clarke had been the Director of the anti-submarine Division of the Admiralty in August 1942, and was identified as the man behind the anti U-boat campaign during the worst days of the Battle of the Atlantic.

Ten days after leaving Plymouth the cruiser arrived at her destination Horta, on 8th December. Here, quite extraordinarily, the ship had to be lit up at night in harbour but on leaving her berth the cruiser had to "darken ship " again.

In Horta a local storekeeper, known as "Smokey Joe," sold bottles of banana flavoured liqueurs which were not available in wartime Britain. One of *Glasgow*'s officers, Sub Lieutenant Davison, bought a bottle, intending to take it back home with him. Unfortunately, after tasting it back aboard, he left the bottle uncorked and by morning the contents had evaporated. When the ship next returned to the port the officer went looking for "Smokey Joe" only to learn that the storekeeper had succumbed to his own enterprise!

Hugo Huntington-Whiteley also recalled "that the hooch sold on the Island was so strong that a contingent of Royal Marines had to be lined up with stretchers on the Quarterdeck at night to collect returning libertymen!" Further proof of the strength of the local alcoholic beverage was provided when a group of sailors returning to the ship purchased a small donkey for 20 escudos and tried to take it aboard. The inebriated matelots were prevented by the Corporal of the Gangway from boarding, and the following morning a local peasant found himself the proud owner of a donkey for free.

Between the 12th to 22nd December *Glasgow* engaged in two patrols of four days duration, and there was an air of contented expectancy among the crew when the warship returned to Horta for Christmas. On Christmas Eve thoughts turned to those left behind in Britain and, conscious of the fact that this was a time for youngsters, the ship's crew quickly made arrangements for a Christmas party, complete with festive tree, to be given for the local children. No sooner had the arrangements been made when orders came, from the Admiralty, for the ship to proceed to sea and intercept a blockade-runner which had been reported, approaching the Bay of Biscay, by a Coastal Command aircraft. Modern warfare is a more and more merciless affair and neither the Christmas tree nor the decorations lovingly put up to mark the season of goodwill could conceal the fact that the existence of *Glasgow's* crew was at stake at all times and that would include Christmas Day as well.

David Dixon, who was Midshipman of the Watch on the Quarterdeck at about 10.0 pm that night, recalls that the deck was suddenly alive with rats running to jump overboard and swim ashore. His thoughts were that they seemed to know something more about what was to come than the ship's company did and were taking no chances!

An hour later *Glasgow* left Horta and set course to intercept the German blockade runner the *Alsterufer,* a fast modern ship of approximately 5,000 tons, which had passed undetected through the South Atlantic narrows. The blockade runner was first sighted at 10.15 am on Monday, 27th December, by a Sunderland flying boat (T for Tare from No. 201 Squadron) in a position about 500 miles west-northwest of Cape Finisterre. The enemy ship, with a gun mounted on its poop deck and others on its bows and amidships, was proceeding, unescorted, in an easterly direction at fifteen knots inbound for a port on the west coast of France. The Sunderland signalled that it had spotted a suspicious looking vessel and, as it moved closer to investigate, was engaged by the enemy ship's gunners, forcing it to keep its distance. The cruisers *Glasgow* and *Enterprise* were dispatched to the area together with aircraft from Coastal Command. For the next two and a half hours the Sunderland continued to shadow the German ship, broadcasting its position, before being joined by other Sunderlands: Q for Queen of No. 422 (RCAF) Squadron and U for Uncle from 201 Squadron. Pending the arrival of ships and aircraft, a Sunderland aircraft of the R.C.A.F shadowed the enemy ship maintaining visual contact with it, in spite of the adverse weather conditions that prevailed at the time, until a sister aircraft arrived to launch an attack.

Although the Sunderland was damaged during the run in, by anti-aircraft shells fired by the blockade-runner, it succeeded in dropping a bomb close to the German vessel. After the attack it withdrew from the target area to make way for a Liberator, H for How, flown by Pilot Officer Dolezal of No. 311 (Czech) Squadron. The Czech pilot, at his point of longest endurance, made an approach from the south and dropped two bombs, one of 250 pounds and one of 500 pounds. One bomb hit the stern of the enemy ship and, as it detonated, the force of the explosion rocked the aircraft, flying at 600 feet above sea level, forcing the pilot to exercise all his skill to control the plane. H for How circled to enable a crew member to take photographs of the enemy ship, as flames poured out of the after hatch. More explosions followed and soon the *Alsterufer's* bridge and superstructure, together with the whole after part of the vessel, was ablaze. The German ship was later seen stopped in the water listing heavily to port with thick oily smoke pouring out of holes in her decks, and flames leaping into the air above the masts. The crew of the stricken vessel had abandoned ship and approximately seventy survivors could be seen in lifeboats or on rafts.

In the early evening the glowing hulk sank beneath the waves approximately 750 miles from her destination. Two days later fifty-two survivors were rescued by British corvettes with a further twen-ty- two being picked by other ships.

Aboard HMS *Glasgow* her captain had received a warning that there was a possibility that warships from the German Bordeaux flotilla, could be protecting the *Alsterufer* and that five ships might be encountered.

Tension and excitement prevented some of the younger men from eating, but the hardened veterans ate more heartily than ever. They new from experience that a man could face whatever tribulations were ahead of him much better on a full stomach. At the same time long hours of duty required a properly strengthened inner man.

The ship raced forward in radar silence, except for the surface warning set. At 35,000 yards distance on 28th December west of Ushant in the Bay of Biscay, where the German Bordeaux and Brest destroyer flotillas had teamed up the radar set picked up a signal identifying several targets. As soon as contact had been made the gunnery radar started up. At 1.00 pm, the ship's company was advised over the Tannoy that the encounter was imminent. As the DCT swung, "targets" were appearing all over and someone called out "Bloody hell! We've got half the German navy here!" From a range of 19,000 yards the Germans fired salvoes at the *Glasgow* and the *Enterprise*. A shell hit *Glasgow* and exploded below the forward fun-nel. The usual smell of cordite and cries of wounded men came from where the shell had exploded on the port pom-pom gun deck, leaving two members of its crew dead and others wounded.

The British cruiser responded from a range of 18,000 yards to engage the enemy with the T.S table tuned to radar ranging. Those manning the 284 sets were able to watch six-inch shells leave *Glasgow*'s turrets as they sped on their way towards the enemy and Bob Craig, a Leading Radio Mechanic, recalls that at times he could actually watch those German shells, which were on target, coming in. This added to the interest!

The weather conditions were bad as *Glasgow* and the *Enterprise*, commanded by Captain H. T. W. Grant, RCN, closed at full speed for the encounter, with heavy seas running. From the look-out came a shout "Smudge of smoke on the horizon bearing green five zero".

The "Action Stations" alarm was sounded raising a great wave of excitement and activity. Doors slammed, heavy footsteps thudded along companionways, men raced up ladders and there were irate shouts of "Keep to the Left", "Keep to the Right blast you" and within a few minutes every fighting station on the ship had reported its complement "All present and correct." The *Glasgow*'s captain, with the aid of his binoculars, could make out the smoke trails stretching thinly over the horizon.

HMS *Glasgow*, in her rush forwards to engage the enemy took on board a lot of water that flooded the Royal Marines' mess deck. Eric Baker, a young stoker, was a member of the Damage Control Party sent to clear the water with buckets. Running along a gangway, intending to throw the water overboard, he slipped, decanting the contents of the bucket all over him. Just as he picked himself up "Action Stations" sounded and this bedraggled seaman had to return to the engine room soaked to the skin!

Meanwhile the Yeoman of Signals reported "Enemy in Sight" and started to count the enemy ships off. Masts were visible over the horizon now, a whole forest of masts. Instead of the expected five there were eleven. This took the smile off the face of the *Glasgow*'s Commander, Lloyd-Davies, as he went aft to take his post in the after control, where he could take over in the event that the ship had been badly hit. Captain Clarke remained in the forward control.

The next Tannoy message was "Nelson said England expects," which gave rise to some sniggers among the lower deck!

The engagement commenced at about 1.30 pm and *Enterprise* was ordered to take up position astern of *Glasgow*. Almost immediately the British cruisers came under fire and enemy shells began to find their range. Shells started to fall alongside *Glasgow* and suddenly, a heavy column of water rose amidships and a shower of spray slashed the faces of those on the bridge, who tasted salt on their lips. That shell had exploded not more than 20 yards from the ship!

Naval gunnery is not merely a matter of shooting at moving targets, the gun turrets themselves are also moving up and down as well as forwards and these various movements greatly complicate the ballistic calculations involved. In addition the movement of the target is probably irregular. The captain of an attacked ship will try to upset the accuracy of his enemy's fire by suddenly changing direction and speed. In short he is no sitting target and the speed with which he can alter course can make it difficult for naval gunners to find their target.

*HMS Glasgow turning away from HMS Enterprise during the encounter   (IWM)
with the German Brest and Bordeaux Flotillas*

Captain Clarke not only ordered changes of course and speed but also used another ploy to confuse the aim of the German gunners. He issued orders for the cruiser's four-inch armament to be depressed and shells to be fired into the sea nearby. If the German shells fell short then *Glasgow's* were fired long and vice-versa. The Germans were unable to make the necessary adjustments and both *Glasgow* and *Enterprise* were spared much damage.

In the boiler room for hour after frightening hour, with ears popping from the air pressure, the stokers knew and heard little of what was going on apart from the near misses and the scream of the boiler room fans. On their alertness, as they watched for orders to open or shut off oil sprayers to the furnaces, depended the precise supply of steam available to meet the sudden changes of speed ordered from the bridge. One of the stokers, whose duty was to inspect the gland spaces, was aware of the Engineering Officer who, having one foot on the companionway, had to be asked to move every time someone had to go up top. The thought that went through that stoker's mind at the time was that the officer would be well placed to mount the companionway quickly in the event of an emergency.

At 2.23 pm a torpedo passed astern and the ship altered course to miss two others, which passed ahead. In the heat of the action it was estimated that the Germans fired about sixty torpedoes at the ship. Clever evasive action taken by *Glasgow's* Commanding Officer meant

152

that the nearest torpedo to pass the ship was approximately 400 yards away. The ship was turned back into the action, by which time the Germans had effectively given up, preferring to head for home, Brest. At 2.55 pm an enemy destroyer was engaged. By this time the six-inch guns had shot themselves in and a steady hail of bursting shells was falling in and around the target. Salvo after salvo screamed over and no sooner had one gone on its way than the gun barrels moved forward from the recoil position to send the next hurtling after it. Brownish yellow coils of acrid smoke enveloped *Glasgow* now making it difficult for those not under cover to breathe. By 3.05 pm the enemy warship was stopped in the water with its forward funnel missing. Within half an hour *Glasgow*'s 'A' and 'B' turrets had run out of ammunition and by about 4.30 pm the fighting was over and the battle won. Not only had the turrets run out of ammunition but the paint had also peeled off the guns because of the heat. By this time the big *Narvik* class destroyer *Z.27* and two smaller destroyers, about half its size, the *T.25* and *T.26*, had been sunk. An additional four more ships had been put out of action including another destroyer which was stopped with a boatload of survivors close by, and an abandoned *Elbling* class destroyer.

When two ships are in action together, shells with colour incorporated are used to help distinguish the fall of their respective shot. In this action the *Enterprise* had shells aboard which produced red splashes while those on *Glasgow* produced yellow ones. A German sailor rescued after his destroyer had been sunk said that his captain, on seeing yellow splashes, thought that the *Glasgow* had fired gas shells and ordered all hands to wear gas masks. This effectively reduced the enemy's fighting efficiency by 50%.

There was a sense of elation about the ship when the crew saw a battle ensign streaming out in the wind, but the sight of a blackened hulk floating motionless in the water quickly tempered this.

When the naval engagement was broken off *Glasgow* came under an enemy air attack during which fifteen German planes launched "glider bombs," nicknamed "Chase me Charlies," against her. These were jet-propelled and fitted with small wings to provide stability when launched and guided, by radio control, from a "launching parent." Fortunately, the bombs missed and with night closing in, the enemy was only able to mount one strike.

Although HMS *Enterprise* was also involved in the attack her main gunnery control equipment failed and *Glasgow* very much fought the action on her own.

Mosquitoes and Beaufighters provided fighter cover while those killed in the action, Ordnance Mechanic R. Andrews and Able Seaman J Smith, were buried at sea in the afternoon of 29th December. Each body was weighted and placed on a sloping stretcher by the guard rail. The assembled crew listened to the melancholy notes of the last post sounded by the Royal Marine bugler as their shipmates splashed into the water below and wreaths, made up from the Christmas tree intended for the children's party at Horta, were tossed into the sea to mark their resting place. Following naval tradition, their effects were auctioned off before being thrown over the side and the proceeds were sent to the next of kin.

The ship then returned to Plymouth, later that same day, where the injured were brought ashore.

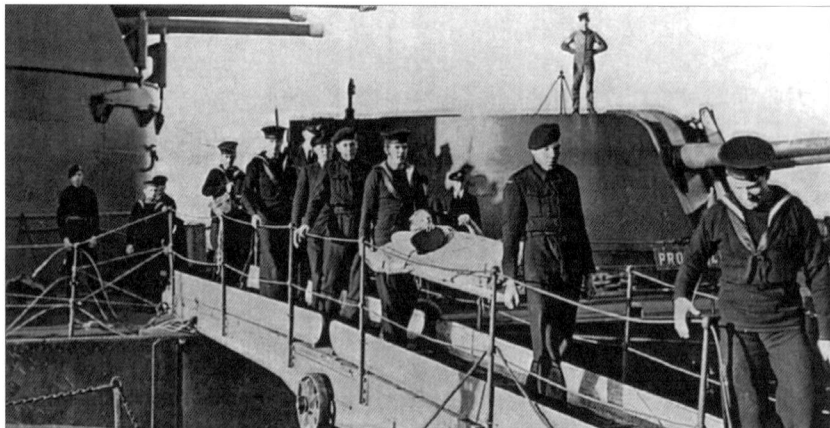

The injured are brought ashore from HMS Glasgow after the Battle   (IWM)

Following a damage survey which was undertaken after the ship docked a decision was taken that the ship was too badly damaged to go to sea again because of holes in the sides of the ship caused by near misses. At the time the "Cease Fire" order had been given some six-inch shells were still rammed home, which became stuck in the gun barrels as they cooled down, and had to be recovered by the dockyard workers. The crew was given a fortnight's leave before preparing to go to sea again.

Commander Lloyd-Davies, the cruiser's second-in-command, considered that with the benefit of

154

hindsight the Germans had made an error of judgement and should have attacked all at once. Having eleven ships available they could have brought the British ships under very heavy fire, with the odds heavily against the British. However, the German ships were knocked out one after another, and he further gathered that the Admiralty had been quite pleased with the outcome of the battle, although they had had slightly cold feet at the thought that just the *Glasgow* and the *Enterprise* had fought the Germans. The flotilla was effectively destroyed as a fighting force and had this not been the case then the allied landings at Normandy in June 1944 might well have been disrupted. Commander Lloyd-Davies admitted "the officers were not always aware of everything going on. The guns just kept firing under the direction of the gunnery officer."

When the *Glasgow* and *Enterprise* had safely docked after the battle Captain Grant, captain of the *Enterprise*, was welcomed aboard the British cruiser.

Captain Clarke welcomes Captain Grant aboard HMS Glasgow
Sub Lieutenant Davison 2nd from right looks on.

After the battle the following were recommended for the award of decorations:

1) Lt.Cdr. R.E. Hutchins, (Gunnery) who showed great coolness and professionalism during the attack. He was credited for the damage inflicted on the enemy and the defeat of the attempted attack by German aircraft and was awarded the DSC for his efforts that day.

2) Cdr. (E) E.J.H. Kirby, who was credited with maintaining the ship's efficiency after she had been hit in "A" boiler intake.

3) Lt. D. Harris, RNVR who by his leadership, initiative and knowledge kept the ship's Radar sets working.

4) Chief Petty Officer J.V.Lovell, BEM.OOQ of 4" guns and Chief Gunner's Mate of the *Glasgow* who showed conspicuous leadership and unfailing cheerfulness under fire and was an inspiration to his men. T.D. Atkinson RM OOQ 'X' Turret who showed fine leadership and initiative to his men

5) Chief Stoker S.R. Baber, who set a fine example to his men when the shell exploded in the air intake.

6) A/Leading Seaman (Radar) J.H. Moore, who gave the first detection range and bearing of the enemy and later by brilliant operation, when one of the sets was put out of action, kept the bridge and ADC of ranges and bearings of attacking aircraft, which led to their defeat.

7) Petty Officer K.J. Ludwig, who showed great coolness and courage after the port pom-pom was hit, bringing the gun back into action by local control.

Having completed his Midshipman's training on *Glasgow* David Dixon transferred to the Hunt class destroyer *Brissenden* that was also based in Plymouth. Soon after joining his new ship the destroyer and *Glasgow* engaged in an "aim off" practice shoot, in which the *Brissenden* was to act as the target ship. Acting as a spotter to report the splashes of the shells, he vividly remembers the close grouping of the fall of shot, all of which fell directly astern the destroyer. For the first time he fully appreciated what the ship's companies of the German destroyers had faced only a few weeks earlier.

The Normandy Landings and D-Day

Captain C.P.Clarke, DSO, RN

Following the return from her encounter with the German Flotillas in the Bay of Biscay HMS *Glasgow* remained in Plymouth during the early part of 1944, often exercising with the *King George V*, in Cawsand Bay off the Cornish coast. On 10th February, the cruiser proceeded to sea to escort convoy MK28A en route to Gibraltar, before returning to Devonport on 22nd February. Two weeks later, 90 RAF and two army personnel were embarked and the ship steamed out of the naval base bound for the Azores, via Angra (Terciera), for Horta

(Faial), where the passengers were disembarked on 8th March. Two days later *Glasgow* set sail, acting as an escort for convoy MRK 29, for a return to the UK where she and the merchant ships arrived safely at Greenock on the 15th March.

Relieved from escort duties *Glasgow* exercised with the U.S. Rangers off Lamlash, on the Isle of Arran. The exercises required half charge shoots at targets selected by grid reference, set up on the Scottish Isle. In the light of what was to come the practice was put to good use. For the next two months the *Glasgow* continued to exercise between Greenock and Plymouth.

In 1943 the Allies, fearing an invasion of Europe would have been premature, contented themselves with landing in Sicily and Italy, and chose instead to postpone the invasion of France until 1944 when more troops and landing craft would be available. Those planning the invasion eventually decided that the landing should take place in the region of Normandy. The plan called for simultaneous landings to take place on beaches, two of which were allocated to the Americans, one to the Canadians and the remaining two to the British. The two assigned to the Americans were given the code names "Utah" and "Omaha." The latter's area stretched from St. Honorine to Vierville-sur-Mer. Of the two beaches, "Omaha" was the most critical because of its position between "Utah" and those allotted to the British. Failure at "Omaha" would mean two separate invasions and an opportunity for the Germans to defend the isolated beaches in detail. Although the topography and defences at "Omaha" caused some misgivings amongst the planners they believed that it could be successfully assaulted. Information received suggested that the German troops manning those defences were of lacklustre quality. On paper the plan looked good, but many of the predictions as to the enemy's strength and the proposed fire support would prove to be tragically wrong.

D-Day was scheduled for 5th June when tidal conditions dictated that H-Hour would be in the area of the American beaches. In preparation for the planned invasion land and naval forces were moved, in great secrecy, to pre-designated locations and on 22nd May *Glasgow* sailed from Plymouth for Belfast Lough, where she arrived the following day.

Belfast Lough is a relatively recent name for the curving stretch of sheltered water twenty miles long that takes ships up to the port of Belfast and was an important rendezvous point for convoys, the focus of activity being a point some four miles north of Bangor. From the arrival of the US Ships *Texas, Nevada* and *Arkansas* in late April, the fleet gradually grew as more and more warships arrived and were allocated anchorages on the grid plan of the Lough. The US cruisers *Tuscaloosa* and *Quincy* appeared in mid-May, and all through that month the British representation built up with the cruisers *Glasgow, Bellona, Black Prince, Enterprise* and *Hawkins*; the sleek French cruisers *Montcalm* and *Georges Leygues* (George's Legs' to the English) arrived. Dozens of destroyers and smaller craft added to the scene.To commemorate the assembly of the Allied Fleet in Belfast Lough a plaque was set into the North Breakwater.

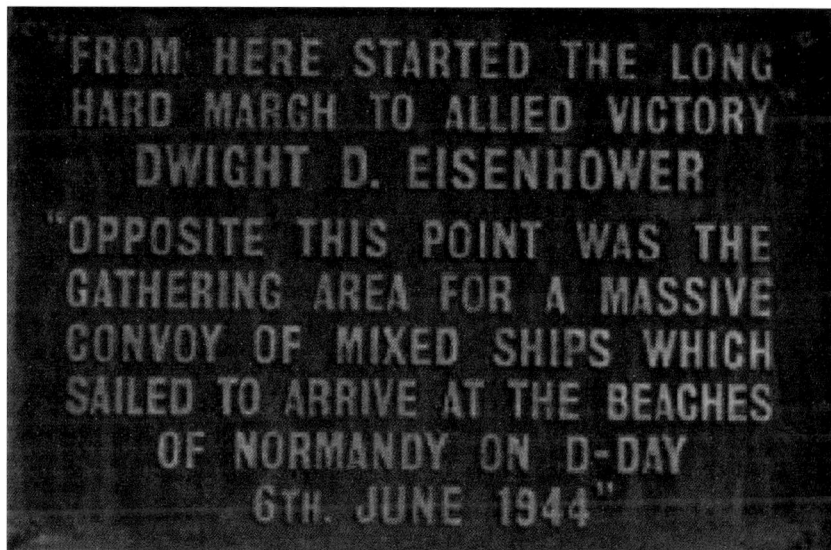

Plaque set into the North Breakwater, Bangor, Co.Down, N.Ireland

George Bygate, a stoker from Sheffield who was caught up in his youth in history's biggest military drama recalls "I was an eighteen year old stoker aboard HMS *Glasgow* when we entered Belfast Lough for D-Day training. I thought that I was miles away from home, being the first time that I had been outside England and Wales. I remember the lush green hills around the Lough and I recall a run ashore in Bangor, missing the last liberty boat back to the ship and sleeping the night in a fairground. Sailor's caps always did make a good pillow! I also recall on my first shore leave in Bangor with a shipmate, also from my home town, deciding to find out what Irish girls were like and on seeing two ATS girls we stopped to chat, only to find out that they also came from Sheffield! We found the local people very friendly, and although I have never returned to Bangor since 1944 and visited many countries during my naval days my memory of Bangor will remain forever."

Aboard HMS *Erebus* a young seaman, James Conroy, recalled "I had never seen so vast an armada of ships. They were anchored on both sides of the Lough facing each other." Later he was reminded of the occasion by something Erwin Rommel had said when he had stood on the French coast, pointing out to sea, saying to his fellow officers, "A monster is out there waiting to be released."

A detailed model of a proposed landing site, "Omaha" Beach, was set out in *Glasgow*'s hanger and on 31st May the ship was 'sealed' ready for the planned Normandy Invasion, as were all others in the Western Task Force, with mail neither coming aboard nor going out. On 2nd June the Task Force 129 Movement Order was received ordering all ships of the bombardment group of the Western Task Force to get underway from Belfast on 3rd June, according to schedule, and proceed via British War Channels to their specified rendezvous points. The ship remained at her assembly port, awaiting further orders. At 8.06 am on Saturday 3rd June the *Tuscaloosa* formed a column in order: *Glasgow, Bellona, Enterprise, Hawkins, Quincy, Black Prince,* screened by the US destroyers *Butler, Herndon, Schubrick* and *Murphy*. The ships left the Lough into the Irish Sea and steamed south at 17 knots. For the next two days *Glasgow* passed up and down the north Cornish coast, heading first up towards the Bristol Channel before returning between the Island of Lundy and Trevore Head, maintaining radio silence.

As the 5th June the date nominated by the Supreme Allied Commander General Dwight D. Eisenhower approached, activity in the ports of southern England was frenetic with thousands of men being embarked aboard hundreds of vessels to await the moment of departure. The number of ships involved without taking account of smaller craft was impressive, 931 for the Western Task Force and 1,796 for the Eastern one. To load these vessels to enable them to be ready for sea during the night of 3rd or in the early hours of 4th June required first rate organisation. The ships were loaded with men and equipment and Eisenhower confirmed the sailing orders. It was at this point that a weather system was to intervene and disrupt the plan. A great depression advanced across the Atlantic north-eastwards, carrying with it strong winds which would raise a difficult sea. The cloud base became so low that the majority of aircraft would be unable to complete their missions, and the sea became so rough that the smaller landing craft could not be certain of reaching their allotted beaches. The weather was atrocious with a gale blowing in the English Channel and it was touch and go as to whether or not the planned operation could proceed. In deference to the views expressed by officers of the RAF, USAAF and Admiral Ramsay, General Eisenhower decided to delay the invasion by twenty-four hours. In consequence, those vessels that were already at sea were turned back at 5.00 am on 4th June. The return of ships to port posed a series of problems, with many of them failing to find shelter from the storm adding to the misery experienced by the infantry aboard. Had the bad weather continued many of the warships would have needed re-victualling and the landings delayed until possibly 19th of the month. The large ships of the Bombardment Force, including *Glasgow*, merely turned in the Irish Sea and steamed up and down the Welsh coast all day until they were eventually ordered to resume their original course. It is worth noting that had this happened, the landings would have ended in a terrible fiasco when, between 19th and 21st June, the English Channel was swept by one of the worst summer storms in its history.

At 3.30 am on 5th June the wind was high and the rain fell almost horizontally but the forecast was at least promising, in fact the Meteorological Office anticipated a thirty-six hour improvement, beginning in the morning of the following day. The wind was to moderate and the wave height off Normandy was predicted at 60cms high. In response to this news General Eisenhower laconically announced "OK. We'll go." At 4.15 am Admiral Sir Bertram Ramsay issued a special "Order of the Day" to every officer and man of the Combined Naval Forces which read: "It is a privilege to take part in the greatest Amphibian Operation in History; the hopes and prayers of the Free World and all the enslaved People of Europe will be with us; we cannot fail them. I count on every man to do his utmost to ensure the success of this great enterprise which is the climax of the war in Europe; good luck to you all and God speed."

The crossing of the Channel, when it began took place at the height of the storm and station keeping in convoy was to become a major problem, particularly for those in the landing craft. Despite this none of the 2,000- plus ships and craft engaged in the operation sank as a result of collisions. On arrival in the Bay of the Seine the crews of the ships were astonished to see the two flashes of the lighthouse on the Barfleur headland which could, as in peacetime, be seen for 29 miles. Clearly the Germans were not worried!

To suggest that the enemy remained totally at ease is, to be sure, not entirely true. Although certain facts began to arouse suspicion amongst some officers within the German High Command, no one appeared to be capable of forming a precise opinion as to what was happening. In fact, despite the Luftwaffe weather forecasters regularly predicting possible Allied invasion opportunities, other experts stated that the enemy had already let three good periods of favourable weather pass without landing and their chances in the weeks to come seemed to be very uncertain. Any potential airborne assault for 5th and 6th June was also ruled out. This accounts for the fact that the Commander of the 1st SS Panzerkorps, Sep Dietrich, was in Brussels, far away from the eventual front and Feldmarshall Erwin Rommel was at home in Germany, endeavouring to obtain Hitler's authority to station the 12th Panzerdivision ('Hitlerjunend') closer to the coast.

Late into the evening of 5th June messages to the French resistance units, from the BBC, increased twofold and radar stations sited between Le Havre and Cherbourg were heavily 'jammed' whilst those to the north of the Seine, deceived by "Operation Fortitude", reported hundreds of 'aircraft' and ships approaching towards the Pas de Calais. A message broadcast by the BBC quoting the following lines from Paul Verlaine's Chanson d'Automne (Autumn Song) : Blessent mon coeur. D'une longeur (wound my heart with monotonous langour) signalled to the French Resistance that the invasion would take place within 48 hours.

The Germans became uneasy and the 15th Army, based north of the Seine, was put on full alert. The confusion created by the Allies resulted in alarm amongst the enemy being only partially raised.

At 2.00 am on 6th June the coastal defence battery at Saint Marcouf reported Allied parachutists landing. In turn other reports quickly followed but again remarkably little credence was attached to them. Finally, at 6.45 am Rommel's staff were informed " The depth of the aerial landings in the region of the Orne and in the southern Cotentin seem to indicate a large scale attack. The aim of the coastal bombardments is not yet clear. They seem to be a measure of protection in concert with actual attacks at other points. Our air and sea reconnaissance since dawn had not discovered anything new." The Germans had been thoroughly mystified.

The British cruiser *Glasgow* proceeded to her assembly point at point 'Z', 13 miles south-east off the Isle of Wight (nicknamed "Piccadilly Circus"), before falling in station with the US battleships *Texas* and *Arkansas* ahead of her, and with the Free French Ships

Georges Leygues and *Montcalm* astern. In line they then passed through the war channels off the north coast of Cornwall, before making their way across the English Channel to take up positions in the Baie de la Siene off Vierville. Under the command of Rear Admiral J.L. Hall, USN, these ships made up Bombarding Force "C", in support of Assault Force "O" which was the force destined to make the assault on St Laurent-sur-Mer in the United States Sector. Force "O" was made up of twelve destroyers plus the major warships: the heavy cruiser USS *Augusta*, flagship of the Western Force, carrying Lieutenant General Omar N. Bradley, USS *Arkansas*, a Wyoming class battleship, USS *Texas*, a *New York* class battleship and HMS *Glasgow*. The force, as the initial indicates, was responsible for "Omaha" beach and the area to be covered by the ships extended from Port-en-Bessin in the east to Signy to the west.

From the first hours of 6th June the fleet deployed without difficulties. The Germans had failed to lay delayed action mines in the sector, and the Allied bombardment group was able to manoeuvre without difficulty in those areas swept by the mine-sweepers. The Allied bombardment group, which consisted of the two veteran battleships *Arkansas* and *Texas*, HMS *Glasgow*, the Free French cruisers *Montcalm* and *Georges Leygues* and three American and three British destroyers took up their positions, the big ships six miles off the coast while the destroyers were just 5,000 yards offshore. The bombardment commenced according to plan and in order to retain the element of surprise it was to last 35 minutes, barely enough. The *Texas* using her 14" guns to great effect, pounded a heavy gun battery at Pointe du Hoc to score a number of direct hits on the casements and create enormous craters with those shells that missed their intended target. Inshore the destroyers took on machine gun nests and radar stations. A mile and a half to the east the USS *Cormick*, FF *Georges Leygues* and the destroyer HMS *Tanatside* launched a fearsome attack on the beach access route leading to Saint Laurent. The hamlet of Les Moulins, believed to be occupied by entrenched Germans, received particularly careful treatment from *Arkansas* and *Glasgow* which both expended powerful broadsides upon it. Further along the *Montcalm* and an American destroyer fired on Port-en-Bessin and other targets to contain the enemy and prevent them from participating in the battle that was to follow. Apart from the batteries at Pointe du Hoc, the Allied bombardment was above all designed to destroy the defending infantry and their machine gun nests.

OPERATION 'NEPTUNE' — THE NAVAL BOMBARDMENT

In advance of the Normandy landings the *Glasgow*'s Captain wrote a prayer.

The Prayer written by Captain C.P. Clarke, DSO, RN before the Normandy Landings:

"Lord, bless this enterprise to restore peace with freedom to the peoples of Europe. We give thanks for the privilege of taking part in it. We are a mighty company, but having done all we can, the fate of this operation is in Thy hands."

"For ourselves in the *Glasgow* we offer our lives and ask Thy blessings on our endeavours. Give to each of us quiet confidence, courage and endurance, that our ship may give her best."

Finally, if some of us should be taken, we ask for the comfort and care of those who have loved and depended upon us."

AMEN

This was used, together with the following one, written by Admiral Lord Horatio Nelson on the eve of the Battle of Trafalgar, before HMS *Glasgow* went to enter the conflict.

Prayer written by Admiral Lord Horatio Nelson on the eve of the Battle of Trafalgar:

"May the great God, whom I worship, grant to my country, and for the benefit of Europe in general, a great and glorious victory; and may no misconduct in any one tarnish it; and may humanity after victory be the predominant feature in the British Fleet.

For myself personally, I commit my life to Him that made me, and may His blessing alight on my endeavours for serving my country faithfully. To Him I resign myself, and the just cause, which is entrusted to me to defend."

AMEN. AMEN. AMEN.

6th June 1944

The military planners believed that two American Regimental Combat Teams (RCT's), followed by the 1st and 29th Infantry Divisions, could overwhelm the enemy and advance into the beach's five bluffs via five draws which led from the beach to the high ground in the vicinity of Vierville, Colleville and St.Laurent.

Each RCT had four rifle companies in the first wave, and would be assisted by naval gunfire, heavy bombing of the German defences by B-24 Liberators, support of the 741st and 743rd DD (amphibious) tank battalions, backed up by several battalions of engineers and naval demolition personnel and howitzer battalions. Immediately before H-Hour, 329 B-24 Liberators began to bomb the "Omaha" enemy beach defences. As they flew in to drop their bombs fate intervened to obscure the Normandy coast with low cloud. Fearing that they might drop their bombs on landing craft below the pilots delayed the drop by several seconds to ensure they were over France. Tons of high explosive fell from the sky to strike the ground several miles inland, leaving the coast defences untouched.

The attack prevented the Germans from moving more men to defend the beaches but gave no assistance to the troops who were about to land.

At 5.54 am, H-1, on the morning fn the 6th of June 1944, Naval bombardment of the coastal defences in the "Omaha" beach area commenced. Those ships assigned to this task included the US battleships *Texas* and *Oklahoma*, the Free French cruisers *Georges Leygues* and HMS *Glasgow*. The British cruiser swung her six-inch armament and proceeded to engage her designated target, Les Moulins. The bombardment ceased at 6.30 am to allow the first troops to be landed on "Omaha" beach. Although the naval gunfire was much more effective than the bombardment from the air, burying some enemy gun emplacements and destroying numerous rocket units, it failed to inflict crippling damage on the Germans because of the short duration of the engagement. The Allied navies had argued for a longer period of bombardment but were over-ruled by the commanders of land forces, who feared that this would allow the enemy to heavily reinforce Normandy against attack. The element of surprise was considered to be greater than that of a longer naval assault.

Visitors walking along the Normandy coast in peacetime cannot fail to notice the difference between the "Utah" and "Omaha" beaches. "Utah" presents a totally flat hinterland, varied only to the north where hills offer views out to sea. In contrast, "Omaha" has a continuous line of yellowish-brown cliffs which give way seawards via a narrow band of marram grass and sand dunes to a beach which is exposed, at low tide, for 300 yards distance. It is the uniformity of the cliffs that is striking, making access routes up them difficult to differentiate. Beyond the cliffs, inland, villages can only be identified by the shape and design of their church towers, thereby creating an impression of hostility.

For the American Assault troops dawn came at 5.58 am on a grey, grim, windy day, with waves five to six feet high in mid-channel being whipped up by a fifteen-knot wind as landing craft, containing men of the American Divisions under Major General Clarence R. Heubner, approached their designated Normandy beach. These were among the first of the American assault force and, from behind, above and ahead they heard the sounds of shells being fired from the warships, including *Glasgow*, to pound the German fortifications.

At 6.30 am, on schedule, thirty six landing craft lowered their ramps to discharge 1,450 of the assault force into water which was waist deep. The troops waded ashore, 100yards distant, to encounter a four mile sweep of sand and shingle, scattered with angular obstacles, which extended a quarter of a mile to the land beyond.

For the Germans this was an easy beach to defend, where 'Hedgehogs,' concrete anti-tank traps and mined obstacles had been sited on the beach, and 75mm and 88mm guns could rake the beach from walls three feet thick. Facing the beach was a line of strong points — eight big gun emplacements, 35 pillboxes, 18 anti-tank guns and 85 machine gun nests. Behind the beach stood German strong points of pillboxes, machine gun nests, and big gun emplacements strung out along the coast.

Unknown to the Allies, the Germans had patiently moved the 352nd Division from inland positions to coastal defence positions, which included "Omaha" beach. Instead of being met by a defence force of perhaps a thousand men from the German 716th Infantry Division, made up of mainly Poles or Russian conscripts who were not expected to adopt a fight to the death attitude, the invading force was met by part of the German 352nd Infantry Division, under the command of Lieutenant General Dietrich Kraiss. These were veterans of the tough Eastern Front and the strength of the defenders had been increased from four battalions to eight. Failure to detect the presence of this division was to prove very costly.

The naval bombardment was directed further inland as the first wave of the 16th and 116th RCT's approached the beach. A strong lateral current was now playing havoc with the inbound craft to push them eastwards at varying rates. Rifle Companies were now approaching the wrong landing areas and in some case their platoons were no longer together. Heavy seas were making the troops very ill, and many of the landing craft shipped water, several of them being swamped. Planned to land ahead of the infantry, the DD tanks also experienced difficulties in the seaway, as the waves caused the struts supporting canvas flotation skirts on the vehicles to collapse. Deprived of support the tanks sank and many of their crews drowned. Of the original thirty-two tanks that were launched only five made it safely ashore! Similarly, the rough weather prevented DUKW's, carrying artillery weapons, from landing, thereby further depleting the much needed backup.

The 743rd battalion fared better because the skippers of the LCT's decided to take their craft up to the waterline rather than risk an earlier launch. Although many of the tanks were destroyed or damaged as they landed, sufficient numbers reached the beach to provide the required fire support for the landing infantry. Troops shore-bound in the landing craft witnessed the fierce naval gun and rocket fire being put down on the beaches. While some wondered why the enemy had failed to respond others prayed that the Germans had pulled back or had been pounded into submission. The answer came when the landing craft were approximately four hundred yards from shore. The eerie silence of the beach broke when German forward observers called in pre-targeted retaliation from rocket pits and the emplacements of the enemy's 352nd Artillery Battalion. Simultaneously well sited anti-tank weapons, some of which were in heavily fortified casements built into the edge of the cliffs, began to pick off targets on the sand. Pre-sited machine gun emplacements joined in to send a withering stream of bullets into the advancing Americans. Not only were the Americans very seasick, they were weighed down with heavy uniforms (impregnated to resist a feared gas attack), assault jackets with pockets stuffed full of ammunition and grenades plus weapons and helmets. In some cases the men jumped out of the landing craft into water over their heads and drowned as a result. Those who did not were blown apart by machine-gun and mortar fire. Shocked survivors sought the comfort of the obstacles placed there, in the water, by the Germans. There was no quick charge up the beach to storm the enemy defences, whose fire was too effective. It took many minutes for men, exhausted, overloaded and soaked through, to reach a line of water- worn rocks that ran parallel to the sea wall. Many weapons and radios were lost and communication between the units was impossible. Losses amongst the troops were very heavy and entire companies were decimated. Successive waves of infantry units landed with varying success, some making it to the beach with relatively few casualties.

The Germans continued to saturate the beachhead from all directions, pinning down the invaders, lowering morale and leaving many of the Americans in shock.

Between 7.30 am and 8.15 am three American command units had landed and it was quickly realised that the original plan would have to be aborted. The German defences had proved too strong to be taken by a frontal attack and would have to be assaulted from the rear. This meant that the infantry had to climb the bluffs. The American commanders shouted, cajoled and cursed the men, urging them forward to attack the enemy in their trenches. This rallying of the troops gave rise to one of the famous quotes of the day spoken by Colonel Taylor of the 16th Infantry Division who said, "Two kinds of people are staying on this beach, the dead and those who are going to die. Now get the hell out of here!"

Throughout that morning *Glasgow*, with the assistance of air spotter aircraft, continued to engage selected targets ashore. In the afternoon, halfway through the Afternoon Watch, the cruiser moved closer inshore to open fire on enemy transport convoys, making their way along the coastal roads, before shifting position yet again to engage other selected targets. The assembled American battleships and French cruisers continued to put down a barrage of shells, aided by destroyers which were close in, seeking out targets in support of the flanking attack by the infantry. Direct targeting was difficult because of the smoke and haze so the naval gunners simply fired where they saw enemy tanks and infantry retaliating.

The naval bombardment, involving battleships, cruisers including *Glasgow*, destroyers and rocket launching assault craft, had done its job of knocking out many of the enemy positions to complete a task which the aircraft failed to achieve. By evening, the US army had established a beachhead on "Omaha", having lost over 3,000 men, 50 tanks, 26 artillery pieces and 2,300 tons of supplies. Fifty landing craft and ten larger vessels were lost in the sea. "Omaha" beach must be counted as a hard won victory for the US forces to establish an essential beachhead between "Utah" and those assaulted by the British forces. It was won and held at great and unexpected cost.

With the approach of evening, just before 8.00 pm a naval barrage of blind fire was put down on shore batteries suspected of shelling those troops already ashore on the beaches. When the cease-fire order came *Glasgow* withdrew to a safe position offshore where she remained overnight. During the bombardment HMS *Glasgow* had fired over five hundred rounds of six-inch high explosive shells.

Colonel S.B.Mason, Chief of Staff, 1st Division later said, "The German defences should have been impregnable. I am firmly convinced that without the naval gunfire we positively could not have crossed the beaches. We encountered on the beaches German pillboxes, fortified houses and gun positions, and it was apparent that the naval guns had worked them over. General Huebner concurred."

On Wednesday the 7th June, dawn came at a little before 7.00 am and *Glasgow*, in company with the USS battleship *Texas*, returned to take up a position from which she could continue the offensive. The British cruiser fired a total of 270 HE shells at the enemy positions as she bombarded Formigny, and provided fire support for US infantry advancing towards Isigny.

Throughout the day the cruiser frequently changed her position to maintain a bombardment of identified targets ashore in Trevies and Formigny. By opening fire on enemy positions near Grandchamps les Bains, on the following day, 8th June, the British cruiser continued to support the American invasion land forces. During the next two days German heavy gun batteries at Saint Marcouf, Crisbecq and Quinville continued to shell the landing beaches and had to be destroyed one by one. (By 14th June all the casements had been reduced to rubble). HMS *Glasgow* received more than a dozen calls from the ground forces for fire support against enemy troop concentrations, vehicle convoys and mobile gun batteries south of Vierville. She responded and bombarded the French coastline, expending a further 423 rounds of HE shells in the process. Five days after the successful Allied landing at Normandy *Glasgow* left the "Neptune" area and sailed for Portsmouth in order to replenish supplies of ammunition before returning, the next day, to anchor in the Baie de la Seine to fire more rounds at selected targets near Grandchamps.

Bombardment of Cherbourg

On 17th June the *Glasgow* returned to take up a position off St Vast in the "Utah" beach area, and between the 18th and 21st June she patrolled off that Normandy landing beach, moving inshore to a position 3.7 miles off St. Marcouf, to anchor in the fire support channels during daylight. From this position she engaged enemy tanks, trenches and flak batteries ashore, withdrawing to a safe position at night before making passage to Portland.

General Dwight D Eisenhower, Allied Supreme Commander, when formulating the invasion plan, considered the port of Cherbourg to be at the crux of the Allied offensive and unless the enemy could be removed from the town the Germans would be presented with an opportunity of hemming in the invading force. This could be further exploited so well that the invasion might be neutralised.

Eighteen days after the D-Day Offensive the port of Cherbourg remained in German hands and on 20th June Lieutenant General Bradley, commanding the First US Army forces, called for naval support. The following day, at 10.45 pm the cruiser *Glasgow*, under the command of Captain Clarke, rendezvoused at Portland with US Ships the heavy cruiser *Tuscaloosa*, flagship of Rear Admiral Morton L. Deyo USN, battleship *Nevada* and heavy cruiser *Quincy*, and HMS *Enterprise* with a screening force of US Ships, the *Benson* class destroyers, *Hambleton*, *Ellyson*, *Rodman*, *Emmons*, *Murphy* and *Gherardi* to set sail as the Bombardment Squadron, Group 1. The Squadron's task was firstly to neutralise the coastal guns on the northern and eastern horns of the Contenin Peninsula by which Cherbourg was defended, and secondly to assist the advancing Allied troops by destroying tanks and artillery batteries inland. However, a violent storm arose, the worst June storm for forty years, which raged for four days, stranding eight hundred vessels on the beaches and wrecking "Mulberry Harbour A" off Arromanches. It scattered the bombardment fleet, and the earliest date that the bombardment could be laid on was deemed to be the 24th of June. General "Lightning" Collins, aware of the importance of capturing the French port said "We've got to get to Cherbourg in a hurry, this must be one of the first major efforts of all Divisional commanders."

The French port was defended heavily by determined Germans who were entrenched in twenty casement batteries, fifteen of which had guns of 150mm calibre or greater, including three 280mm. In addition, there were a considerable number of batteries of 75mm and 88mm guns, some of which could be trained inland as well as out to sea. Unknown to the Allies some 40,000 troops were occupying the town under strict orders from Hitler to hold it at all costs. In order to break the resistance of the principal enemy batteries the fleet was tasked with bombarding them. Prior to this offensive Rear Admiral Deyo had commanded a bombardment group, which had demoralised the enemy, in the assault against the Japanese-held island of Iwo Jima in the Pacific Ocean.

On Sunday 25th June HMS *Glasgow*, in company with CTF (Commander Task Force) 129 Rear Admiral Deyo, aboard his flagship USS " *Tuscaloosa*," and other ships set off to take part in the assault on Cherbourg as part of Group 1. Prior to this offensive Rear Admiral Deyo had commanded a bombardment group, which had demoralised the enemy, in the assault against the Japanese-held island of Iwo Jima in the pacific Ocean. The group was preceded by a flotilla of minesweepers which swept specific channels, along which Group 1 was to approach the designated FSA (Fire Support Area), whilst overhead the Ninth USAAF provided aerial protection cover.

As Group 1 approached the French coast, at a distance of fifteen miles offshore, Rear Admiral Deyo received a message from General Collins, commanding his VII Corps, which was to alter the original role set for the fleet. The American infantry commander had called upon the ships to fire on German 150mm and 280mm coastal batteries on the eastern and north-eastern horns of the peninsular, and other smaller targets selected and assigned by the army, instead of those which had been selected as priority by the Task Force Commander. General Collins's message did not please the naval commanders! Following some discussion a compromise was reached, and the bombarding group were permitted to open fire on a number of specified coastal batteries. For an hour *Glasgow* and the other ships approached Cherbourg behind the minesweepers. Nothing happened. Eventually *Quincy* launched a spotter plane which reported that two of the priority targets on the Cap de la Hague had been totally destroyed, probably by the Germans themselves. The news was hardly encouraging. Had the fleet come for nothing?

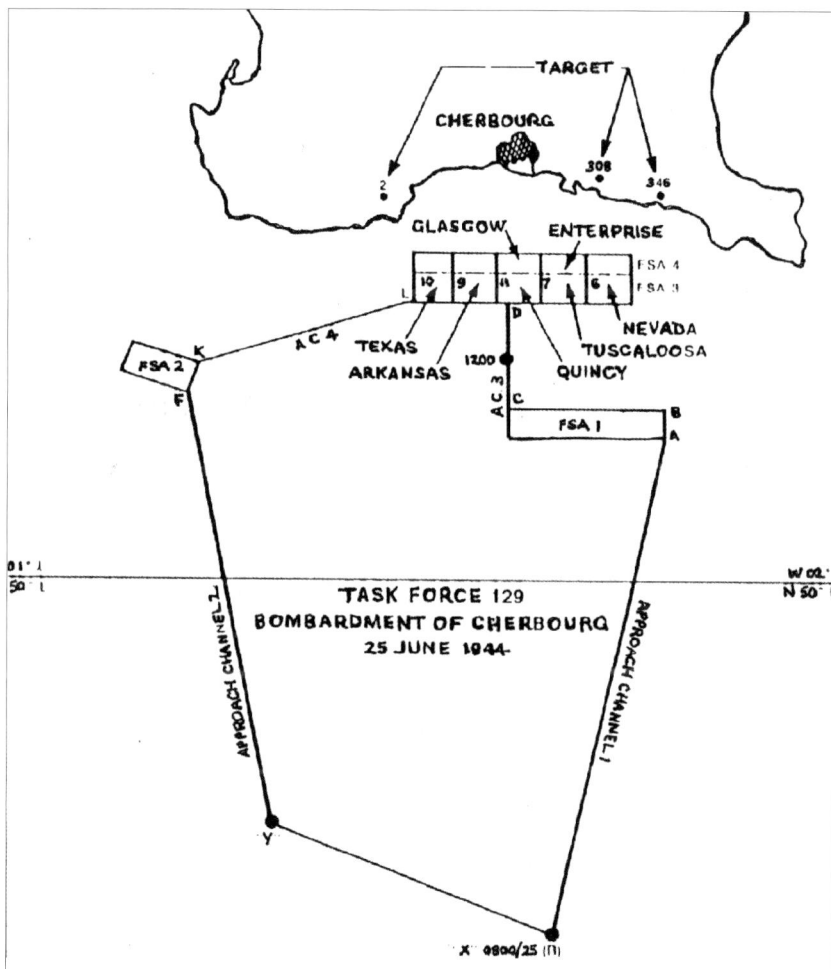

Task Force 129's Bombardment Positions

Just after eight o'clock in the morning *Glasgow* reached position "X" at the southern end of the specially swept "Approach Channel 1." At 10.07 am orders were issued for *Glasgow* to act independently and proceed to FSA 1, to the north of the remainder of the Squadron, followed by HMS *Enterprise. Glasgow* stemmed the tide, with engines stopped, to remain in position waiting for the attendant minesweepers to sweep Approach Channel 3. The two warships *Glasgow* and *Enterprise* manoeuvred to the northward of the swept water back and forth partly in, and on occasion partly to, the north of FSA3 providing support for each other. Ten minutes before noon the minesweepers turned to begin sweeping FSA 4 to the westward and *Glasgow* stemmed the tide to keep the ship in swept water. Noon, the hour planned for the commencement of the bombardment approached; no calls had been received from the shore control parties, nor had any shells been fired from the German batteries. As the tension mounted brilliant flashes of light were seen beside the village of Querqueville, and a salvo of 150mm shells burst close to the minesweeper HMS *Sidmouth*, at the head of Group 1. The minesweepers quickly turned north to escape and Admiral Deyo ordered *Glasgow* to fire on the enemy battery, and seven minutes later, at 12.14 pm, she opened up with her main armament, soon to be joined by HMS *Enterprise*. However, the haze which hung over the land and the smoke and dust raised by the falling six-inch shells hampered air-spotting assistance and observation by SFCP's (Shore Fire Control Parties) and prevented the enemy battery from being correctly located. The Germans, profiting from a lull in the bombardment, fired more salvoes at the minesweepers, forcing Admiral Deyo to order their retirement.

HMS Glasgow Bombarding the German Shore Defences – Cherbourg June 1944
(IWM)

174

The German commander of the battery, named 308 by the Americans, focussed his attention on *Glasgow* and fired a salvo at the British cruiser. Twenty minutes later shells fell close astern, and *Glasgow*'s stern contour plate was perforated, forcing the warship to take evasive action.

When one of the larger warships was being hit the others would close her and draw the enemy's fire. This generally proved to be effective because the fire being returned from the coastal guns decreased in accuracy. Often the gunners became confused by the multiple targets being presented and by the manoeuvres completed by the naval vessels. The enemy shore batteries continued to fire on the warships and more shells continued to fall close by.

HMS Glasgow Straddled by 105mm Shells – 25th June 1944   *(IWM)*

At 12.51 pm, *Glasgow* took a direct hit in the port hanger.

HMS Glasgow Taking a Direct Hit on the Port Hanger   *(IWM)*

Damage to the Port Hanger

When "Action Stations" had sounded a Royal Marine rushed to his post, scrambling as he did so down the steel ladder leading to the shell room of "X" turret, several feet below the water line. Suddenly, there was a loud explosion and he was hurled against the racks holding the six-inch shells. Violent and distinctly alarming shudders reverberated along the hull for the whole of the ship's length. As he and his "oppos" squatted in the small compartment, totally surrounded by tier upon tier of highly explosive shells he knew the full meaning of unadulterated fear. Those who were in the TS, situated right down near the bottom of the ship below the armour plated deck, controlling the main armament, were also aware of the danger that threatened to destroy their existence and take them and their shipmates to a watery grave.

One minute later, after turning away and increasing speed, the ship was hit again, this time abreast the After Director Control position.

Damage control parties sprang into action and First Aid personnel took the wounded to the Sickbay where they received attention and treatment.

176

Damage caused by second shell

Having expended 96 rounds of high explosive shells, the cruiser ceased its engagement with the target (308) on the shore. Moving eastwards *Glasgow*, having identified a second target at 1.11 pm, continued to bombard the shore battery number 346, firing a total of 54 high explosive rounds.

In "X" turret manned by the Royal Marines, where the guns were named after biblical characters Shadrach, Meschach and Abednigo. the men did not need to recognise each other. They had worked together for so long and were so well trained that each man could do his job with his eyes closed. In a closely-knit environment the men had become more than nameless cogs in a great machine. Their names were no longer McLintott, Smith or Jackson, but numbers of the gun's crew 1,2,3,4 and so on, each with a specific duty to perform. For the next half an hour the cruiser remained under a steady attack from the enemy shore batteries.

Glasgow broke off the combat in order to escape the punishment and speeded up in a swept channel, under cover of a smoke-screen laid down by US destroyers *Ellyson* and *Emmons* to enable her captain to consider the damage to the cruiser caused by the German shells. Having determined that the ship's steering gear was unimpaired and satisfied she could continue the fight, Captain Clarke asked to be allowed to regain his position in the line. Admiral Deyo duly gave his permission.

The duel continued and around 1.00 pm *Enterprise's* spotter plane reported that two of battery 308's four guns had been destroyed. *Glasgow* returned to the conflict to re-engage the second enemy target, 346. Initially the destroyers' actions had distracted the German gunners, but the enemy fire intensified and soon enemy shells were falling ahead of the cruiser, forcing the ship to alter course towards the south-east. Further salvoes from the shore batteries were fired and it was not long before shells, forcing a change of course to withdraw to safety, straddled the cruiser. Aboard *Glasgow* the order to "Cease Fire" was given.

Although the cruiser was no longer within range of the shore battery (target 346) she became under accurate fire from target 308 and, at just before 2.45 pm, the ship was again very closely straddled, with evasive action quickly taken at full speed. During this action *Glasgow* received several near misses and some shells which caused damage to "Y" turret, the mid port side and aft areas of the ship. The bombardment continued and by 2.50 pm the battery had been temporarily neutralised at the expense of 318 six-inch shells.

During a period of ninety minutes which had been allotted to them, all the ships had fired on various targets without major results; the German batteries were not yet muzzled. Admiral Deyo, conscious of this, had asked General Collins if the fleet should continue firing. After a delay of forty-five minutes General Collins replied in the affirmative and asked for the bombardment to be maintained until 3.00 pm it being then 2.05 pm. The conflict was not over yet; battery 308 had returned to life, firing several salvoes at the US destroyer *Murphy*. The *Tuscaloosa*, two destroyers and the cruiser *Quincy* joined in the fray to put a third gun out of action. Several 14" salvoes from the *Nevada*, which was also called in, finally reduced the enemy battery, it seemed, into silence. In fact it resumed firing the moment the fleet left the area. Thus, the combined efforts of one battleship, four cruisers and numerous destroyers had not been conclusive; no more so, perhaps, than the battery itself which had failed to score a major hit on any of the Allied ships throughout the battle. At three o'clock that afternoon Rear Admiral Deyo signalled the bombardment fleet to withdraw, and soon afterwards *Glasgow* was ordered to break off the engagement.

The British cruiser, low on ammunition, turned to head for Portland to off-load the wounded and to re-provision. As she steamed northwards the following signal was received from Admiral Deyo: "Please extend my sympathy to your wounded and praise yourself and ship in quickly getting back into action. Though badly handicapped by poor spotting conditions ashore and seriously threatened by enemy gun batteries you gave a fine performance of the greatest value to the army at a critical time-all the ships did their full duty." This was followed with one from General Collins which read: "I witnessed your bombardment of the coastal batteries and covering points around Cherbourg; the results were excellent and did much to engage the enemy's fire whilst my troops stormed into Cherbourg."

At 3.30 pm Group 1 ceased fire for good and left with regrets that the German batteries had not been destroyed. This does not mean that the naval bombardment of Cherbourg was useless or ineffective. Although few direct hits had been registered the morale of the German troops, already hard pressed by the Allied infantry, had been lowered and the majority of the enemy batteries had been subdued. All naval firing ceased at 3.40 pm and the Squadron retired to regroup at Portland.

The only Group 1 ship to be damaged, other than superficially, despite blistering fire from the German defences, was *Glasgow*. This damage resulted from a spirited duel between the protagonists *Glasgow* and *Enterprise* for the Allies and the battery guns of the Germans, during which the enemy had concentrated its fire on the two British ships. Examination of the damage sustained by the first hit revealed that the enemy shells hitting the ship had been of the high explosive type, which had detonated on impact, causing numerous splinter holes over large areas in the vicinity of each hit. The outer side of the Port Hanger had been punctured by a hole approximately seven feet long by six feet high, the jagged edges of which had been turned inwards like the petals of a flower, with further damage in the form of holes, varying in size from half an inch to two inches in diameter, peppering an area approximately twenty four feet by twelve feet. The hanger roof was also distorted and perforated with splinter holes.

A large number of splinter holes had damaged the inner bulkhead of the hanger extending over an area of approximately thirty feet by twenty feet. Additional damage was caused to kit lockers near the hanger. Hit number two struck the Carley floats stored on the port side and peppered the plating, also scoring the hardwood decking nearby. The After Director Control Tower suffered similar damage, as did the Radar Office and port galleys. One near miss astern of the ship, on the port side, holed the Captain's cabin in two places through the stern contour plate and caused numerous strikes along the ship's side for a distance of up to sixty feet from the stern.

General Eisenhower stated after the bombardment that the final assault on Cherbourg had been materially assisted by heavy and accurate naval gunfire, which had inflicted tremendous damage to the shore batteries. Some of these were never active after the bombardment and remained pointing out to sea, even though they could have been turned inland. From the enemy's perspective the German General von Schlieben, in reporting to Feldmarshall Erwin Rommell, stated that the heavy fire from the sea was a major factor in rendering defence useless. This was a view shared by the German Admiral Kranke, former captain of the commerce raider the *Admiral Scheer*, who commented that the naval bombardment had been of a hitherto unequalled fierceness and had been a contributory cause of the loss of the port of Cherbourg.

At 9.00pm. that day Rear Admiral Deyo went aboard *Glasgow* to attend a Captain's conference hosted in Captain Clarke's well ventilated cabin, at the conclusion of which the order "Splice the Mainbrace" was given. Admiral Ramsay endorsed the gratitude to the commanders of the Bombardment Force and in his dispatches relating to "Overlord" he stated: "This operation was carried out with the greatest skill and determination."

The 29th June saw the German surrender of Cherbourg, during which more than 39,000 prisoners of war were taken. However, the port was now in ruins, destroyed by explosives and its waters non-navigable with ships that had been scuttled and sown mines. It would not be in use until 16th July!

From Portland, on 1st July, *Glasgow* set course to sail up the West Coast of England, rounded the top of Scotland and made her way down the East Coast heading for the River Tyne. Two days later, she was accepted into Palmer's Yard, Hebburn, to undergo a major refit. Although there were no fatalities resulting from the action bombarding Cherbourg, fifteen members of the crew were injured and these were taken ashore and sent to the Naval hospital at Cullercoats, and the remainder of the crew went on leave. After the leave period and before the ship "paid off" there was a farewell 'Booze-up' in Newcastle Town Hall, paid for in the main by NAAFI, and a good time was had by all!

New crew members joined the ship and Dockyard Routine was worked. On 28th December 1944, the First Anniversary of the Battle of the Bay, the acting Commanding Officer posted Daily Orders to remind the crew of the significant victory achieved by *Glasgow* and *Enterprise* the previous year.

DAILY ORDERS
THURSDAY 28Th DECEMBER 1944
TODAY IS THE FIRST ANNIVERSARY OF GLASGOW'S VICTORY OVER ELEVEN GERMAN DESTROYERS IN THE BAY OF BISCAY.
DUTY COMMANDING OFFICERLIEUTENANT EDRUPT.

OFFICER OF THE DAY	MR INSTANCE.
DUTY P.O	P.O. HART.
DUTY R.P.O	P.O. SHORT.
DUTY L.SEA	L.SEA. FOXALL.
EMERGENCY PARTY L.SEA	L.SEA. TEASDALE.
DUTY WATCH	RED WATCH.
DRESS OF THE DAY	REFITTING RIG.
ROUTINE	DOCKYARD ROUTINE.

SPECIAL PARTIES:		
	Extra Gunners Party	1 plus 6
	Messdecks (A.M. only)	4
	Shipwright's Party	1
	Torpedo Tube Chipping Party	3

LEAVE: - To the BLUE and WHITE watches from 0615 until 0730 Friday 29th December, Chief and Petty Officers 1800. Usual Watchkeepers leave.

NOTE: - On December 24th Glasgow left Harbour to intercept a German Blockade-runner. This was sunk on the 27th Dec. by the R.A.F. just before we reached it. Information we received of a force of German Destroyers and Glasgow and Enterprise proceeded at high speed into the Bay of Biscay to intercept them.

At about 1330 on the 28th Dec. 11 German Destroyers were sighted and as we were between the Germans and their base a hot action developed. At about 1530 we were running out of ammunition, and having sunk three disabled destroyers we altered course out of the Bay.

At 1830 we were attacked by 15 German Heinkels with Glider Bombs without success and finally returned to Plymouth.

The result of the action was,

Three German Destroyers sunk.
One severely damaged   (In dock 7 months)
Four fairly severely damaged (In dock over 3 months).

Our casualties were 2 killed.
                   11 wounded.

Forces engaged	Glasgow	12	6"
	Enterprise	7	6"
German forces	5 Narvik Destroyers	25	5.9"
	6 Elbing Destroyers	24	4.2"

Germans had about 80 Torpedoes to our 12.

IN MEMORIAM

Ord. Mechanic ....Roy W. Andrews.

Able Seaman ....John Smith

Killed in action on the 28th December 1943 on board this ship

COMMANDER

On 16th June 1945, her refit successfully completed, *Glasgow* departed from Palmers Yard and made passage to Rosyth. One month later, on 15th July, she left the naval base and headed for Scapa Flow before making her way into Thurso Bay, on the north-eastern coast of Scotland, where the newly fitted radars were fully tested and calibrated. The warship, now fully ready for sea service, proceeded to Greenock. After leaving Greenock *Glasgow* was engaged in an exercise which involved the RAF.

Off the Isle of Arran, three Beaufighters carried out a low level "attack" on the cruiser and, as he stood under "A" turret, Arthur Beards recalls the guns being swung round to line up on the incoming aircraft in order to test the firing circuits. Suddenly, both propellers on one of the planes stopped as though it had been hit. The pilot struggled to gain height and head for land but the aircraft plunged into the sea and the crew perished. The exercise was immediately called off and, with an air of sadness about her, *Glasgow* continued to make passage towards Portsmouth, where she arrived at the beginning of August.

During her refit in Hebburn *Glasgow* had been fitted with a "Y.E." beacon, which transmitted a coded signal in various sectors that aircraft could use to home in on the ship. Following the German surrender the cruiser was due to sail and lay off the Japanese coast, with Allied aircraft carriers laying off even further out to sea. Planes from the carriers would then carry out bombing raids on the Japanese mainland and make their return by using the beacon aboard *Glasgow* to guide them before following a different code out to the home carrier. However, with the surrender of the Japanese forces the plan was changed.

The Post War Years

During the years following the cessation of hostilities *Glasgow* fulfilled a much-needed role "showing the flag" in numerous foreign ports throughout Europe, the Adriatic, the Balkans, the Middle East and the West Indies to maintain a British presence. Often these duties were by nature ceremonial. However, when International unrest occurred in these theatres of operation she was deployed to deal with them as part of the peacekeeping role entrusted to Britain.

After the crew returned from leave the Captain mustered the ship's company on the foc'sle to inform the crew that the original programme was fortunately now no longer necessary and the ship was to go to the East Indies for a period of three years. On 23rd August 1945,a week after the VJ Day celebrations, *Glasgow* set sail for the Far East. As she made passage to Malta, three days out from the U.K, a small boat was spotted; its occupant in a state of collapse.

Glasgow stopped and a seaboat was lowered so that assistance could be given to the small boat's solo occupant, a Spaniard, who was suffering from sunburn and a shortage of water. The boat and its distressed owner were taken aboard the warship and a course was set to meet up with HMS *St.Austell Bay*. The Spaniard and boat were transferred and *Glasgow* continued on to her destination, Malta, where she entered Grand Harbour at the end of the month. Malta had taken a pounding during the war and the Island was in a state of turmoil, with most of the streets littered with the masonry from bombed buildings. In the harbour lay the sunken merchant ship *Ohio*.

Libertymen were ferried ashore by "Liberty-boat" to the Customs House Jetty where they were able to use the fernicula lift up into Valletta . Fresh from UK, those going ashore had to contend with the local paper currency, which had denominations of sixpence (2½p) one shilling (5p) and so on, which confused some of them especially when they had drunk some of the local brew. The only land transport ashore was the 'Garry', a horse drawn trap, while that on the water was provided by the Maltese 'Dghaijes,' or as Jack would say "Diso," and the fare between shore and ship was three pence (1½p). Most went for their run ashore down the "Gut," a street lined with dozens of bars having enticing names like the "Silver Dollar"and "Gypo Queen." All the bars provided some form of 'entertainment' and the matelots were able to drink copious quantities of bottled beer, called 'blues'. The most famous of these was the bar run by a couple of gays "Bobby and Sugar." Bobby played the piano while 'Sugar' was a female impersonator. Any matelot or marine causing trouble was rapidly dealt with by the Naval Patrol or the Maltese police. One policeman in particular, nicknamed 'Tiny', who was massive in stature was able to pick up a sailor under each arm and carry them of to the cooler. (In 1999 he was retired and living in Gozo.)

For nearly three weeks *Glasgow* engaged in gunnery and torpedo exercises, using her new radar to good effect, before weighing anchor and heading first for Aden before voyaging to Colombo, where she joined the East Indies Fleet under the command of Vice-Admiral Pallister, as C-in-C, on 1st October. In Trincomalee *Glasgow* joined up with the colony class cruiser *Jamaica* and the two aircraft carriers *Glory* and *Theseus* which had already been on station for more than two months before *Glasgow's* arrival.

Shortly after her arrival *Glasgow* was engaged in exercises with the carriers and Guy Cook recalls " a number of the older naval officers were unfamiliar with Radar. Whilst I was in the Air Direction Room, during an exercise with *Glory*, watching the display screen I counted 7 aircraft taking off from the carrier, which was below the horizon line. I reported this to the bridge where the C-in-C 'pooh-poohed' the suggestion that this was possible and he was not best pleased when, moments later, they roared over *Glasgow's* upper deck." This incident proves that the navy had its share of 'Colonel Blimps'.

It was during the same exercise that an unfortunate accident occurred. Two brothers were serving aboard *Glory* as Lieutenants, one a pilot the other a Deck Landing Officer. The latter was at the end of the carrier on the flight deck with his 'Bats' guiding the in-bound pilots aboard when his brother came in too low and crashed into *Glory's* stern to die instantly in the crash. The exercise finished on a sad note.

Glasgow's next port of call was Singapore where, in company with *Jamaica*, she swept the Malacca Straits for mines using 'Paravanes' and those which came to the surface were destroyed by gunfire.

After five days *Glasgow* and *Jamaica* returned to Singapore harbour in time to witness the departure of a Hospital Ship full of British troops, who had been PoW's, on their way back to 'Blighty'. Little did *Glasgow's* crew realise as they lined the rails, cheering them on their way, that the Hospital Ship was to hit a mine two days later, as it cleared the Straits and passed the Nicobar Islands. As soon as the news reached *Glasgow*, she immediately set sail at full speed to assist but when she reached the area all survivors had been rescued by HM Ships *Orion* and *London*. The only evidence of the incident that remained was the burnt out hulk of the Hospital Ship on the beach.

Barely one week later a large number of camp beds were taken on board and the cruiser was engaged, in company with *Jamaica*, in ferrying troops of the 14th Army from the naval base in Singapore to Colombo, where they awaited repatriation to the UK.

After she re-provisioned and took on ammunition in Colombo, on 20th November, she continued to patrol the waters between Colombo, Trincomalee and Mandapan until she entered Singapore, on 23rd December, where the crew was able to celebrate Christmas.

Safe from threat and the restrictions of wartime rationing in Britain, the crew was able to enjoy a veritable feast aboard as the first post-war Christmas was celebrated.

Ye Xmas Fare

On board ye Goode Shippe GLASGOW

The Forgotten East Indies Fleet

Two days after Christmas 1945 the *Glasgow* sailed for Colombo and on 13th January 1946, Captain Clarke relinquished command to Captain A.G.V. Hubback, OBE. In keeping with naval tradition Captain Clarke was rowed ashore before the ship sailed from the port to engage in troop transportation, taking 350 servicemen from The Sussex Regiment to Singapore.

As she patrolled the waters surrounding Trincomalee, Singapore and Surabaya, a decision was made that the crew's diet should be supplemented by a supply of fish, and a depth charge was dropped over the stern. The depth charge detonated and much to the disappointment of the onlookers only half a dozen 'tiddlers' floated to the surface. The experiment was not repeated!

With the Japanese surrender and cessation of hostilities those on board *Glasgow* were looking forward to returning to UK and demobilisation. This was not to be because, on 27th January 1946, the cruiser was dispatched to Java's largest naval base, at Surabaya, in support of British troops who were there to contain a local rebellion. The murder of Brigadier Mallaby, Commander of the 49th Indian Infantry Brigade, by Indonesian rebels resulted in General Sir Philip Christison, Allied Commander, Java, calling on the rebel leader, Dr. Soekarno, to hand over the assassins or face military intervention. Dr. Soekarno failed to respond positively and the Allied Commander, having no alternative, took the appropriate action which involved all branches of those armed forces based at Surabaya. After a naval bombardment, aided by air strikes carried out by the RAF, troops of the 5th Indian Division moved into the city to release 3,500 Dutch Prisoners of War, including women and children, due to be shipped home via Singapore. It is not commonly known that the military

"Spike" Window

forces were obliged to employ Japanese prisoners to assist with security operations until Dutch armed forces were able to take over their former colony from the British Task Force.

It is customary for those members of the crew crossing the Equator for the first time to be summoned by the "Court of King Neptune" to participate in the "Crossing the Line" ceremony. On 23rd January as the ship made its way to Surabaya, Drummond "Spike" Window received such a summons:

SUMMONS TO ATTEND FOR INITIATION

*Neptune by grace of Mythology, Lord of all the waters, Sovereign of all the oceans, Lord High Admiral of the Bath, Grand Knight Captain of the Trident with Oak Laurels, Baron of the Bath Tub Etc. Etc. Whereas it has pleased us to convene a Court to be holden on board His Britannic Majesty's Ship **GLASGOW** on the Fxle thereof, at the hour of 09.00 on the 24th day of January, in the year one thousand nine hundred and forty six.*

By those present we summon you DRUMMOND WINDOW to appear at the said Court to tender us the usual homage and to be initiated into the mystic rights according to the ancient usage of our Kingdom. Hereof, nor you, nor any of you may fail, as you will answer at your peril and to the delight of our trusty Bodyguard, given at our Court on the Equator this 23rd day of January 1946.

During one of the patrols a seaman had fallen asleep on top of one of the four-inch gun turrets only to fall off into the water.

His life was saved thanks to the presence of mind of the Lifebuoy Sentry. When it came to the "Crossing the Line" ceremony he was the first to be initiated!

HMS *Glasgow* arrived at Surabaya but she was not involved in quelling the uprising. Her presence off-shore acted as a deterrent to the rebels. *Glasgow* returned to Singapore on 5th February 1946 to engage in "Full Power" trials before entering a Floating Dock a week later for maintenance work to be carried out.

Crossing the Line Ceremony 23rd January 1946

On 18th February HMS *Glasgow* left the floating dock and steamed for Colombo where she received orders to proceed at full speed to Bombay to intercede in the mutiny of the Royal Indian Navy. According to a stoker on board at the time "every rivet on the ship

HMS Glasgow in Floating Dock Singapore February 1946. (AB)

was vibrating. Down in the engine room as the ship sped towards its destination an incident was about to happen. Fuel oil was being transferred from the main tank into an auxiliary tank, to be pre-heated prior to injection into the boilers, by a reciprocating pump. The Stoker Petty Officer set the pump to maintain a steady supply of oil to the thirsty boilers; unfortunately the supply exceeded the demand with the result that excess oil found its way up the breather tubes to be discharged and cover half of the ship. The crew was not amused, especially those who were given the task of cleaning it off.

Glasgow arrived at her destination after a two-day passage to face an assembled fleet of Royal Indian Navy cruisers and destroyers, with 12,000 RIN (Royal Indian Navy) personnel aboard their warships. These were being supported by the Communist party and local strike committee led by Vitab Kumar. The citizens of the city of Bombay were gripped with fear of such a magnitude previously unknown. The heart of the City was paralysed; even the renowned Taj Mahal hotel came under the threat of shelling from the guns of the Royal Indian Navy and assault from the mobs of local supporters.

On arrival in Bombay harbour *Glasgow*, with her two escorting destroyers, took up station near the "Gateway to India", where her guns were uncovered and preparations were made to take action against known targets ashore and afloat. Ashore, Vice Admiral J.H. Godfrey, Flag Officer Commanding the Royal Indian Navy, called on all RIN ratings to surrender. Failure to do so would result in the British warships being ordered to open fire.

The first indications that the RIN were ready to surrender came when Mr. Jinnah, from Calcutta, offered his services to act as a mediator for the rebels. The deadlock was broken, and with it came the surrender of the RIN and the Strike Committee. The local population made their way down to the "Gateway of India," an archway similar to Marble Arch, during the day to see if, in fact, their navy had surrendered and listen to speeches given by members of the Strike Committee.

The Royal Indian Navy as seen from the "Gateway to India"   (SW)

The speeches were impassioned and aimed at creating a bond between those in the Services and those who were civilians. "Our strike has been an historic event in the history of our nation. For the first time the blood of men in the Service and the man in the street flowed together in a common cause. We in the Services will never forget this, we also hope that you, our Brothers and Sisters, will not forget — long live our great people — Jai Hind."

Vice-Admiral Godfrey, aboard his Flagship the *Navada,* accepted the formal surrender and ordered all Royal Indian naval personnel to co-operate with the authorities pending the outcome of talks, which aimed to reach a solution to the problems raised by the uprising. He informed the surrendered mutineers that passive resistance would not be tolerated but their grievances would be fairly and fully considered by the Courts of Inquiry. Representatives of the ratings, in their response, stated "The RIN will not hesitate for one moment to come out on strike again if the authorities make any attempt to victimize a single striker." The following day, 26th February, all Royal Indian naval ships had run up the "Black Flag" of surrender, and the ringleaders were arrested and held for further questioning. Troops had secured the Naval Shore Stations and removed all ammunition and firearms. Naval boarding parties were put aboard the ships, to render the guns safe and hold the crews under guard pending further action by the naval authorities.

Two hundred people died and more than one thousand were injured in the Mutiny and civil riots which followed in its support, with extensive destruction and damage being caused to property in the city.

In the volatile India of that time the event was a "Nine Day Wonder." When an atmosphere of calm had been restored in the city, and before returning to Trincomalee, the *Glasgow* held two "Open Days". These gave the local people of Bombay the chance to witness for themselves that the crew were not "The filthy Imperialist pigs" as described by the Strike Committee in their press releases during the civil unrest.

Guy Cook, Boy Seaman, recalls "if hadn't been serious it could have been amusing. There we were one single ship against the whole of the Indian Navy, about four cruisers and countless Destroyers and Frigates. We would have stood no chance at all!"

Having successfully completed her mission *Glasgow* left India, on 3rd March, to return to Colombo. Here the cruiser, after re-oiling, embarked some political prisoners to be taken down to Zanzibar. The prisoners were held in the Port Hanger under Royal Marine guard and exercised daily on the boat deck.

Upon arrival at the entrance to Zanzibar the Port whaler was lowered, and manned by six Boy Seamen under the command of Lieutenant Balfour, the boat followed *Glasgow* into the harbour. For the remainder of the commission Lieutenant Balfour was responsible for the production of the ship's concert parties and pantomimes.

Next port of call was Port Louis, in Mauritius, to again 'Show the Flag' and soon after her arrival the ship was opened to visitors, which proved to be a popular local attraction.

Amongst those who went ashore in Port Louis was Stoker William Wright who, on seeing a street vendor selling 'lovely, luscious strawberries,' was tempted to buy some before a well dressed European informed the hungry matelot that the crop had been grown on human sewage. The strawberries immediately lost their appeal!

From Mauritius the warship made her way back to Simon's Town where she was destined to undergo a major refit and have one of her rolling keels, which had been ripped off, replaced.

HMS Glasgow entering Simon's Town 22nd March 1946

On 9th April 1946 she entered dry dock and when it had been drained hundreds of fish were found in the bottom. The Catering Officer quickly ordered their collection and these were stored, for future use, in the fridges.

Since the days of Nelson little alteration had been made to the living quarters of naval ratings — they had eaten, written letters and slept in the same small deck space and Captain Hubback decided that the refit provided an ideal opportunity to make improvements to the living conditions of the crew. The mess tables were removed, the mess decks were converted to 'lounges' and the starboard hanger became a cafeteria and cinema. These novel catering arrangements and comfortable mess decks, planned by the officers in consultation with the men, were deemed to be an unqualified success. One rating was quoted as saying, "This is far more like home." The venture had Admiralty approval but only on condition that no materials were obtained from Britain. Upon completion of the much needed internal improvements the ship was repainted, white hull and superstructure with buff coloured funnels, in the same colours as had been used by the pre-war East Indies Fleet. For the crew it was no joke keeping the ship 'Spick and Span.'

Being familiar with the layout of a ship is very important, particularly so in wartime, when going to action stations but italso had its advantages in times of peace. While *Glasgow* was in port one of her Midshipmen went aboard the aircraft carrier HMS *Colossus* and removed a life buoy as a souvenir. The absence of the life buoy was soon noticed by Sub Lieutenant Davison who, as OOW on the carrier, was loath to report the removal to the Commander and admit that he had lost some of the ship's property. The Sub Lieutenant, having served aboard HMS *Glasgow* 1943–1944, completed his Watch and, using his past knowledge of the cruiser's layout, went aboard *Glasgow* accompanied by a Royal Marine. The couple headed for the Gunroom where the cruiser's "trophies" were kept, and they not only recovered the life buoy but also, for good measure, removed another of *Glasgow's* souvenirs, a barber's pole, before returning to the carrier!

HMS Glasgow in Dry Dock Simon's Town for Major Refit

HMS *Glasgow* left the dry dock on 29th May and berthed alongside the jetty for the remainder of her refit, which was completed on 5th July. Having completed her fifteen week refit the cruiser proceeded out to sea, for sea trials, and as she did so a tragedy was about to unfold. It would appear that an officer on the Quarterdeck, noticing a hawser trailing over the side, ordered a Midshipman to get it pulled in. Instead of pulling the hawser in himself the 'Snotty' went looking for a seaman to do it and in the meantime the hawser became entangled around the port outer propeller and the ship stopped. The regular diver, Petty Officer Starley, was in the Sickbay, suffering with an ulcerated leg, and Chief Petty Officer Richards (Shipwright), who needed to validate his certificate to dive, was asked to go down to carry out an inspection and clear the obstruction. Chief Petty Officer Richards went over the side, attached to a lifeline, with two air bottles and wearing a facemask and nose-clip. The sea was calm at the time but as Roy Dixon recalled the "Old Girl" was rolling in the ground swell and subjected to strong tidal currents. When the diver failed to appear at the surface after completing his task, concern was expressed as to his safety. Those on deck were unable to pull the "chippy" back round the shaft and up to the surface. On learning of the accident Petty Officer Starley leapt from his cot in the Sickbay, ran aft, and with minimal delay fitted his equipment and went down to try and rescue the unfortunate trapped diver. He managed to locate CPO Richards, who had been knocked off the propeller shaft to fall on the wrong side of it, losing as he did so, his facemask. CPO Richards was brought to the surface where willing hands carried him onto the Quarterdeck and resuscitation was attempted. Unfortunately this was unsuccessful and the man was later buried ashore in 'Dido Valley', the Naval Cemetery in Simon's Town.

HMS *Glasgow* steamed out of the South African port resplendent in her new colours to undergo further sea trials, before making her way to Trincomalee via Port Louis, Mauritius. Here in Port Louis the C-in-C, Vice-Admiral Sir Arthur E.F. Palliser, KCB, DSC, took the salute as a ship's Detachment marched past him and the Governor of Mauritius.

Vice-Admiral Sir Arthur Palliser takes salute at the March Past

Once again when the ship was open to visitors, in Port Louis, she attracted a lot of local interest. Having completed the required ceremonial programme the *Glasgow* set course, in August 1946, to visit Rodulgez, Port Victoria and eventually Dar-es-Salem where, to the great delight of the local crowds, the Royal Marine detachment 'Beat a Retreat.' On leaving Dar-es-Salem HMS *Glasgow* continued her circuitous route via Tanga, Kilindini Aden, and Male, in the Maldives, to return to Colombo.

In the Maldives, Guy Cook, now an impressionable Ordinary Seaman, recalls that the Queen of the island, was paddled out to the ship in a dugout canoe to pay her official visit to Vice-Admiral Palliser. Her Majesty arrived on board wearing a large multi-coloured gown and spectacles which had no lenses. As a gift to the Admiral she brought a suckling pig which broke loose on the Quarterdeck and ran in and out of the lines of the assembled Royal Marine Guard, messing all over their boots as it did so. Having vented its stomach the pig dived overboard and swam back to the safety of the shore. When the C-in-C went to return the Queen's visit he found that she lived in a tree house. The only way in was by way of a tree trunk, which was set at an angle with notches cut into it. Finding it impossible to mount the 'staircase' he had to settle for holding the visit in a boat-house on the jetty.

By the end of the year the cruiser had made her way back to the naval base in Trincomalee where the crew spent Christmas. No doubt they would have preferred to spend it back home but the Pantomime entertainment provided by the S.O.D.S. "Ginbad the Failure" and the fare that was made available partly compensated them.

Christmas Menu

Breakfast
Fruit
Bacon, Kidney and Egg
Bread Rolls, Marmalade and Coffee
Dinner
Tomato Soup
Roast Turkey and Stuffing
Roast Pork, Roast Potatoes
Green Peas
Christmas Pudding, Rum Sauce
Dessert

Tea
Christmas Cake
Supper
Ham, Cold Roast Pork
Pickles
Fruit Jellies, Blancmange
Biscuits and Cheese
Tea and Coffee

Trouble in Colombo

HMS *Glasgow* set out from Trincomalee during January 1947 to visit Rangoon. As she entered the mouth of the Irrawady River at the mouth of the Delta, heading for Rangoon, the early morning sun rose above the horizon, east of the inbound cruiser. To the west stood the Shwe Dagon pagoda, with its gold leaf covered dome. The sun's rays struck the dome to be reflected back and give the illusion that two suns were rising to the heavens.

During *Glasgow's* absence Colombo had experienced the effects of civil unrest, and shortly after the cruiser's return an armed guard was landed, under the command of Lieutenant Commander King, to protect the Stanley electrical power station and the Anglo-American Oil compound at Kolonnawa, about five miles outside the Capital. At the oil depot hot air balloons made out of paper bags, under which were little trays full of oil and a burning wick, floated over the wall of the compound towards the tanks, which contained petroleum, oil and gas. As the bags burst into flames, scattering burning oil, the British seamen had to douse them before they could set fire to the tanks. Guy Cook, a member of the guard, recalled that on one particular day the local protesters grew angrier and an armed detachment of police formed a cordon across the road, linking the two sites, with men from *Glasgow* behind them, to deter a protest march. The protesters, on reaching the cordon, harangued the police and an inspector, using a megaphone, ordered that the crowd be silent before a local magistrate addressed them. The magistrate stood on the bonnet of a police Land Rover and read out the Riot Act to the crowd three times, after which they were ordered to disperse. The protesters refused to move. An order was then given for the police to load their weapons and fire one volley into the crowd. Shots rang out and people fell to the ground. Someone among the protesters returned the fire to which the police

197

HMS Glasgow in Calcutta in East Indies livery, painted white with yellow Funnels

responded by firing three more volleys. The crowd quickly fell silent and the only sounds that could be heard were the cries of the wounded. Eventually the naval guard was recalled to the ship and *Glasgow* sailed for Calcutta, before returning to the Ceylonese Naval Base.

The next month HMS *Glasgow* sailed to Bahrain, a Middle East archipelago in the Persian Gulf, east of Saudi Arabia. There are no natural water resources so that only ground water and seawater are available for use. The terrain is mostly low desert plain rising gently to low central escarpments. *Glasgow* remained here until March, when she set off to "Show the Flag" in Basra (where shore leave was restricted) and Kuwait. The state of modern Kuwait traces its history back to the eighteenth century when members of the Utab clan, from what is now Saudi Arabia, settled in the area. Over the years those and other Arabs, traditional sons of the desert, who settled in Kuwait adapted themselves to a life revolving around the sea: trade, fishing, pearl diving and boat building.

In clear skies the sun measured its way upward, like a bubble slowly rising from the bottom of a bottle of champagne, matched by increasing temperatures. For those in the ship's engine room the conditions were barely tolerable, with the temperature often being in excess of 120° F. Only with an adequate supply of liquids were the stokers able to counter the effects of dehydration. On one occasion access to a supply of water was denied by the Engineering Officer, with the result that stoker William Wright passed out and had to be taken topside and laid on the torpedo tubes to recover. Once recovered he had to return to his duty.

Passing through the Gulf the cruiser ran aground on a sandbar, which caused a degree of consternation amongst the occupants of the engine room. Leading Stoker Redman, conscious of the fact that cooling water was drawn from the bottom of the ship, and aware of the dangers associated with a shortage of such water to the generators, hit the emergency button. He then quickly switched off the steam supply and yelled a warning to the remainder of the men who, without further ado, vacated the engine room in double quick time! A similar incident affecting the *Cleopatra* had resulted in a generator exploding, killing a number of men.

From Kuwait *Glasgow* steamed south-eastwards for Karachi where, during a period of civil unrest, rioting had occurred. In 1942 discussions relating to the future constitution of India led to the Indian National Congress, led by Mahatma Gandhi, starting the "Quit India Movement." This movement required that British Government of India should cease and that power should be transferred to Hindu Raj. The Muslim population, who were in the minority, would become mere subjects of the new adminis- tration. The Muslims quite clearly were not happy and the All-India Muslim League, led by Quaid-e-Azam Mohammad Ali Jinnah, demanded that the right of self-determination should be guaranteed and that a sovereign state with two constitution-making bodies should be set up. This was to be in those Muslim majority areas, in the north-east and north-west of India which was to become Pakistan. There followed a period where Hindu was set against Muslim and Muslim against Hindu. Friction amongst opposing factions had led to the death of a number of the city's inhabitants.

Shortly after the cruiser's arrival in the Pakistani port Guy Cook, now Able Seaman, recalled seeing bodies, which had been thrown off the 'Ugli' bridge, floating in the river.

It is not only the lower deck seamen who fail to abide by the rules and it was here in Karachi that two officers were reported for being AWOL, between 8.00 pm on 5th June and 1.00 am on the 6th June, and improperly dressed. They were still dressed in tropical dress in a public place after dark!

On 12th June *Glasgow* returned to Trincomalee before yet again making passage to Singapore, where she paid off on 6th August.

In September 1947 the cruiser returned to Portsmouth, via the Suez Canal and Gibraltar, to enter dry dock in the Hampshire port for an extensive refit. During the refit living conditions aboard deteriorated and Miles Huntington-Whiteley, younger brother of Hugo Huntington-Whiteley, a Writer in the Captain's office, recalled that the ship was over-run with workmen, power and compressed air cables, dirt and deafening drilling machines. In the broadside messes conditions were far from pleasant and men slept where they could — several of the hammock hooks were unavailable due to them being used to carry loose thick cables [Miles slept on one of the side benches].

The crew aboard was also deprived of the use of heads and ablution areas having to use dockside facilities instead — showers (where the water was always hot) and latrines built in the eighteenth century (a row of bum holes and newspaper). At night, for bladder relief only, an old rum fanny would suffice and the task of emptying it usually fell to the youngest in the mess.

There was some compensation for the discomfort experienced by those on board in that while the ship was in dry dock evening shore leave was generous and, apart from those on watch, most of the crew went ashore after the workmen had left for the day. For those who could afford it hostels, such as "Aggie Weston's," provided welcome overnight accommodation at the cost of a shilling (5p) per night.

Upon completion of her refit *Glasgow* was moved to a berth at the Railway Jetty where she remained until September the following year.

Aggie Weston's

- **Dame Agnes Weston (1840-1911) was the spinster daughter of a successful barrister and a fervent temperance crusader.**
- **She devoted her life to those she called 'my bluejackets' and established the famous Sailors Rest hostels at Pompey, Devonport and Keyham, Plymouth where jack could get a cheap clean bed even, or especially, when too drunk to return on board. The Rests were always known as 'Aggies'.**

"Any Old Iron" – Glasgow Relieves "Shiny Sheff"

Captain C.L. Firth DSO, MVO RN

On 1st August 1948 Captain C. L. Firth, DSO, MVO, RN assumed command of the cruiser.

In 1940 he had been the Commanding Officer of the destroyer HMS *Imogen* which was sunk in a collision with HMS *Glasgow* off the Pentland Firth.

At the time of Captain Firth's appointment, ashore in naval and Royal Marine barracks personnel were receiving drafting instructions. At

Eastney Barracks the Royal Marine Detachment were hard at work practising drills for the forthcoming "Showing the Flag" cruise in the West Indies as the Flagship of Admiral Sir William G. Tennant, KCB, CBE, MVO. Admiral Tennant had been captain of the *Repulse* when she was sunk and as such was very much in demand when the ship made her courtesy calls. A ceremonial drill squad was formed and practised a routine that was to hold them in high regard as the ship went from port to port during the forthcoming months. The Detachment was under the command of a liberally minded officer Major P.R. Matters, RM who, after seeing his troops turned out on parade, in the tropical kit which had been issued wanted to get away from knee length shorts and decided that they should be shortened. As he walked along the assembled ranks he would say "shorten" whenever it became appropriate. All went well until he came to one musician who was well endowed and had decided to parade without underwear. On inspecting him Major Matters looked down and said "lengthen!"

Following the embarkation of the new commission of seamen and "Royals" the crew was continuously engaged in working up exercises in the sea area off Portland, until mid-October, when the ship set sail for Bermuda to relieve her sister ship, HMS *Sheffield*, as Flagship of the West Indies Squadron. This was to be the last full commission of the West Indies Squadron.

Glasgow battled her way across the Atlantic and during the passage the cruiser was hammered by gales to eventually arrive on station looking decidedly the worse for wear, with hawse pipes covered by rust and rust stains dripping down her sides. When the crew of the *Sheffield*, known colloquially as "Shiny Sheff" because she was painted 50/50 enamel courtesy of an allowance from Sheffield City Council, saw the state of the *Glasgow* they burst out laughing and ribald comments were exchanged.

The *Glasgow* was ordered by the C-in-C America and West Indies, Admiral Sir William G. Tennant KCB, CBE, MVO, to proceed and anchor near Warwick Camp and get cleaned up. While the *Sheffield* waited to be relieved the crews of each ship were able to request records to be played and sent across the airways to be heard by the crew of the other ship by the use of SRE. During one of these good-natured exchanges the SRE operator on the *Sheffield* sent the message "From ship's company HMS *Sheffield* to ship's company of the *Glasgow*" before playing the record "Any Old Iron".

Soon after her arrival the ship's crew were set to work engaged in painting the ship to restore it to a condition befitting that of a flagship.

Every stage in the ship was put over the side, manned by ratings with long paint brushes, with short paint brushes, with brushes that were thick and bushy, with brushes that were thin and straggly. Pots of paint were hung over the side above the stages, and then the stages, ratings and paint were lowered or raised by leading hands whenever a patch was completed. A short time later the *Glasgow* returned to duty all spruced up and, on 15th November 1948, she relieved "Shiny Sheff" as flagship of the America and West Indies. The day coincided with the birth of HRH Prince Charles being announced and, not only was a twenty one gun Royal Salute fired but much to the delight of the crew this was followed with the order to "Splice the Mainbrace."

John Chiverell, PO Fo'c'sle, recalls "we had on that commission one of the finest skippers I have ever served with, Charlie Firth, a communicator by trade, with Bill Tennant as the Admiral to start with. Tennant and Firth had been the perfect combination and under them *Glasgow* must have been the happiest ship in commission. Firth could turn the *Glasgow* on a sixpence and to see him berth her in Bermuda was a dream."

Able Seaman John Behan fought as *Glasgow*'s representative in the welterweight division, in the America and West Indies Fleet boxing championship. Following his success as a boxer, he was asked by the Warrant Officer guns to go baby sitting for the Gunnery Officer, Lieutenant Commander M. Pollock, (later to become Admiral of the Fleet) who was living ashore on the island. When he was told that the officer's boat would take him there and collect him later John didn't know whether to laugh or cry. It would appear the Nanny who normally fulfilled this function was afraid of being in the house alone, until the early hours of the morning, when the local coloured lads came round selling water. John baby-sat while Lieutenant Commander Pollock and his wife attended a dinner or cocktail party on board *Glasgow*. Upon their return the boatswain of the officers' boat would be instructed to wait for John and take him back to the ship. One night Able Seaman Behan missed his way and went to the wrong jetty. The boatswain, thinking John was stopping over left. Sitting on the jetty until 7.00 am without a top coat was decidedly uncomfortable.

Baby-sitting did however, have some compensation in that John was able to get free time when it was the Nanny's afternoon off. The couple often took a picnic basket made up by Mrs. Pollock down to the beach where they were able to swim and sunbathe. John believes that he is the only Able Seaman who can claim to have baby-sat for an Admiral of the Fleet.

In addition to having a number of competent boxers aboard, HMS *Glasgow* was able to field a very strong football team which played in the Bermudan league.

Football Team HMS Glasgow 1948-1950

The team received a lot of support from its supporters who provided musical accompaniment from the touch lines.

Ship's Comic Band provide support

Life was never dull aboard *Glasgow* and in December when a rating was reported as being missing overboard from the MFV 344 powerboats from the British cruiser assisted in the search for him. It is not known whether or not the rescue mission was successful.

Glasgow Visits South America

Following a visit by the C-in-C to the ship on 2nd January 1949 *Glasgow* sailed for Trinidad where she carried out radar calibration exercises. Next on the agenda was a passage to South America, and a week later course was set for Rio de Janeiro, the first port of call for a number of "Showing the Flag" visits. Just over an hour after the cruiser had crossed the equator her speed was reduced, and for the next ninety minutes most of the ship's company assembled on the fo'c'sle to witness several of their shipmates meet King Neptune, his Royal Court, Guard, Police, Heralds and of course the all-important Barber.

King Neptune about to hold Court (GB)

205

On 18th January a 21-gun national salute was fired before the ship secured alongside the Praca Mava pier in Rio de Janeiro's harbour. In 1502 Portuguese explorers sailed over to Brazil and as he sailed into the bay which is known today as Guanabara, Andre Goncalves mistook it for the mouth of a river, Rio in Portuguese. The month was January (Janeiro) and he brightly concluded Rio de Janeiro! The name stuck. The first economic activities were sugar cane farming and whaling, with native Brazilians and African slaves from Angola doing all the heavy work. With the discovery of gold Rio became the second capital of Brazil; however, the country experienced instability until the mid-nineteenth century, which prevented its cultural development. Political stability did eventually come in the mid–1800's and the city received major improvements with access to gaslights, plumbing, a sewage system, telephone and telegraph. In 1888 the African slaves were freed and a large migration from the country fields to the city took place, and the first favela (shantytown) was spawned. With a military coup in 1889 the first republic was born and Rio became the capital of Brazil.

During the four day visit, which coincided with the renowned Carnival, *Glasgow's* Royal Marine Guard and Band were involved in a number of ceremonial parades and Sergeant Frank Agass, RM recalls "the visit was a constant sleepless period and although we had to provide our drill display every night the runs ashore afterwards were ample reward. It was out of this world." Those of the ship's company who were not involved in the ceremonial duties ceased work at the end of the forenoon watch and libertymen were able to enjoy the available social life, with Copacabana and Sugar Loaf Mountain dominating the scene. Three days after the ship's arrival the crew organised a party for some of the local children. Those who were able to attend thoroughly enjoyed the festivities and fun. The next day, 22nd January, the cruiser was open to visitors, which proved to be a very popular attraction.

Having ensured that all the locals were safely ashore preparations were made for the ship's departure and, on the 25th, the British cruiser sailed out of the harbour bound for Buenos Aires. Special sea dutymen were piped to their stations in preparation for the long passage to the Argentinian capital. The ship's arrival three days later heralded a round of official visits, including one made to the ship by the country's president, His Excellency the President of the Republic, General Juan Domingo Peron, on 3rd February. The President accompanied by his wife Sra. Maria Eva Duarte de Peron and a number of

206

The Perons on board HMS Glasgow   (GB/GS)

other distinguished guests including HBM Ambassador Sir John Balfour KCMG, was welcomed on board *Glasgow* by Admiral Sir William Tennant, and Captain Firth. A Guard of Honour was provided by the Royal Marine Detachment. This was possibly the last overseas guard seen by Eva Peron who died in 1952.

That evening the Royal Marine Band 'Beat Retreat' on the quayside whilst the officers and guests attended a cocktail party on the Quarterdeck. The hard work that had gone into rehearsing the drill programme, paid dividends as the Drill Squad and Band formed up in the darkened area of the jetty where they awaited a signal which caused the searchlights, signal lamps and added illumination to be turned on. As the lights came on the band struck up with a rousing march and the Royal Marines all marched forward together until a pre-determined position was reached. At this point the band stopped and the ceremonial drill squad continued to march through the ranks of stationary musicians to halt on the jetty opposite the Quarterdeck. To the accompaniment of music the drill squad marched and counter-marched until they had completed their programme which concluded with "Sunset" and the "Evening Hymn". Those on the Quarterdeck were overcome with emotion and many a weeping eye could be seen. Sergeant Frank Agass RM recalls "the programme never failed to impress the local dignitaries at the ports we called at during our tour of duty."

207

Allan Mercer second from the left in the "Apostleship of the Sea"   (AM)

Ashore in the "Apostleship of the Sea"

For the lower deck, entertainment was provided at the 'Apostleship of the Sea' where beer and a buffet supper was laid on followed by a floor show and dancing.

Most of the crew was able to find entertainment in the city while others managed to explore further inland. Buenos Aires is a complex, energetic and seductive port city, which stretches south to north along the Rio de la Plata, and has been the gateway to Argentina for centuries. Porteos, as the multinational people are known, possess an elaborate and rich cultural identity and value their European heritage highly. The city has no dominating monument, no natural monolith that serves as a focal point. Instead it is composed of many small places where the city's neighbourhoods are highly individualised. The spirit of the country is present everywhere, from its 19th century Victorian houses to its tango bars hazed with the piquant tang of cigar smoke.

The visit over, *Glasgow* sailed on 4th February to the Falkland Islands where, like her predecessor thirty-five years earlier, in 1914, she anchored in Port Stanley.

Those who were able to explore the local terrain were convinced it was not the place to live, a fact brought to mind during the most recent conflict. Royal Marine Blackwood described Port Stanley as " just a run ashore for a walk, a few jars and a talk to the sheep".

Port Stanley 1949 (GB)

On the 13th February the cruiser slipped from her anchorage and made a voyage to the whaling station at Grytviken, South Georgia, and en route the crew sighted icebergs and finback whales. *Glasgow's* crew were able to visit the whaling station and witness at first hand the nature of the industry.

Whaling Station, Grytviken, South Georgia   (GB)

The Royal Marine "Mountaineers" practising at Grytviken   (FA)

Sergeant Frank Agass recalls that "we decided to experience the Antarctic and a party of us "kitted out" in what warm clothing we could find and set off on a mountain climb.

After climbing the mountains overlooking the bay without the proper mountaineering equipment we descended a slope overlooking the whaling station and came across a grave.

The grave was that of Sir Ernest H. Shackleton, the British explorer who died at South Georgia in 1922 while on a fourth Antarctic expedition and is buried in Grytviken.

Grave of Sir E. H. Shackleton   *(GB)*

When the 'Royals' mentioned the find to those who were employed at the whaling station the workers showed a degree of ignorance, as to its presence.

From Grytviken, *Glasgow* carefully made her way to the capital of Uruguay, threading her way between icebergs, some of which she passed within five cables to port.

Iceberg off South Georgia (GB)

Having successfully avoided the dangers presented by the icebergs, on 24th February, *Glasgow* entered Montevideo's harbour, which lies on the broad mouth of the river Rio de la Plata, behind which is the city in which over half the country's population live. While moored in Montevideo, the principal port and Capital of Uruguay, the ferry *General Artigas* collided with the port quarter of the stationary warship, buckling plates four feet below upper deck level. There was however no damage to the ferry! The following month, on 3rd, *Glasgow* departed from Montevideo heading towards Bermuda. Next on the agenda were visits to be made to Punta del Este, which is a narrow strip of land which juts out into the South Atlantic, Port of Spain, Antigua, discovered by Christopher Columbus during his second voyage from Spain in 1493, and Guantanamo in Cuba, which was an American naval base. The accent was on relaxation rather than ceremonial and the crew took full advantage.

On 5th April *Glasgow* arrived in Bermuda, where her three months stay was marred by the death of Able Seaman William James Dawson, who was found drowned in Riddells Bay, having died between 9.20 pm on 31st May and 7.00 pm on 1st June.

R. J. Ayres, Royal Marine, recalls "that while climbing up Malabar Bastion, in Bermuda, during a simulated Commando Assault on a sailor's home day he lost his footing and fell all the way back down.

In the local paper next day he noticed, as he read a report on the event, a comment stating how realistic the dummy had been as it was thrown from the top!"

In July it was time to move on to "Show the Flag" in Canada and North America. *Glasgow* left Bermuda on 11th July to travel first to Portsmouth (New Hampshire) where she arrived two days later. On Sunday 17th July the ship was opened for visitors and a large number of local people turned up to look around her. One of the guests at a cocktail party held on board was light fingered. He or she removed a silver globe decorated with a figure of a lion, which was used to decorate the top of a flag pole, from the Wardroom. Once the news got out concern was expressed as to what the British would think of the locals and the matter was reported by the port naval authorities to the local police force. [It is not known whether or not the globe was recovered.]

Three thousand men, women and children crowded the pavements and streets off Market Square to witness "Beat the Retreat", presented by the Royal Marine Detachment and Band under the supervision of Lieutenant Peter Williams, RM.

Royal Marine Detachment Beat Retreat 19th July 1949 Portsmouth, New Hampshire

The ceremony was, according to a British spokesman, "an appropriate conclusion to a week during which the cruiser's crew had been entertained by navy and city officials and the people of Portsmouth." It was a traditional sunset programme which has its origins in days of old when drummers in England "beat the retreat" to call wanderers back to a city before the gates closed for the night.

Captain Firth issued the following statement of thanks to the people of the city " The Admiral, myself and all the men of the *Glasgow* were overwhelmed by the hospitality extended to us by the people of Portsmouth. The feeling of friendliness was genuine and came from everyone we came in contact with, from those who entertained us, the shopkeepers, police and all. They went out of their way to express a friendly attitude. The co-operation between the American military personnel and ourselves was especially pleasing. We are leaving many friends behind us. If this demonstration of goodwill and friendliness is a reflection of feelings between the United States and Britain, we will always be friends. Our thanks are genuine and come from our hearts"

On 19th July before *Glasgow* left for St. John's Newfoundland, crowds that had welcomed the cruiser on her arrival on 13th turned out again and lined the harbour walls to bid "bon voyage" to newly made friends.

Once clear of the harbour the cruiser headed for Newfoundland and made the 770-mile passage to Cornerbrook.

Cornerbrook was a small settlement which had its economy based around a paper mill, owned by Bowaters Ltd, and offered little in the way of entertainment. During the four day stay *Glasgow's* crew had to exercise a degree of caution to avoid falling into the water which was heavily polluted. Any dip would have resulted in an immediate visit to the sick bay! Royal Marine Blackwood described Cornerbrook as " a typical "wild west" town with sidewalks, a bar but no gunslingers, with sulphur fumes from the factory turning the ship a mustard colour. We had to spend several days washing the ship down before she continued on her way."

Welcome to Cornerbrook (GB/GS)

214

This was the beginning of the scheduled Autumn Cruise during which visits were to be made to ports throughout Canada and America, the purpose of which was to maintain relationships with the Canadian and U.S. navies and, in particular to give the C-in-C the opportunity to meet and discuss his business with the diplomatic and international authorities who would, in time of crisis, be closely involved with his force of cruisers and frigates. The whole operation was a re- establishment of the pattern of pre-war relationships, responsibilities and authority and part of the traditional military/political "Showing the Flag" cruises world wide by the Royal Navy. It quickly became apparent that these relationships, diplomatic patterns and shifts in the balance of power had been changed by the war to become largely meaningless and, in some cases negative in their effect.

Sailing onwards *Glasgow* made the short voyage of 120 miles to St John's, which is unlike any other city in North America – where a new arrival at this great seaport can expect to be greeted with affection, laughed at without scorn, treated with respect, and even insulted with humour and gentility - perhaps all at the same time!

On 4th August *Glasgow* left Newfoundland and sailed to her next port of call; Halifax (Nova Scotia), where many of the victims recovered from the seas following the sinking of the liner *Titanic* are laid to rest in three of the cemeteries.

Glasgow's visit coincided with the bi-centenary celebrations and the Royal Marine detachment took part in the nightly Tattoo.

The Royal Marine Detachment were kept busy and Beat Retreat on the quayside.

As part of the celebrations a boat pulling regatta was arranged in which the ship's boats competed against those of Canadian fishermen in the local harbour, for a cup which had been donated especially for the occasion. *Glasgow's* boats won the event overall and the cup was exhibited for all to see in a jewellers shop window in Barrington Street.

In the forenoon of 15th August *Glasgow* commenced her 680-mile journey from Halifax to Murray Bay and anchored two days later, for an eight-day long visit.

Five hours after leaving Murray Bay on 25th August, *Glasgow* arrived in Quebec for an eleven-day stay. *Glasgow* moored beneath the Heights of Abraham where the Royal Marine detachment Beat Retreat to a tumultuous reception.

Having completed her courtesy visit the cruiser made her way 139 miles upstream, via the St. Lawrence river, to Montreal where she remained until 12th September. That day *Glasgow* departed from the Canadian port and set course and speed for the 1,470-mile passage to New York where she arrived five days later.

Royal Marines Beat Retreat on Heights of Abraham (FA)

During the time spend in Canada little thought was given to what was happening back in UK, where the country after the withdrawal of Lend Lease, was virtually bankrupt however, the crew was given a sharp and painful indication of this when the rate of exchange was cut by a half and the crew members suddenly found they were only getting $2.40 to the pound instead of $4.80: overnight they became paupers when ashore. For most it was a severe blow to national pride and the morale of the crew plummeted. After nine days spent in New York *Glasgow* set off towards her penultimate stop Annapolis MD. where the crew found it was easier to disguise and accept their new found poverty. However, the shattering collapse of the pound led to the realisation that Britain's standing in the post war world had been greatly reduced. In spite of this reduction in world standing the welcome the ship received in each of the ports she visited was in no way diminished.

Glasgow remained in Annapolis for eight days before she steamed the short distance of 150 miles to her final destination of the tour, Norfolk (Virginia), on 5th October. It was here in 1917, during the First World War, that 600 German sailors, crew of the interned raiders *Kronprinz Wilhelm* and *Prinz Eitel Friedrich* were held in the Navy Yard. To while away the time, they built a German Village, in Portsmouth, from which baked goods and souvenirs were sent to the German Red Cross. However, following the entry of the United States into the war, the sailors became prisoners of war and were sent to POW camps in Georgia and the U.S. Naval Operating Base and Training Station was established. Upon its completion, 1,400 American sailors marched in to occupy the new base. During World War II, in 1941, with heightened defence activities, hundreds of families moved into the area to double Norfolk's population. It was here that troops practised embarkation and landing exercises, on the shores of Chesapeake Bay, in preparation for the successful invasion of North Africa (Operation Torch). By the end of the war, Norfolk Naval Base and Air station became the largest military installation in the world.

While *Glasgow* was moored alongside the jetty in Norfolk, a carelessly discarded cigarette caused a fire in the ship's motor cutter, which damaged the boat's stem post and deck beam and destroyed its compliment of lifebuoys and oilskins. This was quickly brought under control and a major incident was avoided.

Having completed her tour the British warship left Norfolk on 12th October for the two-day passage to Bermuda where she entered dry dock the following month for routine maintenance. *Glasgow* remained in Bermuda for the remainder of the year and at Christmas-time the SODS put on their traditional pantomime.

Ships Pantomime Christmas 1949   *(AM)*

A Second Royal Tour

Vice-Admiral Symonds-Tayler, C.B., D.S.C.

Early in 1950 HMS *Glasgow* became the Flagship of C-in-C America and West Indies Station, Vice-Admiral R.V.Symonds-Tayler CB, DSC, who succeeded Admiral Sir William Tennant, KCB, CBE, MVO.

In February 1950 the ships of the America and West Indies Squadron dispersed from Bermuda to the various sections of the enormous station with the Flagship heading for the Caribbean Islands. In 1950 they were all Crown Colonies with Governors or, in the case of the smaller ones, Administrators. Calls were made to as many of them as possible to boost the standings of the Colonial representatives and to give the various authorities the opportunity to discuss with the C-in-C their problems and possible emergencies for which they might need the rapid support and military capability which only his ships were capable of providing. Again in the changed post war climate the Islands were all themselves beginning to chafe at colonial rule and, without regard to the economic facts of life, demand independence. The atmosphere relating to the indigenous population was not as easy going and friendly as it had been and here, as in so many other aspects of British international relations, the changed world status of the British Empire intruded into the daily conduct of affairs.

Admiral Sir Michael Pollock, GCB, LVO, DSC, Admiral of the Fleet (Then a Lieutenant Commander) recalls "our first specific example of this occurred just before *Glasgow* arrived in Jamaica. Signals arrived saying there was the likelihood of major civil disturbances sparked by the usual militant trade unions in the island and that we might be required to re-inforce the army manpower available from the battalion actually stationed in Jamaica.

Members of the local Trades Union Movement (FA)

220

The Royal Marines girded their loins for the type of operation for which they were carried on the ship and the ship's company landing party of sailors and stokers dug out khaki webbing and the mass of other "field service" equipment stored in remote areas of the ship, and planned to show the 'Royals' that they too could be just as good soldiers as any bootneck-in the role of "aid to the civil Power", let me hasten to add, rather than true military operations! Fortunately we were not put to the test: as we approached the island the trouble fizzled out and by the time we arrived, all was once more quiet and peaceful. It was a good exercise because with an additional spur behind it the action could have been for real."

On February 20th 1950, Vice-Admiral R.V.Symonds-Tayler transferred his Flag to H.M.S. *Snipe* to enable *Glasgow* to accommodate Her Royal Highness the Princess Alice, Countess of Athlone and her husband the Earl as they conducted a Royal Tour of the West Indies from Thursday 23rd February until Sunday 12th March 1950.

Three days later at Kingston, Jamaica, half way through the Morning Watch, the Royal Guests were welcomed aboard the cruiser by a Royal Marine Guard and Band. Once the party was safely aboard the ship slipped and proceeded slowly to sea. Two days later, on 25th February, having settled in their quarters the Royal couple toured the ship. It was during the tour that they were able to witness the issue of "Grog" and promptly ordered "Splice the Mainbrace", a gesture warmly welcomed by the crew.

Grog Issue witnessed by HRH Princess Alice (JY)

221

HRH Princess Alice being presented with birthday cake on her 67th birthday   (JY)

The day of the tour coincided with that of the Princess's 67th birthday and a special cake, baked to mark the occasion, was presented to her.

The cake was cut at dinner in the Wardroom that evening and distributed among the officers who, in turn, made a presentation of a silver salver to the Countess.

The following day, 26th February, the Governor of the Windward Islands and his wife, Mrs Arundel, boarded the cruiser prior to anchoring in Dominica where, once the ship had anchored, the Earl and Countess disembarked, with the Governor and his wife, to reside in Government House for the duration of the ship's stay.

That evening, at Government House, a Royal Garden Party was held with officers from *Glasgow* attending to act as hosts for the 500 invited guests. Having enjoyed the hospitality of the Governor the Royal party returned to the ship two days later. After weighing anchor at 9.00 am the ship made passage to St. Lucia, the next port of call, where it arrived, off Castries, five hours later.

HMS *Glasgow* rapidly became a hive of activity as preparations were made to host a dinner party aboard that evening, attended by the Governor of the Windward Islands and eight others. The Royal

HRH Princess Alice and her husband landing to attend a Royal Garden Party (JY)

couple, faced with a demanding programme of social occasions to ful-fil, left the ship after dinner to stay overnight at Government House where a second Garden Party was to be held the following day.

Just after midnight on 2nd March HMS *Glasgow* sailed for St. Vincent to arrive there as the Morning Watch changed. The Royal party attended their third Garden Party of the tour that evening. As the bells signalled the start of the Forenoon Watch on 3rd March *Glasgow* sailed from St. Vincent and, after a seven-hour trip, arrived off Grenada. Once more the Royal party disembarked to stay at Government House for the duration of the ship's stay. Having attend-ed yet another Garden Party on Monday 6th March the Earl and Countess returned to the cruiser. The necessary arrangements were made and the cruiser set sail for Barbados at 11.00 pm.

David George, on the Quarterdeck as Midshipman of the Watch, recalls that Her Royal Highness came up for a breath of fresh air. He saluted and made to leave the deck available for her use but, as he started to go, she started to talk to him. The only part of the conver-sation he remembers is that being young and foolish, he asked her how she managed to endure one Garden Party after another and withstood all the shaking of hands. Her reply was simple: "Breeding, young man, breeding."

Most of the following day was spent at sea before landfall was reached off Bridgetown at 4.00 pm on 7th March. Once the ship was secured the Princess and her husband disembarked to spend the night ashore before attending the last Garden Party arranged in their honour.

223

On Thursday 9th March the Earl and Countess went to a Race Meeting held at the Savannah Park Racecourse, where they enjoyed a friendly, welcoming reception from the race-goers.

In the early evening of the following day the *Glasgow* weighed anchor and made her way at a leisurely pace to Man of War Bay,

Members of the Ship's company enjoying a Banyan.

Tobago, where she anchored off shore to allow the Royal party and the ship's company to enjoy an informal "Banyan" on a secluded beach. This was purely recreational with emphasis on swimming and beachcombing.

Having enjoyed a relaxed day everyone returned to the ship where the Earl and Countess enjoyed a "Royal Command" film performance on the cruiser's quarterdeck. Some of the crew found that they had sunbathed too long and as a result were afflicted by very red and sore torsos. When the Royal party had retired for the night the crew quickly cleared away the quarterdeck and the *Glasgow* weighed anchor before steaming southwards towards Trinidad. That evening was a memorable one as the sinking sun cast a glistening veil over the sea so that it looked like silk embroidered with blue and red with touches of gold and violet. However, when the sun finally sank below the horizon the light turned cold and hard and the colour drained out of the sea.

The ship made steady progress through the night to pass, on Sunday 12th March, through the "Dragons Tooth" into the Gulf of Paria, Port of Spain, as the Morning and Forenoon Watches changed.

HMS *Glasgow* proceeded to moor alongside HMS *Snipe*, with the C-in-C aboard, which fired a 21-gun salute as the cruiser approached.

At 9.30 am Vice-Admiral Symonds–Tayler embarked and bid farewell to the Earl and Countess before they departed Port of Spain for British Guyana, in the *Lady Nelson*, that afternoon. Once the Royal Party had left, *Glasgow* reverted from yacht back to warship, in preparation for combined exercises with the Canadian Navy and the C-in-C hoisted his Flag to reinstate the cruiser as his Flagship.

The Royal Party posing for a Farewell Photograph

Post-war the Canadians were, whether deliberately or fortuitously, gradually taking over the task of providing guidance and protection- a duty previously fulfilled by Britain as a colonial power. Canadian money now provided much needed and improved docking and cargo handling facilities ashore in Halifax from whence a reduced level of shipping, compared with pre-war, through and to the islands now operated. It was fast becoming evident that the Canadians within the next few years would take over many of the British colonial responsibilities in the area: all this against the background of a Canadian government whose overt policy was as anti-colonial as that of the USA.

Although the number of merchant vessels making passage between the islands was reduced those that did were very important to those in the Royal Navy and in particular for those on the

Glasgow. Where the merchant ships came from in the waters around the West Indies was of great importance because they were the only source of mail for those in the Royal Navy. It must be remembered that at this time there was no transatlantic airmail service although Pan-Am flying boats occasionally flew to Bermuda and the Caribean Islands. 'Mail' in 1950 meant "sea-mail" and the sight of a long, single funnel and traditional cargo boat outline of one of the Harrison Line started a wave of activity aboard the cruiser where outgoing letters, already started, were hurriedly finished or, in some cases quickly begun before a special boat transported the Royal Marine "Postie" to the merchantman to collect in-bound mail and deliver that which was to be sent on to the British Isles. Having completed his duty he returned to the warship with his much-awaited consignment of letters from loved ones in UK, after which the letters were sorted out, in a cluttered mail office, by mess and name. Finally the bugle sounded "Mail Call" followed immediately by the pipe "Hand of a mess for mail" and the leading hand of each mess went to fetch it. When he got back to the mess deck the mail was then sorted it into individual piles. Some of these were bigger than others. Their owners scooped them up. "I've got twelve called one." "Well I've got fourteen cried another." They tore open envelopes reading

Winning
Whaler Crew
Inter-Part
Championship

Mne M Cunningham
(2nd Stroke)
Cpl C.Fry
(Stroke)
Mne V. Farrington
(Midship)
Mne G.Kelly
(2nd Bow)
Sergt F. Agass
(Cox)
Mne D. Cooper.
(Bow)

bits of the contents until they reached the last one then they settled down to read each letter thoroughly. Soon all their troubles were forgotten and the mood of the men changed and the mess deck was alive with smiles and banter.

In Trinidad, whilst awaiting the commencement of the manoeuvres *Glasgow*'s boats crews practised hard for the forthcoming fleet regatta which had been arranged to take place on the 15th March. After seeing them in action the Royal Marine whaler crew was adopted by a local rich Indian businessman who sent fresh oranges aboard for them every day while they were training. After the 'bootnecks' team had won the final in record time they were taken out on the town by their benefactor and when the time came for the men to return to the ship Sergeant Aggass, RM recalls "we were fairly shot away and the businessman wanted to show his appreciation by writing an open cheque. I suggested that he just wrote 'Many thanks to the RM team'."

The following day, Thursday 16th March, HMS *Sparrow* arrived from South America to collect the Earl and Countess from British Guyana and take them to Trinidad where they were due to conduct a ten-day official duty. HMS *Glasgow*, released from royal duties, made a brief visit to the large United States base at Guantanamo in Cuba where the British ship was able to make use of practice facilities so singularly lacking on the America and West Indies station, before making for Nassau. *Glasgow* entered Nassau harbour on 1st April and within two hours of berthing the C-in-C went ashore to visit the Governor of Bermuda. The following day the ship was open for visitors and attracted a good response from the locals who turned up just after 2.00 pm. The Bermudan people were friendly and the crew enjoyed having them aboard. Two days later the C-in-C and *Glasgow*'s Captain entertained 361 guests at a cocktail party held on the Quarterdeck. On 6th April *Glasgow* weighed anchor and set course for Bermuda where she arrived on the 8th. After a four-day stay she set sail again to take part in a number of exercises, some of which involved aircraft, and the crew were kept hard at work. The men were pleased to return to the friendly atmosphere and environment of Bermuda to enjoy the runs ashore.

Captain Firth relinquished command to his successor Captain Yendell, and a presentation of a silver salver was made to him on behalf of the ship's company by Boy Seaman Fairless, who later went through the hawse pipe to become a Lieutenant Commander (Provost) RN.

Mrs Firth accepts a silver salver on behalf of Captain Firth from boy Seaman Fairless.

On 26th April Captain W.J. Yendell, RN (later to become Rear-Admiral W.J. Yendell, CB) assumed command of the warship and carried out an inspection of the ship. He quickly settled in and the ship's company went about their business of maintaining equipment and fittings.

Captain W.J.Yendell RN   *(FA)*

One of the training requirements for a sailor has always been that should be able to act as a "landing party" when needed, so that the completion of an "Annual Musketry Course" was a requirement of the training year. The Musketry course when carried out, as in so many parts of the world in cold and wet weather, was often a dreary affair. However, in Bermuda in spring weather it was quite the opposite and gave the ship's company, who tended to be under employed, bored and with few leisure outlets or friends ashore, an opportunity to get out of the ship for a weeks virtual picnic in idyllic surroundings. On the south shore of the main Island, flanking some half mile of perhaps the most perfect beaches in the world, the local Army Garrison and the Bermuda Volunteers had a rifle range among the sand dunes, long established and not used to capacity. Accommodation for both officers and ratings alike was provided in the form of Army tents, and a beer canteen provided liquid sustenance for those who needed it. Within a quarter of a mile of the camp was an effectively private beach of pink coral sand with a warm sea beyond. During the period that the ship's company were in the camp a "tropical routine" was worked which meant that the men turned to at 6.00 am, worked through until 1.30 pm on the ranges and, after dinner, packed up for the remainder of the day.

After a relaxed fortnight a Royal Guard, representing the flagship, then embarked on a training programme in preparation for the forthcoming King's Birthday Parade - always a great occasion in overseas colonies as it was in the UK at this time. This took place in Bermuda on some large playing fields near to the military barracks in Hamilton, the capital of the Island. This ceremony was attended by the Governor, the Naval Commander-in-chief, the Army Commander, and as many members of society and the local population as could be fitted in, for it was the local equivalent of the "Trooping the Colour" ceremony in London. This Parade provided a major shop window for the British forces in the Island and the local volunteer detachments, – which were substantial at the time. The Royal Guard numbered 100 and was accompanied by a Colour Party with its own close escort. For Lieutenant Commander M. Pollock, the officer charged with the responsibility of co-ordinating the Naval arrangements tied in with those of the local and Army organisation the task was considerable. Transport to the Dockyard from the ships had to be by boat and bearing in mind that all were wearing white uniform, which does not stand up well to being rain soaked, a fine day was a pre-requisite for success. Even in Bermuda this could not be guaranteed in June. The task of co-ordination was further complicated by the fact that contingents from HM Ships *Snipe* and *Sparrow* had to be included in the guard to indicate that it was not solely for the benefit of the Flagship but the Royal Navy in Bermuda.

The Royal Navy when parading ceremonially always marches at a slower pace than most regiments and, as both *Glasgow* and the Garrison had a band present there was plenty of scope for conflicting tempo. In spite of a terrible rehearsal on 6th June a triumphant performance was achieved on 8th June which was the actual day. Little did anyone realise at the time that this was to be the last King's Birthday Parade of the century as King George VI died the following winter.

Travelling around had taken its toll on the paintwork and during 13th and 14th June the ship's company 'turned to,' to paint ship. Painting a ship, from stem to stern and from truck to waterline was done quite often in peacetime, when the ship's programme and her paint allowance permitted. This was particularly the case on foreign stations where warships tended to do a lot of rust-streaking sea-time interspersed with 'flag showing' to foreign ports when the ship was on display. This is one of those activities in which all available seamen are required to take part.

"Both watches of the hands" was piped and the boatswain's party provided bosun's chairs and 'stages' which were hung over the ship's sides. The boatswain also arranged for a 'bowsing-in wire' to be rigged in preparation for painting the forrard part of the bows where they flare. The queue that formed at the paint shop-hatch was noisy with much banter between the men. Each man in the painting party drew a pot of ship's-side crab fat paint, brush, wad of cotton waste plus a length of spun-yarn to hang the pot on. The drawing of materials was often interspersed with loud, and often obscene remonstrations from the painter. Having collected their materials, each man would find his appointed place over the side, two men to a stage. The men began to paint, beginning at the top and working down. After they had completed the section or 'fleet' – a width of paint work corresponding to the width of the stage plus the distance a man could reach with an extended arm on either side – the men would lower the stage by unbending the lanyard, one side at a time paying it out carefully. When the 'fleet' down to the waterline had been completed each pair was retrieved by the killick of the boatswain's party, in a small skittish dinghy, and ferried to the gangway where the painters would climb inboard to begin another fleet. Occasionally the painters would fail to paint small areas of the ship's side would be missed by the painters, which was easy to do, with one's nose barely inches away from a flat, grey uniform surface. In the Buffer's book these were known as 'holidays' and those unfortunate to commit this 'crime' were sent back over the side to complete the job, often getting smeared in paint in the process. Men under punishment undertook final touches and stowage of gear.

All smartened up by her new coat of paint *Glasgow* slipped from her berth and in company with HMS *Snipe* left for Christobar. After a

230

short stay the cruiser was on her way again, this time to Kingston, Jamaica, securing there on 3rd July for a four-day visit. In company with *Snipe, Glasgow* returned to Bermuda on the 10th.

A week later passage was made to Halifax Nova Scotia, again with *Snipe,* where the ships entered the dockyard during the First Dog watch on 20th July. The crew barely had time to get their bearings in the Candian port before they were off again to visit Montreal, calling once again in Cornerbrook for a two day visit, en route. Once again the ship had to be cleaned down.

PO John Chiverell recalls " because of the Korean War which commenced in June that year our planned cruise up the West Coast of the United States was cancelled and we had to substitute a second one of the East Coast. That gave a dabtoe a bit of a shock as a very irate daddy was waiting at the bottom of the gangway when *Glasgow* berthed in Montreal. The dabtoe thought we never went to the same place twice. I remember Montreal as being a beautiful city where the crew were extended much hospitality." In Montreal the crew was entertained by an unusual display of ritual Indian dancing performed on the fo'c'sle by "Big Chief Poking Fire" and fellow braves from the local reservation. Captain Yendell was initiated into the tribe as Chief "Fire Cloud".

Captain Yendell initiated into the tribe as Chief "Fire Cloud"(GB)

On 14th August *Glasgow* made passage to Quebec where she tied up below the Heights of Abraham. On the following day news reached the ship that Her Royal Highness Princess Elizabeth had given birth

231

to a baby girl. That afternoon a 21-gun salute was fired and permission was sought from *Glasgow*'s Captain to "Splice the Mainbrace"

The port of Quebec had the timber industry to thank for its growth when much lumber was transported to England in the late 1700's. Its growth also owes much to the massive arrival of Irish immigrants who fled the potato famine. These had sailed relatively cheaply to Canada from Ireland in freighters, which had discharged their cargo of timber in England and needed weighing down during the return journey to help their navigation. The immigrants provided the required ballast and between 1800 and 1850 some 30,000 immigrants landed in Quebec each year and it prospered. However, the opening up of the St Lawrence seaway, which allowed ocean shipping to sail up the river to the port of Montreal meant that Quebec had competition and it suffered as a result. The lack of a link across the St. Lawrence river added to Quebec's problems but in 1917, when the Quebec Bridge was built, the Port of Quebec and its area were able to rejoin the principal railway artery of the country and its future was assured. Although many of the *Glasgow*'s crew considered Quebec to be a magnificent city most remember that the local populace were French speaking and some were not particularly friendly towards them.

From Canada the warship travelled back to the Caribbean where, on 28th August, a courtesy visit was made to Ciudad Trujillo in La Espanola Island.

The lads enjoy a beer in Ciudad Trujillo   *(GB)*

When the ship had docked in Ciudad Trujillo the MO and Master-at-Arms went ashore. After they had returned members of the crew were advised to avoid certain establishments ashore. Most of the men heeded the advice but some didn't only to find out the reason for the warning when they had to see the Doctor again!

Ciudad Trujillo was known as Santo Domingo until 1936 and is not only the capital but is also the largest city and port of the Dominican Republic.It is believed to be the oldest continuously inhabited settlement in the Western Hemisphere, having the oldest cathedral in the Americas. Just outside the city stands the world's largest lighthouse. The crew was able to enjoy a relaxed stay before the ship set off on 4th September for Kingston, Jamaica, where she arrived the next day.

Jamaica, at the top of a submerged mountain range, is the third largest island in the West Indies, situated south of Cuba and west of Hispaniola. The land above sea level is mainly plateau with the 7,402 feet Blue Mountains rising in the south. It has many white-sand beaches and clear seas ring the island. Jack felt very much at home here although, at the time of the visit, it was the rainy season. After an all too short four days *Glasgow* slipped and on the 9th set course and speed for Vera Cruz in Mexico. She reached the Mexican port after a four-day passage on 13th. September 1950.

In Vera Cruz the Mexican Navy challenged the *Glasgow's* boats crews to a pulling match in which the Mexicans used the British cruiser's boats whilst *Glasgow's* men were seated in boats of American design. Stoker George Stemp a member of the Stoker's boat, representing *Glasgow*, recalls " the contest was held over a course in the harbour, which was approximately one mile in length. The Mexican's boat was fitted with oars like mini tree trunks, which were very heavy to pull and we were decisively beaten by the home team who had no trouble with our whaler, whereas we struggled with theirs."

The city of Vera Cruz is steeped in history, which centres on the ancient people of the Totanacs and the Spanish Conquest of Mexico. It became an important point of contact, politically and commercially between Spain and its new dominions. Mexico regained her independence from Spain in 1823 and Vera Cruz became an important port. In the mid-twentieth century, as part of Mexico's decentralisation policy, the port became a major centre of industry engaged in the production of steel, aluminium, machine tools and equipment for the petroleum industry.

On 16th September the Mexicans celebrate their Independence Day which is a huge military/ carnival occasion of great importance and,

Stoker's Boat crew representing HMS Glasgow versus the Mexican Navy.   (GS)
Stokers: L/R W.Dunstan, Geordie?, G. Stemp, G.Breading, Buzz Breazley, F. Ayliffe.
Geordie Denholme

in pre-war days had been supported by guards and bands from the cruisers in the station one year in four. However, in more recent times Royal Naval or Royal Marine support had been missing because of other commitments but in 1950 diplomatic and national prestige were considered to be at stake and a contingent from *Glasgow* prepared itself for the occasion. Fortunately those who had participated in the King's Birthday parade in June needed no more than a little refresher training to bring them up to the high standard expected of them.

The port of Vera Cruz, on the east coast of Mexico, is connected to Mexico City by rail, an essential ingredient for moving such a large body of men up onto the mountainous plateau on which the capital city is built. Unfortunately the journey was made in both directions at night and thus those who took part in the ceremony were deprived of the opportunity to enjoy the spectacular scenery as the train made its winding ascent over six thousand feet from sea level to the capital or on the returning descent. The men arrived in Mexico City where accommodation and entertainment was provided by the Embassy, - officers staying with ex-patriate families and the guard being billeted in barracks to make sure they did not get lost in the rather violent culture of this very Spanish capital.

Sir Michael Pollock recalls "the march through the city was to be about six miles, – quite a long way for the rifle to be at the "Slope"

234

position or for the officers to march with their swords held out in front of them at the "Carry" – especially six thousand feet above ones own "operating height. However, there was a tremendous will to succeed and present a really smart appearance, no one had to fall out, no one fainted or dropped their weapon, not difficult to do during a long, hot morning, and an excellent impression of smart alertness was achieved. The procession was a heterogeneous collection of different services, organisations and affinity groups with several bands using different collections of instruments and not always wedded to the strict tempo, which alone maintains unbroken step in a large marching body, and finally a whole division of cavalry. Now a division of cavalry is an awful lot of horses and this division could have kept the rose beds in all the Royal Parks in London heavily fertilised with first class organic manure for at least a year. The horses marched past six abreast which filled the whole width of the street; immediately behind them marched the British contingent from *Glasgow* in their immaculate white uniform and initially, shiny black boots. We learned to march lifting our feet considerably higher than required. It was a thoroughly good natured occasion and the Naval and Royal Marine contingents got storms of cheers and handclaps all along the route, — with some justification in view of their excellent appearance and bearing."

The commitment to the ceremony unfortunately left little time for the crew to see the City or visit the surrounding countryside however, the hosts made certain that the name of the great volcano, Popocatepetl, which dominates the skyline was pronounced correctly and the importance of its place in local culture was understood.

The majority of the crew failed to appreciate the history of Vera Cruz, preferring instead to try spicy foods and the locally produced liquor.

On 19th of September she set off again to complete a three-day passage to Belize in British Honduras.

Belize, once a part of the 'Maya' civilisation was probably traversed by Cortes on his way to Honduras but the Spaniards did not colonise the area. Buccaneers, who founded the city of Belize, were followed by British Jamaicans, who exploited its timber. Spain contested British possession over a long period, but in 1859 Guatemala agreed British Honduras's boundaries with Britain. In 1940 Guatemala declared this agreement invalid but it remained a British colony.

The "Showing the Flag" programme was coming to a conclusion with a two-day return to Kingston, Jamaica before *Glasgow* headed for San Juan in Puerto Rico. On 27th September the cruiser docked at the delightful island, which is about 1,000 miles south-east of Florida, close to the deepest submarine depression in the North Atlantic Ocean.

Although most of the crew had a great time touring a part of the world they would normally only dream about visiting, *Glasgow's* crew members often found it difficult to enjoy themselves when they went ashore because they were strapped for cash. John Chiverell recalls "the hospitality enjoyed during the latter part of the commission was often at the American bases which had been in place since the Americans had established them during the Second World War. It must be remembered that the British Government had devalued the pound from approximately $4 to the £1 down to $2.40. which effectively cut all our salaries by one third and no allowances were substituted for forces serving in the West Indies, where effectively the dollar was king!"

After a week's stay in San Juan *Glasgow* returned to Bermuda, meeting up with HMS *Sparrow* en route. During the passage the crew were reminded that they were on a warship when they carried out a bombardment of Culebra Island using the six-inch armament and simulated a torpedo attack on *Sparrow*.

There was an air of excitement amongst the crews of both ships as the approach to Bermuda was made and both warships entered the dockyard on 6th October. Those who were in off-duty watches wasted little time in getting themselves ready to go ashore at the earliest opportunity.

Upon her return to Bermuda the ship settled down to the usual programme of occasional exercises, sports events and a relaxed schedule of maintenance and basic training.

Ten days later the *Glasgow* set off for Pompey to arrive in the Hampshire port on 25th October 1950. Three days after her return to British waters, Captain Yendell left the ship and Commander C. C. Suther, assumed command of the cruiser.

The following month on 9th November *Glasgow* slipped from her berth and made for Chatham naval dockyard, which she entered the next day to undergo a major refit.

Time for a Refit

For most of 1951 the *Glasgow* remained in Chatham Docks, where the Aft Director was replaced. During this period dockyard routine was worked as the normal working day, and with the ship in dockyard hands life on board was barely tolerable, with few places to eat, nowhere to wash and no heating or ventilation.

Upon completion of the refit the warship was expected to join the fleet taking part in the Korean War. However, these orders were changed and she was destined to take over from HMS *Sheffield* as Flagship for the Mediterranean Fleet, based in Malta. News soon followed that the new Commander-in-Chief of the Mediterranean Fleet was to be the great man himself — Admiral The Earl Mountbatten of Burma, KG, GCSI, GCIE, GCVO, KCB, DSO, PC, known throughout the fleet as 'Lord Louis', Lord Louis was to join the ship in Malta; normally flying his flag ashore as Supremo of the whole NATO. fleet organisation of several countries, however for official visits and manoeuvres he and his staff would join the ship.

On 18th September 1951 Captain J. Holmes, a gunnery officer whose bark was worse than his bite, assumed command and for the following two months the crew worked a dockyard routine.

Armistice Day fell on Sunday 11th November and following divisions the memorial service was held on the Quarterdeck. As 11.00 am approached a black ball was hoisted by the Dockyard Tower signal station, and as the hour struck the Royal Marine Bugler sounded the "Alert" and 2 minutes silence was observed, after which the Bugler played the 'Last Post' and 'Reveille' followed by the "Carry on."

At 11.00 am on Wednesday 14th November, on a grey dismal day with the sky filled with rain clouds *Glasgow* slipped to make her way to Sheerness. Orders rang through the ship and the crew responded, attending to their specific duties while ashore dockyard maties loosened springs and securing lines. The cruiser slowly gathered momentum and headed away from the quayside under the control of tugs as she left number 3 Basin and passed through the North Lock into the Medway. The manoeuvre was tricky but safely executed with the aid of springs. Soon the quay behind grew smaller and people became unrecognisable. They were still waving, but that is only because that's all there is to do when a ship moves off, not because they knew where *Glasgow* was heading. No one had consciously turned up to say goodbye and the waving was as empty and uninteresting as the gloomy grey day with its rain-filled sky. The ship then proceeded down the river before securing to a buoy.

Anchoring trials were successfully carried out and two days later, at 2.50 pm *Glasgow* headed for Sheerness where she took on board ammunition. Supervising the loading of shells and cordite for use by the Royal Marine's "B" turret was Major Wright, RM assisted by Lieutenant Smith, RM in the lighter on the starboard side and Midshipman Peter Hinton, working the derrick. Sergeants Dunk and Ackland, two corporals and 25 other ranks completed the working party. The weather was cold but the men soon became warm as they toiled to get the shells aboard. These came up 12 at a time in a net, the grommets were cut off and the shells were put into 'shell bags' and lowered, in lots of 4, to the Shell Room below the turret, where they were placed in the shell ring. Cordite and fuses were then taken aboard from a lighter, which had secured on the port side. The operation was hampered by the fact that the 'Royals' only had one net at their disposal and the crane kept breaking down. Eventually by mid afternoon the following day the task was completed.

On Thursday 21st *Glasgow* slipped and got under way to make passage towards Portland. That afternoon full cruising speed trials were undertaken and the Bofors armament was tested before full power trials took place the following day. All the way down through the English Channel *Glasgow* completed various trials before she arrived off Portland where the cruiser remained secured to a buoy for a further five days before slipping to head for Portsmouth, arriving there at the end of the month.

On 5th December, the cruiser sailed from the Hampshire port bound for Gibraltar. During the passage the ship was put through her paces, with full armament trials being carried out at Portland, before *Glasgow* eventually arrived in the Straits of Gibraltar five days later, to berth alongside the Tower. Soon after her arrival in Gibraltar the crew was soon put to work painting ship in preparation for the forth-coming arrival in Malta.

After an uneventful passage *Glasgow* entered Grand Harbour on 17th December where, in the days leading up to Christmas, the crew was again employed in bringing the ship up to scratch after her long refit in the UK.

HMS Glasgow enters Grand Harbour Malta 17th December 1951   *(JM)*

A welcome break came with the arrival of Christmas and on Christmas Eve the crew was entertained by the S.O.D.S who put on a concert party, consisting of songs and comic turns, much to the amusement of those who were able to see it. Leading Seaman Sam Rowe recalls "although we were able to put on big shows with the help of the Royal Marine Band we also had small SODS Opera's in the mess deck. In our mess we had some talented people, including a lad who was able to hypnotise his 'oppos.' On one occasion when the Bosun's whistle sounded for Rounds we all sprang to attention as the Officer of the Watch, stepped over the coving into the mess deck. As he did so he found two grown men on all fours imitating 'moo-ing' cows, completely unaware of their predicament !"

On Christmas Day, the catering staff excelled themselves to provide traditional fare to a lot of hungry officers and men.

The weather was brilliant after the gloom of an English winter and on Boxing Day a football match was arranged, with a team from the *Glasgow* competing against Rabat F.C. In spite of losing 4-0 the ship's company played well and were not disgraced.

The "holiday" came to an end when the cruiser left Malta for a working up programme which sought to improve the fighting efficiency of the ship and blend the crew into an homogenous ship's company.

In the Med with 'Lord Louis'

As New Year's Day 1952 began, *Glasgow* sailed from Marsaxlokk to calibrate her gunnery radar equipment and engage in a full calibre and full charge bombardment of the island of Filfla before returning to Grand Harbour, Malta. On the Island a series of sports events were organised, and in the final of the Cruiser Squadron football tournament, *Glasgow's* First XI forced a draw against a team from her sister ship HMS *Liverpool* but lost the replay.

Football Team HMS Glasgow   (RP)

Soon the crew was back at work when HMS *Glasgow* participated in Exercise "Horsewhip One", which involved simulated landings by the Royal Marine detachment and a bombardment of shore targets on Filfla. The Shore Spotter credited *Glasgow* with eight hits when only six guns had been fired! **Well-Done *Glasgow.***

241

HMS Glasgow fires her main armament   (GB/GS)

Mid-January was a time of heightened activity aboard the warship as preparations were made to convey Rear-Admiral R.A.B. Edwards, FO2, to Benghazi where he was due to meet the newly crowned King of Libya, King Idris. The First Lord of the Admiralty, the Right Honourable J.P.L Thomas, M. P. was also due to carry out an inspection of the Fleet. This required a Royal Marine guard and a contingent of 100 men from *Glasgow* to join others from HM Ships *Cleopatra* and *Euryalus* on board the aircraft carrier *Ocean*. Initially the inspection was planned to take place on the carrier's flight deck but the arrangements were altered at the last moment, for it to be held in the hanger. As aircraft were being moved up in one lift, the men were transported down in the other, all successfully accomplished in seven minutes!

On 19th January *Glasgow* hoisted the flag of Rear-Admiral R.A.B. Edwards, and when he and his staff were safely aboard, course and speed were set for the passage to Benghazi.

Adverse weather conditions heralded the ship's arrival the following day to prevent the cruiser from anchoring. After firing the national salute she continued to steam nearby throughout the night before returning to the Libyan harbour in the morning, where the salute was repeated. Two days after the ship's arrival Rear-Admiral Edwards went ashore to receive an audience with King Idris.

Rear-Admiral Edwards returned to the ship and on 22nd she weighed anchor and made her way back to Malta where again the

242

Rear-Admiral R.A.B. Edwards addresses the crew of HMS Glasgow

Consul-General Rear-Admiral R.A.B. Edwards   King Idris of Libya   (PH)

weather deteriorated, forcing the ship to remain at sea overnight before she was able to safely enter Grand Harbour two days later.

On 25th January the ship was alive with rumours following receipt of a signal which ordered all British ships in harbour to sail that afternoon. The lower deck was cleared and the Commander told both Watches that the ship was destined to go to Tobruk. The fact that extra provisions had been taken on board during re-storing added fuel to the "buzz" that *Glasgow* was to be used "for trooping". This was further reinforced when 400 camp beds were taken on board.

As she left Grand Harbour, HM Ships *Saintes* and *Armada*, from the Third Destroyer Squadron, formed up astern and course and speed was set for Tobruk. However, in response to a "Flash" signal, informing the Rear Admiral that renewed rioting and arson attacks had occurred in Cairo with some loss of British lives, the cruiser's course and speed were adjusted to ensure that she arrived in the Libyan port at dawn.

During the passage Rear-Admiral Edwards received notice of his promotion to higher rank and on arrival in Tobruk he transferred his flag to HMS *Liverpool*.

Soon after *Glasgow*'s arrival shore leave was granted and some of the crew made the acquaintance of some very potent strong local brew!

Arab OUZO takes its toll! (GS)

On 28th January 1952 a fully equipped 1st Battalion The Devonshire Regiment were embarked on *Glasgow*, and their motorised transport and stores were taken on board the *Empress Baltic*. When the troops were safely aboard the cruiser left harbour and steamed along to allow the troops to become accustomed to life on board a British warship. During this acclimatisation process the troops and the ship's company each went through their respective "Action Station" procedures.

1st *Battalion The Devonshire Regiment embark equipment*   *(GS)*

It was at this time that Their Royal Highnesses the Princess Elizabeth and Prince Philip, Duke of Edinburgh, were due to fly to Nairobi, en route to Australia, and *Saintes* and *Armada* were despatched, as a precaution, to patrol the route of the intended flight path.

The month of February began with a Regatta in which boat crews from *Glasgow* competed against those from the *Liverpool*, and the returned destroyers *Saintes* and *Armada*. Those from *Glasgow* acquitted themselves well. This period of relaxation was soon followed by one of gunnery and torpedo firing exercises.

On 6th February the Fleet received the distressing news of the death of His Majesty King George VI and all ceremonial duties and sports competitions were immediately cancelled. Two days later a 56-gun salute was fired at the rate of one round each minute, to mark each

245

year of the late King's life, followed later by a 21-gun salute fired in honour of the proclamation of Her Majesty Queen Elizabeth II.

Glasgow left harbour on 9th February bound for Malta, and during the passage a force nine gale blew up which caused some structural damage below "B" turret. Temporary repairs were effected which enabled the ship to proceed, at reduced speed, to enter Grand Harbour three days later.

For exercise "Grand Slam" Vice-Admiral R.A.B. Edwards, FO2 transferred his flag from the *Liverpool* to the *Glasgow* and she set sail again. Following the successful conclusion of the exercise *Glasgow* returned to her berth in Grand Harbour from which, on the day of the late King's burial in St. George's Chapel Windsor, another 56-gun salute was fired.

In the full sports tournament which was organised on 22nd February *Glasgow* did well by beating *Liverpool* decisively 8-0 at football, and with her fencing team winning the bayonet fencing.

HMS Glasgow's Royal Marine Bayonet Team practice their skills (MC)

Mike Cobbold recalls the 'Royals' won the 'spring bayonet' event during which he fought an opponent who was six foot two with long arms to match. "I didn't think I had a chance, however he came at me with speed on each occasion and I forgot all about 'spring bayonets' and defended myself as though I had a real rifle and bayonet, winning my bout as he impaled himself on my bayonet every time." He further recalls "the heavy weight championship was won by a young OD who knew very little about boxing and had been pushed forward as the biggest lad on board. He squared up to his opponent from the Home Fleet who promptly floored him with a low blow to the stomach and as the OD could not continue; he was carried out of the ring as heavy weight champion of the Mediterranean Fleet." P.O. Isaacs, of the Cygnet, who had carried the Olympic torch in the Games of 1948, won the cross-country event!

Chuffed with their success the crew of *Glasgow* soon got back to work when she sailed away from the island on 26th February to engage in exercises which aimed to sharpen up the response times of the gun crews as they went to "Action Stations". Much time was spent training and elevating the guns, testing firing circuits, fire controls and communication systems.

On 1st March the cruiser entered Cagliari Bay firing a national 21-gun salute as she did so. The next day course and speed were set for Aranci Bay, on the east coast of Sardinia, where full scale bombardment exercises were to take place. *Glasgow*, in company with *Liverpool*, US Ships *Pittsburgh* and *Roanoke*, French warships *George Leygues* and *Gloire* and the Italian ships *Garibaldi* and *Montecuccoli* made runs up and down the approach course in line astern. Each ship fired salvoes at targets with the results recorded by spotters ashore and in aircraft overhead. Once the bombardment exercises had finished the ships dispersed and *Glasgow* proceeded to Naples.

Naples overlooked by Mount Vesuvius.   (DR)

247

Naples, one of the oldest European cities, is situated at the foot of Mount Vesuvius, 185 km south-west of Rome, in the midst of a volcanic area at the rear of the Bay of Naples. Peter Hinton recalls" the city of Naples is a rather typical naval base, the business area is clean and fairly modern, whereas the back streets are, for the most part rather dirty and sordid. The Neapolitans are very much a distinct type who have a dialect of their own and many customs and traditions, which include the Tarantella dance. One of the highlights of the visit to Naples occurred on Monday 10th March when the crew had an audience with Pope Pius XII.

The crew of HMS Glasgow meet Pope Pius XII   (JM)

During the course of the same visit the crew was entertained by the well-known singer from Lancashire, Gracie Fields who lived nearby on the Isle of Capri.

The return to Malta on 13th March was unusual to say the least in that all the ships that accompanied *Glasgow* on the return trip had Flag Officers aboard:

HMS *Liverpool* — C-in-C Mediterranean Fleet, Admiral Sir John Edelsten,

HMS *Indomitable* — C-in-C Home Fleet, Admiral Sir George Creasy,

HMS *Glasgow* — Second in Command Mediterranean Fleet,Vice-Admiral R.A.B. Edwards,

HMS *Superb* — Flag Officer Flotillas Home Fleet, Rear-Admiral W.G.A. Robson,

HMS *Cleopatra* — Flag Officer Flotillas Mediterranean Fleet, Rear-Admiral F.R. Parham,

HMS *Theseus* — Flag Officer (AC2) Mediterranean Fleet Rear-Admiral Caspar John

Glasgow and the other ships arrived safely in Malta on the 15th but for her crew there was little time for relaxation because trouble was brewing in the Middle East and on the 21st she re-stored in preparation for a tour of duty in the Canal Zone. A "buzz" circulated the ship that she was destined to go to Port Said on completion of the impending exercise "Full Toss". *Glasgow's* captain received his sailing orders but before the ship could set sail for the exercise the First Sea Lord Admiral Sir Rhoderick McGrigor visited the ship and addressed the crew. *Glasgow* set course for Port Said, accomp- anied by the destroyer HMS *St. James* to arrive at the entrance to the Suez Canal on 26th March. *Glasgow* reached her destination after an uneventful passage.

Canal Offices

The local "gulley-gulley" men, who had rowed out to trade with the cruiser's crew, were constantly deterred from plying their wares. On board, additional sentries were posted who completed 'rounds' of the ship every half an hour to ensure that the ship did not come under attack from Egyptian frogmen, nor was it depleted of any equipment fixtures or fittings during her stay in port!

Ashore, the atmosphere was a little tense and such shore leave as was granted confined the libertymen to the compound, where a pub run by ship's personnel, the "Stag Inn", had been opened. This was supplied with vast quantities of beer which had been taken on board in Malta. On the evening of Sunday 6th April the well-known comedian Frankie Howerd gave a concert attended by a third of the ship's company who thoroughly enjoyed it.

Frankie Howerd entertains the crew of HMS Glasgow at the Stag Inn   *(GS)*

Eventually, shore leave was granted to a limited number of ratings to venture out of the compound in order that the Egyptians, seeing unarmed British sailors walking about, would realise that the crisis was over.

Whilst the ship was in port the S.O.D.S put on a performance of "The *Glasgow* Gag Show" to entertain the officers and their guests. This was repeated a few days later at the Scots Guards' camp, where it was declared a great success due to the talents of the ratings who appeared in them.

Leading Seaman Sam Rowe recalls "while we were alongside in Port Said over the ship's Tannoy came the pipe 'Ship's Concert Party lay aft' and when four of us mustered on the Quarterdeck we were introduced to Frankie Howerd. It was not long before we became involved in the production of the Frankie Howerd Show which was recorded aboard *Glasgow* and broadcast as a BBC radio programme at a later date.

Twelve days later *Glasgow* returned to Malta to re-provision and take on ammunition before setting sail again to take part in exercise "Task Force 57," in company with HM Ships *Theseus, Euryalus, Manxman, Surprise, Sluys, Solebay, Vigo, Armada, St.James, Cheviot* and *Saintes*. When the exercise was over *Glasgow* detached and made her way towards Phaleron Bay where she anchored before proceeding to anchor in the port of Piraeus on 23rd April.

Two days later, King Paul of the Hellenes unveiled a Memorial to those of the Commonwealth forces who had fallen in the defence of Greece during the Second World War, and at the conclusion of the ceremony he took the salute as the contingent of Royal Marines and Seamen, representing the *Glasgow*, marched past.

That afternoon two Midshipmen, one of whom was Midshipman Peter Hinton, were detailed to take a group of children on a tour of the ship. As the two officers went with their charges to the Admiral's Dining Cabin for tea they discovered the children were the Crown Prince Constantine of Greece, his sister the Crown Princess Irene and the two sons of the British Ambassador resident in Athens.

The following day, 26th April, the Greek King paid a formal visit to the ship where, after inspecting a Royal Marine Guard of Honour, he was introduced to the officers. That same day Lieutenant General Grigoropoulos (later to become an important member of EOKA) paid a visit to the C-in-C, Admiral Sir John Edelsten.

General Grigoropoulos aboard HMS Glasgow   (JM)

In the evening the Royal Marine Bands from *Glasgow* and *Theseus* 'Beat a Retreat' in Constitution Square which was attended by Their Majesties the King and Queen of Greece and other dignitaries from the resident British community, and from the Mediterranean Fleet. *Glasgow's* visit to Greece, which ended on 28th April, had been a success and the ship returned to her base in Malta.

Early in May, the C-in-C, Admiral Sir John H. Edelsten bid farewell to the Fleet and, in his address to the assembled ship's company, expressed the importance of "showing the flag." He further recognised the part played by HMS *Glasgow* within the Fleet, going on to compliment the men on their conduct ashore saying, "the behaviour of libertymen could make or mar the reputation of the Royal Navy while in foreign ports."

On 15th May he relinquished command to his successor and, in accord with naval custom, was rowed by Admirals and the Captains of ships of the Mediterranean Fleet, from the Customs House out to HMS *Surprise*, which was to take him back to the UK. The newly appointed C-in-C Mediterranean Fleet, Admiral The Earl Mountbatten of Burma, KG, GCSI, GCIE, GCVO, KCB, DSO, PC, hoisted his flag in *Glasgow* and addressed the crew.

Admiral The Earl Mountbatten   (JM)
arrives aboard HMS Glasgow as C-in-C

Lord Louis, as Earl Mountbatten was known throughout the Navy, was an Admiral who, like Nelson, had the welfare of his men at heart. The lower decks were cleared and Lord Louis spoke to the entire ship's company, giving them details of the first programme of fleet exercises and visits. Speaking bluntly of the joys and agonies of being the flagship, he said he was very happy to have the cruiser as his

252

Flagship and promised that the best billets and visits would be reserved for her. On the other hand the ship always had to be immaculate and there would be extra work for all, planning for the number of VIP's who would call on board for various functions. He advised the officers that there would be a great deal of entertaining to do in the various ports visited by the ship, consequently the mess bills would be higher than usual. He also told them that he expected a high standard of dress, with exemplary behaviour being required at all times both ashore and afloat.

On 20th May *Glasgow* entered dry dock where her bottom was scraped and repainted while remedial work was undertaken to unblock scuttles which had been sealed during the refit in Chatham the previous year! Three days later the long spell of good weather came to an end when it poured with rain to explode the myth that it never rains after Ascension Day on Malta.

On Empire Day, 24th May, the Fleet sports were organised to take place. *Glasgow* won the Cruiser Challenge Cup and her "Tug of War" team defeated all comers in straight pulls.

Chart of HMS Glasgow's First Summer Cruise 1952   (AM)

On 20th June the First Summer Cruise commenced with a visit made to Taranto where the base consists of two harbours, the Mar Grande and the Mar Piccolo, joined by a narrow canal across which is a large swing bridge with 'traffic lights' to control the ships entering and leaving the little sea. This had been the scene of one of the most important engagements during the Second World War, in which *Glasgow* had played an important part twelve years earlier -the effective destruction of the Italian Navy.

Vice-Admirals Manfredi, C-in-C Italian Naval Forces, and Juliano Di Negozia were received on board, as was the British Naval Attaché Captain C.D. Bonham-Carter, who was later to assume command of the *Glasgow* for her last commission from November 1955 until November 1956. In the dock area of Taranto the 'girls' wore bikini type undies and could be visited for a few lira, whereas in an uptown mansion evening dress was rig of the day and clients were entertained in special rooms. The local Police Captain was always well received by the "Madames" and several lads were returned gently to the ship — one of them was 'rescued' fast asleep in loving arms whilst a queue had formed!

From the Italian port *Glasgow* sailed on Tuesday 24th June to Rijeka, formerly Fiume, in Yugoslavia. She arrived, to anchor on the following day and fired a salute in honour of the country's self-styled leader Marshal Tito (Josip Broz).

Sir Victor Mallett, British Ambassador arrives on board in Rijeka (JM)

Next day the cruiser sailed for Brione, Tito's privately owned island, rumoured to have been surrounded by a minefield! Shortly after *Glasgow*'s arrival there Marshal Tito was welcomed aboard the cruiser where he inspected the guard provided for the occasion before being introduced to the ship's officers.

254

Marshal Josip Tito inspects Royal Marine Guard of Honour   (PH)

The sight of the Rum Tub caused him some amusement as he continued his tour of the ship, before *Glasgow* continued on her way to make a courtesy visit to Trieste, arriving there on Friday 27th June.

Trieste, a seaport and city overlooked by a castle built by the governors of Venice in 1368, has always been contended because of its position; up until the First World War it was part of the Habsburg Empire and after the Second World War it was reclaimed by Yugoslavia.

A degree of excitement was provided while the ship was in the Yugoslavian port when a car, driven by a lady, ran off

Tito amused at sight of Rum Tub   (JM)

255

the jetty into the water. Fortunately this happened close to where *Glasgow* was berthed and the driver was pulled from the car and taken aboard the cruiser where she was examined by the PMO before being transferred to Trieste hospital.

Vic Smith recalls "Trieste was a good run ashore because drink was cheap which made us happy and we had a field day. However, *Glasgow's* Padre was concerned that some of the crew might be affected by clap, and put a notice on the notice board advising the crew as to the evils and dangers of VD while the ship was in port. Some bright spark requested over the SRE that the song 'There's a Tear in my Eye' be played, which caused great amusement amongst the ship's company, apart from the Padre."

The ship departed Trieste on 1st July and made her way to Argostoli, on the southern side of Kephalonia, for a series of anti-sub-marine exercises.

Argostoli is the capital of Kephalonia with an attractive main square, the Platia, with plenty of bars and tavernas in which to sit and watch the world go by. The visit to the Greek Island produced a liking, in the lads, for the local Ouzo, which was not only cheap but also powerful and made even worse when the sailors returned on board and drank plain water.

During "Rounds" in the Morning Watch on 3rd July, a stoker was found asleep in the CO_2 Room. At the Defaulter's Parade which followed, he was punished, being awarded fourteen days Number eleven's and forfeited thirty days leave!

Three days later hands turned to for funnel cleaning duties and entered the vast cylindrical shaped forward funnel and proceeded to scrub the internal surfaces to remove the accumulated soot. Before long the exposed skin of everyone involved was covered with thick oily soot which also found its way, despite the gauze masks worn at the time, into lungs and mouths. The soot was so thick one could almost eat it!

At the end of the day ratings emerged looking like performers in the "Black and White Minstrel Show." A further day was spent by some, "searching" the pre-heater tubes. This required a brush, connected to the end of a wire stem, to be pushed through the tubes to dislodge the soot within. For the man working at the lower end perched uncomfortably and precariously on top of the Regenerator tubes it was particularly unpleasant as the particles of soot emerged onto him.

A little light relief came two days later when HM Ships *Glasgow, Forth, Euryalus* and *Gambia* competed against each other in the heavy ships regatta. In Home Waters boat pulling and sailing was rarely indulged in, whereas in the Mediterranean and Far East fleets the fleet Regatta was the highlight of the sporting year. Rivalry between HM Ships and shore establishments in the Mediterranean intensified as the annual regatta which included tug of war and bayonet fighting, which could be indulged in aboard or ashore, drew closer. For some reason the boat pulling races had a special attraction and the crews competitively strove to win a special silver trophy which was much prized. All branches were expected to provide a boat's crew to pull against their opposite numbers in the other ships and those who crewed the winning boats and the ship's company to which they belonged crowed about for ever afterwards. After the presentation ceremony the trophy , silver cockerel, would be hoisted to the masthead of the winning ship as a sign of the victory and the ship would take on the title – "Cock of the Fleet."

Often for light relief there would be a comic crew of odds and sods dressed in pirate rig propelling whatever with Carley float paddles deck scrubbers and tin trays. On this occasion ratings were able to place bets on the results of the events at the Tote located on "X" gun deck. *Glasgow's* First crew won the Royalist Cup.

Having completed another series of exercises *Glasgow* made passage to Navarin where one of her predecessors, a frigate, had fought in the Battle for Greek Independence in 1827. During the visit another regatta was organised to take place in which the ship's divisions competed against each other. *Glasgow's* Number one boat won the Custani Cup!

The whole of 16th July was taken up with the Fleet Regatta in which *Glasgow* did not do very well, only coming second in two races. At the conclusion of the prize-giving the *Gambia* and *Euryalus* departed. As they did so a Carley float, fitted with a cabin, square sail and a supported oar as a rudder, rigged up like the Kon Tiki raft drifted by, manned by three men wearing straw wine bottle covers as hats. In the evening post regatta high spirits prevailed and the traditional raiding occurred, during which *Glasgow* lost her motor boat. Don Aldridge, Leading Writer to the C-in-C, recalls that Earl Mountbatten was disappointed with the lack of discipline during the Regatta, which took on a somewhat holiday atmosphere, with relaxed standards of dress and much horseplay. Concern was also expressed that with swimming going on at the same time as the raiding, it would only be a question of time before an accident occurred and a signal was sent instructing all boats to return to their ships and the men to attend Divisions, the purpose being to ensure that none of the ratings were still away swimming. While the ships remained anchored at the Greek port a series of evolutions was carried out which required the Royal Marines to set up a field kitchen, the Midshipmen to construct a thirty-man raft and each ship to send two live cockroaches across to the flagship. The series concluded with all non-essential crew abandoning ship.

Two days later *Glasgow* left to steam to Phaleron Bay, outside Athens, and while the ship was at anchor the C-in-C hosted a dinner party for the King and Queen of Greece on the Quarterdeck. After the meal Their Majesties and the other guests were entertained by the Flag Lieutenant's display of conjuring skills.

News from Egypt two days later caused a degree of concern and the ship was alive with "buzzes" as to what might happen. HM Ships *Striker* and *Dieppe* were despatched to Malta ready to transport troops or equipment as required, and on 23rd July *Glasgow* weighed anchor and headed for Port Said. After an uneventful passage the British cruiser arrived two days later to find that conditions in the port were somewhat similar to those which had existed at the time of her previous visit, apart from the fact that Jim Cairo's laundry had burnt down and the Naval compound was guarded by a few civilian policemen. Sentry duty was again increased.

The Egyptian Situation

On 23rd July 1952 the Egyptian Free Officers Movement, headed by General Neguib, seized control of the armed forces in a bloodless coup d'etat in Cairo. Many of the army officers had become dis-illusioned by the level of incompetence shown by their high ranking superiors, and the corruption which had existed in high places. The appointment of his personal favourites into positions of power by the King, His Majesty King Farouk, together with his interference in military matters added to their displeasure. General Neguib, anxious to avoid military intervention by Britain informed the British Government, via the Americans, that the coup was neither political nor directed against either the King or the country's Prime Minister, Hilaly Pasha. However, in the fullness of time General Neguib sought the resignation of the Prime Minister. Following the resignation of the Prime Minister Hilaly Pasha, Aly Maher Pasha was appointed as his successor and he formed a new Government.

The western world was shocked to learn that, at 10.00 am on Saturday 26th July 1952, the Royal Palace in Cairo had been surrounded by armed militia, and the newly appointed Prime Minister, instructed by General Neguib, had delivered an ultimatum requiring the King to abdicate in favour of his son, Crown Prince Ahmed Faud. This ultimatum further required the King to leave the Country by 6.00 pm local time that same day. King Farouk left Egypt with other members of his family aboard his Royal Yacht and sailed for Naples where he was granted asylum.

Following the King's departure Aly Maher Pasha's Government assumed responsibilities for governing the state until a Council of Regency had been set up and approved. In the fullness of time the Crown Prince was crowned King Ahmed Fuad II of Egypt and the Sudan. Although there was no significant change in policy towards Britain other countries, which had an Ambassadorial or Ministerial presence in Egypt, were forced to declare allegiance to the newly-crowned King.

Soon after news relating to the abdication of King Farouk reached *Glasgow's* captain he received orders to sail for Tobruk. Both Watches turned to and the cruiser slipped in the early hours of the Middle Watch on Sunday 27th, and after an uneventful passage anchored off the Libyan port at 10.00 pm *Glasgow* entered the harbour the next day where, amongst much activity, preparations were made to embark FO2 and senior ranking army personnel.

Military Cemetery in Tobruk   *(GS)*

Tobruk is Libya's only natural harbour and was occupied by the Italians as early as 1911 and subsequently used as a naval and air base for their military operations to the south. During World War II the Italians lost Tobruk, which was the focus of some of the most prolonged fighting in the North African theatre of operations.

After the war the city was rebuilt. The purpose of the *Glasgow's* visit to Tobruk was to impose a restraining influence on the Egyptians. It was successful because no local trouble was encountered.

Despite the unrest in Cairo the off-duty libertymen were able to take advantage of Tobruk's locally available sports facilities. Arrangements were made for the ship's First XI soccer team to play against a team from the RAF and *Glasgow's* players scored an overwhelming victory by beating their opponents 15-0! In the team were several players who later went on to play professional First Division football, including Petty Officer P.Harburn who played as centre forward for Everton.

When orders were received for *Glasgow* to return to Malta the news was viewed with mixed feelings. Married men quite naturally looked forward to returning to base whereas others, who found the island of Malta to be dull and unpleasantly hot, preferred the enjoyment of a cool breeze and the comfort of a pleasant bathing beach in Tobruk. The departure from Tobruk on 11th August was preceded by a period of intense activity when the luggage of over 350 members of the Highland Light Infantry was taken on board prior to their transportation back to Malta. The return journey was devoid of exercises and a speed of 18 knots was maintained, apart from a slight interruption when Able Seaman Lamb fell overboard while ditching expended ammunition. A boat from *Manxman* rescued him, none the worse for his experience, and the passage continued until *Glasgow* secured alongside Parlatorio Wharf on 14th, where the ship went into Dockyard routine.

It was during this spell in the Maltese harbour that the colour of *Glasgow's* boats was changed, from a light grey to that of a much darker shade, to prevent the oily water in Grand Harbour from adversely affecting the external appearance. This brought them on a par with those of *Theseus, Forth* and *Cleopatra*. This action begged the question as to whether it was worth sacrificing the title of the ship with the smartest boats in order to save the thirty minutes required daily to hoist a boat out of the water to clean it.

Soon after her return to Valletta Harbour a conference, attended by the various service commanders in the Middle East SBNOME (Rear-Admiral Stokes), GOCBFE (General Festing), AOC205GPRAF (Air

260

Vice-Marshal Slatterly), OC 19Bde and hosted by the FO2MF was held aboard *Glasgow.*

On 26th August 1952 news reached the crew that the record for the air crossing of the Atlantic had been shattered. A Canberra bomber which had started from Aldergrove airport in Northern Ireland flew to Gander in Newfoundland and back in a total flying time of seven hours, fifty-five minutes. The good news of this fine achievement was tempered on 7th September, as *Glasgow* changed berth, when the crew received word that while performing at the Farnborough Air Show, a De Havilland jet aircraft, the DH110, had broken through the sound barrier and disintegrated in mid-air in front of the assembled crowd with disastrous consequences.

Nearer to *Glasgow's* theatre of operation in Egypt a number of political figures had been arrested by troops under the command of General Neguib who had assumed the role of Prime Minister and Minister of War, and in doing so brought about a virtual military dictatorship in the country. In order to win both the support of the workers employed on the cotton estates and retain power General Neguib set about the process of breaking up the larger estates into smaller units, which brought internal chaos to the country. Although in agreement with the overall plan one man, Aly Maher Pasha, who realised that radical reform could not be achieved "overnight" opposed General Neguib and was forced to resign. With his departure the opportunity to create stability within Egypt was lost.

During the days that followed *Glasgow* participated in exercises, which often involved firing her main armament. In Aranci Bay , on 21st September, before setting off for Naples her role changed dramatically to that of a film star.

Crew hoist "Third Funnel" to convert HMS Glasgow into the   *(GS)*
'German' Cruiser Ziethen

A third canvas funnel was fitted to change the warship's appearance to enable *Glasgow* to become the 'German' cruiser *Ziethen* in the film " Sailor of the King" which was based on C. S. Forester's novel "Brown on Resolution" in which Michael Rennie played the part of Captain R.E.S. Saville-Samarez, commanding officer of the British light cruiser *Leopard,* HM Ships *Cleopatra* and the *Euryalus* were to play supporting roles.

By the beginning of October filming sequences finished and *Glasgow* sailed on to Algiers where she "showed the flag."

Algiers, the capital city of Algeria and the most important port of north-west Africa, has a population of over three million, making it the largest population centre in the country. It is located on the Mediterranean coast, set against forested mountains and overlooking a bay. During the Second World War Algiers played a strategic role as the headquarters of De Gaulle's Free French army, remaining an important centre from 1943 until the conclusion of hostilities.

With her visit over *Glasgow* returned to her base in Malta on 6th October to continue her newly found role in film making. On this occasion she provided the technical team: Director, assistant Director, three cameramen and the Naval adviser Commander Rundle, RN and the platform from which scenes were shot, off Marsaxlokk, to produce the instructional film "Replenishment at Sea."

The ship returned to Malta and preparations were made to receive the King and Queen of Sweden on board. On Sunday 12th October a Church Parade was held, attended by the C-in-C, the King and Queen of Sweden and other dignitaries. (The Queen of Sweden was Lord Louis' sister and he wanted to impress her) The presence of more than 100 ratings was also required to attend to ensure that a reasonable congregation was present! A month later, on Saturday 29th November, His Royal Highness the Duke of Edinburgh present-ed new colours to 40,42 and 45 RM Commando Brigades, with Detachments from HM Ships *Theseus, Cleopatra, Euryalus* and

Glasgow taking part in the ceremony on the Parade Ground at Floriana.

HRH the Duke of Edinburgh arrives to present new Colours to 40, 42 and 45 RM Commando Brigades   (MC)

The following day Prince Philip went aboard *Glasgow* to attend Divine service which was held on the Quarterdeck.

Exercises and evolutions, in and around Malta, became the routine for the remainder of the year. However, as the year came to a close talented members of the cruiser's SODS rehearsed regularly before putting on another show, "The Glasgow Follies", on 17th, 18th and 19th December to entertain the ship's company in the Corradino Canteen Cinema during the week leading up to Christmas.

Cast of SODS Christmas Pantomime 1952   (GS)

Since joining the ship Vic Smith had kept himself occupied by building a table lamp from odds and ends that were "available," which was in the form of a yacht in full sail. When finished the yacht had small cabin lights which lit up the interior and was mounted on a plinth. For Christmas that year the yacht was put in pride of place, surrounded by a hand decorated lifebuoy, on the mess deck and attracted the attention of Earl Mountbatten as he toured the mess decks with his wife on Christmas Day. Turning to Vic Smith 'Lord Louis' said, "I'm not going to ask where you got all the equipment to construct the yacht. I really do not want to know where the materials came from!" Vic was full of admiration for Earl Mountbatten, describing him as a man who "got on with the job without airs and graces and was a pleasure to serve under."

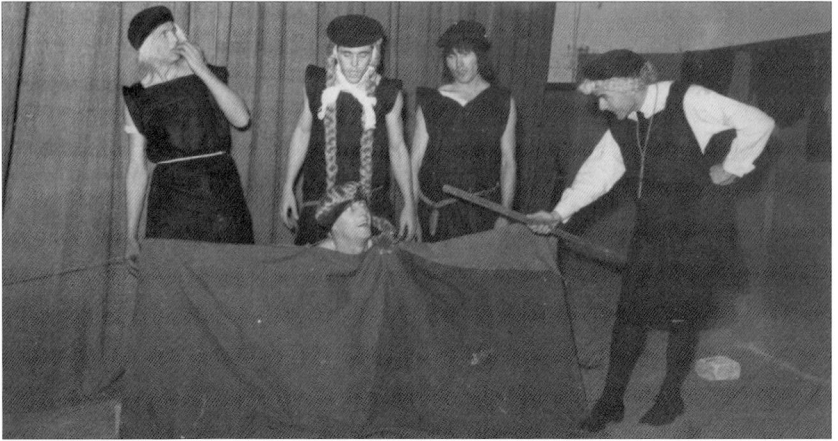

"Girl Guides Go Camping" (SR)
AB Feltham   L/ Seaman Pinder   AB Wheatley   L/Seaman Rowe

Glasgow at the Spithead Review

1953 began badly with the death of Royal Marine G. Wymer occurring on New Year's Day.

For the next two months *Glasgow* was moored in Valetta Harbour Malta, during which time the crew was able to witness a complete eclipse of the sun on 31st January.

At the end of February the Mediterranean Fleet with the aircraft carrier HMS *Eagle*, wearing the Flag of Vice-Admiral J Hughes–Hallett, CB, DSO, and the Sixth Frigate Squadron with HM Ships *Venus, Virago* and *Verulam* assembled in Grand Harbour Malta prior to sailing for Combined Fleet Exercises. These exercises were designed to test the anti-aircraft and anti -submarine capabilities of the Fleet, while at the same time enabling the aircraft carriers to practice air reconnaissance and strike roles.

The assembled Fleet, including *Glasgow*, were joined by: the aircraft carrier *Indomitable*, and HM Ships *Gambia, Euryalus, Manxman, Daring, Chequers, Chieftain, Chivalrous, Chevron, Cheviot, Gravelines, Mermaid, Magpie* and *Cygnet*.

Submarines from the First Submarine Squadron HM Ships: *Forth, Trump, Talent, Token* and *Sanguine*, sailed from the Island, on 1st March, to take up their positions for the impending exercises. On 3rd March, the day the exercises were due to start, HMS *Glasgow* slipped and made the two-day passage to Gibraltar. During her stay in Gibraltar an Inter-Fleet sports tournament was held and it would be fair to say that the Mediterranean Fleet, apart from the soccer, was decisively beaten.

Date	Event		Result
7th March 1953	**Inter Fleet**	**Rugger**	Home Fleet 19
			Mediterranean Fleet 3

10th March 1953	**Inter Fleet**	**Soccer**	Home Fleet 0
			Mediterranean Fleet 1
13th March 1953	**Inter Fleet**	**Hockey**	Home Fleet 4
			Mediterranean Fleet 1
13th March 1953	**Inter Fleet**	**Boxing**	Home Fleet 20
			Mediterranean Fleet 14

Having completed the combined exercises the Home Fleet was detached to enable ships to visit Spanish, French and Portuguese ports to give crews leave, while the bulk of the Mediterranean Fleet sailed to take part in exercise "Rendezvous".

On Sunday 15th March 1953 HMS *Glasgow* slipped from 42 berth Gibraltar and set a course for the Gulf of Lions to exercise with the First Destroyer Squadron consisting of HM Ships *Chequers*, *Chieftain, Cheviot* and *Chevron*. The ships headed, against fresh headwinds, along a route that took them west of Ibiza and fifteen miles to the east of Toulon. As they approached the French coast the weather improved and it remained good until a position south of Crete was reached on the 22nd of the month. Having successfully completed exercise "Rendezvous", on 24th March, *Glasgow* was detached by the Commander, United States Sixth Fleet, and made her way towards Athens.

On Tuesday 24th March the cruiser anchored in Phaleron Bay as the forenoon watch changed. That same morning, at 11.00 am, His Majesty King Paul of the Hellenes boarded the ship and, as an Honorary Admiral in Her Majesty's Fleet, his flag was broken from the main mast marking his arrival.

King Paul of the Hellenes inspecting (RP)
the Supply Division HMS Glasgow

266

After carrying out an inspection of the ship His Majesty was invited to lunch with *Glasgow's* Captain, Captain Holmes, and invited guests. When the Royal Party had departed the ship weighed anchor and moored in the port of Piraeus. The cruisers gunners were kept very busy that day, firing a total of five salutes: three 21-gun, one 19-gun, one 17-gun, and one of 15-guns.

The following day, Wednesday 25th March, a contingent from *Glasgow* - a Colour Party of three with the White Ensign, six Seamen ceremonial buglers, a company of sixty-six Seamen and Stokers and the Royal Marine Band, - took part in the Independence Day Parade in Athens where His Hellenic Majesty King Paul took the salute.

Contingent from HMS Glasgow march through Athens on Independence Day (RP)

The contingent showed great bearing and discipline as they marched along and the ship's Captain received numerous compliments from His Majesty King Paul and both Greek and United States Senior Naval Officers. These included a letter from the King.

To the Commanding Officer of HMS *Glasgow*,

After my visit to HMS *Glasgow*, when I first hoisted my flag as Hon. Admiral of the Royal Navy in one of Her Britannic Majesty's Ships, I wish to convey to you and to your Officers and Ship's Company an expression of My satisfaction at your fine turn out. I was greatly pleased with what I saw. It was an honour and a pleasure to me to accept the invitation, which I received from Her Majesty, Queen Elizabeth to assume the rank of Hon. Admiral in the Royal Navy. I greatly enjoyed My visit to you and I am glad to think that the seamen and the Royal Marines from HMS *Glasgow* will take place in the parade which will celebrate the anniversary of that day when My Country achieved its freedom and on which enduring friendship between Greece and the United Kingdom was first sealed.

The Queen joins me in wishing all good fortune to H.M.S. *Glasgow* and all who sail in her.

Signed Paul R

The Royal Palace, Athens, 24th March 1953.

British Embassy

ATHENS.
25th March 1953.

(Captain Holmes)

I am desired by His Majesty, The King of the Hellenes, Admiral of the Royal Navy, to express to you his pride and satisfaction in the splendid bearing of the seamen and the Royal Marines under your command who took part in the ceremonial parade this morning, when His Majesty took the salute.

His Majesty is more than ever pleased that he now has a special relationship with them.

Signed Charles Peake
H.M. Ambassador.

The Commanding Officer
HMS *Glasgow*.

On 26th March the death of Her Majesty Queen Mary was announced which led to the cancellation of all public entertainment.

The following day two Maltese canteen assistants were arrested by Customs Officials trying to smuggle 108 cigarette lighters ashore. Use of tact and diplomacy by the British Consul resulted in the sentence of twenty-five days imprisonment being reduced to that of a fine, of Dr 4,000,000, which was paid by the Canteen Manager to secure their release.

The ship was opened for visitors for a period of two hours on Saturday 28th March and departed from Piraeus on the following Monday morning to sail for Malta. HMS *Glasgow* arrived in Grand Harbour on 1st April and five days later Captain B. Bryant, DSO, DSC**, OBE, assumed command of the warship.

That month the C-in-C Mediterranean transferred his flag to "*Lascaris*" and on 17th April *Glasgow* slipped from her berth and proceeded first to Toulon and then Athens. Having completed the visits the cruiser returned to Malta where preparations were made for the forthcoming Coronation Review which was to be held at Spithead on 15th June 1953.

HMS Glasgow lit overall in Valletta Harbour in Preparation for Spithead Review (RP)

Captain Bryant received his sailing orders and *Glasgow* left the island of Malta and made her way back to Pompey via Gibraltar to participate in the review. During her passage across the Bay of Biscay Midshipman Brown, was reported overboard on 9th June and a search for him was quickly carried out. Fortunately for him he was picked up out of the water at fifteen minutes past midnight none the worse for his experience.

On 11th June 1953 *Glasgow* anchored at Spithead, in readiness for the forthcoming Review, dressed overall in honour of Her Majesty the Queen Elizabeth II's Birthday. The next day her crew witnessed the arrival of the Norwegian Royal Yacht with King Olav aboard.

Aboard the cruiser Captain Bryant received an AFO concerning the drill to be followed when the monarch passed by in review. Caps were to be removed and held at arms length above the head and flourished in a clockwise motion three times in phase with the cheers, which were to be preceded with three hips rather than two and followed by 'Hooray' and not 'Hoorah.'

Three days later, on 15th June, Her Majesty Queen Elizabeth II reviewed the assembled Fleet aboard the Royal Navy's last remaining battleship, HMS *Vanguard.*

Ships as seen from Left to Right with liner Mauretania passing between them

Furthest Lane HM Ships	– *Cleopatra*	*Dido*	*Redpole*		
Centre Lane HM Ships	– *Superb*	*Sheffield*	*Swiftsure*	*Gambia*	*Glasgow*
Nearside Lane HM Ships	– *Theseus*	*Illustrious*	*Indefatigable*	*Implacable*	
	Indomitable	*Eagle*	*Vanguard*		

The Coronation Naval Review was an unforgettable experience. From the time when the Royal yacht HMS *Surprise*, preceded by the Trinity House vessel *Patricia*, slipped her moorings in Portsmouth Dockyard and steamed out of harbour towards the assembled company of ships, until she dropped anchor after completing the review passage, was a bare two hours. It was a majestic two hours, during which the Queen in white and the Duke of Edinburgh in the uniform of Admiral of the Fleet, from the specially built viewing platform just ahead of *Surprise's* bridge, acknowledged the salutes and loyal cheers of the great fleet as the Review procession traversed its four main lines. The *Surprise*, smartly painted and decked out with awning, was wearing the Royal Standard and the Board of

Admiralty flag in deference to the Queen's presence, for in olden times the Sovereign was the Lord High Admiral. Behind the *Surprise* came a long line of ships, HMS *Radpole*, the Admiralty yacht for the occasion, carrying the Board of Admiralty, followed by other naval vessels and three great liners in gleaming new colour crowded with official guests. It seemed all too short, too sudden a climax for what had taken months of preparation and immeasurable effort to achieve. It is difficult to say what stood out most from an outstanding day — whether it was the great line of aircraft carriers, headed by the only battleship, HMS *Vanguard*, Flagship of the Fleet, or some of the smaller ships with their greater sense of individuality.

The carriers, especially HMS *Eagle*, gave a tremendous feeling of sheer power, looking like huge leviathans that had shouldered themselves out of the deep, aggressive in their bulk. The fast patrol boats with their graceful lines seemed deceptively quiet when one remembered the power pent up in them and the dash of which they were capable. The long low submarines, sleek, streamlined and sinister, like watchful alligators showing little of themselves, with their crews linking hands against the skyline, as if they were about to break into a hornpipe.

Destroyer upon cruiser, frigate upon destroyer, line upon business-like line, their grey shapes bright in the sunlight, swung half-broad-side by the wind against the tide, the small wave-crests playing impertinent slap and tickle against their unfeeling sides. All the 300 ships and numberless small craft were dressed-overall, the flags of the International Code in streaming line from bow to masts, from masts to stern, in a quivering display of colour. The commemorative fly-past, impressive alone for its compressed timings - 300 aircraft of varying speed and types, from helicopters to the latest prototype jets - flashed by in perfect formations in a matter of five minutes. That night the assembled ships were illuminated so that their outlines were picked out strong and starkly, and against this backdrop fire-works soared high into the night to mark the finale of the Royal Navy's greatest day for many years.

The day following the review many of the ships dispersed and *Glasgow* weighed anchor and headed back to Gibraltar for a four day stop-over before returning to her base in Malta, where she arrived on 26th June. For two weeks the crew were able to relax in familiar surroundings before the cruiser left for another visit to Athens, via Vatika Bay where a series of "Evolutions" was undertaken.

The Mediterranean Fleet in Vatika Bay (MC)

From 21st July until the 25th the crew were able to enjoy Greek hospitality before the ship headed towards Istanbul for a week's visit. Roy Palmer went ashore in Istanbul and asked a local taxi driver to take him to see the barracks where Florence Nightingale nursed the wounded during the Crimean War. The taxi driver first took Roy to the Nightingale hospital, where an English speaking nursing Sister was delighted to point out the barracks nearby. As soon as the Turkish officers discovered Roy was English they took him to see the building where Florence had worked.

Roy recalls "as I walked through the corridors and climbed the stone tower, which she had climbed with her lantern, I got the feel for how it must have been all those years ago.

Royal Marine Band Beat Retreat in Istanbul 30/07/1953 (MC)

At the conclusion of the visit to Turkey *Glasgow* returned to Malta on 6th August 1953. The ship remained briefly in Malta before *Glasgow* sailed once more on 10th to the Middle East to arrive in Port Said three days later. During the time *Glasgow* was in Port Said, Royal Marine Underwood regrettably died here and was buried in the Military Cemetery at Fayid with full military honours.

Royal Marine Funeral Party Fire Farewell Salute to a Comrade   (MC)
in Fayid Cemetery Port Said

The warship maintained a presence in Port Said until 8th September 1953 when she returned again to Malta. Ten days after her return to base *Glasgow* was on the move again, this time for short visits to Navarin, where a regatta was held, and Piraeus.

Navarin Bay in the Ionian Sea, in the southwestern Peloponnese area of Greece is also known as Pylos Bay after Homeric Pylos. It is small, deep and almost landlocked and was the scene of a decisive battle in 1827 that consolidated the Independence of Greece. Here the combined fleets of Great Britain (including the frigate HMS *Glasgow*), France and Russia destroyed the Turko-Egyptian fleet. Two years after the battle the French built a small town on the bay's southern shore. The bay is one of the safest anchorage's in the Mediterranean, protected as it is by the island of Sfakiria which acts as a giant breakwater for the bay's inner lagoon, leaving a broad channel to the south and the Sikias Channel to the north.

On 9th October she departed from Piraeus for Malta to re-provision and carry out routine maintenance before sailing again to Port Said, Fayid and Aqaba, in Jordan. Aqaba is Jordan's only port with its history dating back to 4,000 BC when it became important as a result of its strategic position at the junction of trade routes linking Asia, Africa and Europe. As the trading routes connecting Aqaba with southern Arabia and Yemen developed it grew from a town into a thriving city.

The Jetty at Aqaba 1953 (MC)

However, by the beginning of the 6th century it became part of the Ottoman Empire and went into a decline to become a simple fishing village of little significance. During the First World War, however, the Turks were forced to withdraw from the town after a raid by Lawrence of Arabia and the Arab forces of Sheriff Hussein.

In more recent times archaeologists unearthed what they believe to be the world's oldest building built specifically to be a church - slightly older than the Church of the Holy Sepulchre in Jerusalem and the Church of the Nativity in Bethlehem. During the three days spent in Aqaba King Hussein visited the ship to see her put through her paces. This visit was celebrated by the issue of the Jordan Service Medal (JSM), which was approved by the British Government (who did not pay anything towards it). Members of the commission are entitled to wear it and money raised from the sale of these medals is donated to deserving charities and the King of Jordan Memorial Fund.

King Hussein on HMS Glasgow's Bridge

On 2nd November *Glasgow* sailed from Aqaba to make a four-day passage to Massawa (in Eritrea), where she stayed for five days before returning to Malta via Port Said. During her stay in Massawa a number of matelots and "royals" fell in love with the local dusky maidens and went AWOL, forgetting that in the community they stood out like beams of torchlight on a dark December night. Soon all were returned to the ship! *Glasgow* departed from Massawa on 11th November and entered Grand Harbour, Valletta five days later where she remained until after Christmas.

In keeping with tradition it is customary for the Captain of a warship to assist the cooks in preparing the traditional Christmas pudding and make a wish for the safe keeping of the vessel and her crew. As the festive occasion approached Captain Bryant lent a hand to stir the mixture before it was cooked.

Captain Ben Bryant, RN stirs the Christmas pudding December 1953

While the *Glasgow* was in harbour that year the crew enjoyed a traditional naval Christmas with good fare and entertainment provided by talented members of the SODS, the Pantomime "Sinbad".

On Christmas Day 'Lord Louis' and his wife Edwina upheld the tradition of visiting the mess decks to wish members of the crew the compliments of the season.

Earl Mountbatten and his wife Edwina visit the mess decks at Christmas 1953 (RP)

The year ended with the C-in-C entertaining Their Royal Highnesses the Prince and Princess of Hesse on board the cruiser on New Year's Eve.

Fit for a Queen

HMS *Glasgow* continued to be based in Malta and on 22nd January 1954 she hoisted the Flag of the C-in-C Mediterranean.

During February that year the cruiser left Malta for Cyprus where she engaged in gunnery exercises before going on to Morphou Bay and Port Said where she remained until March returning back to her base in Malta.

On 13th March HM *Submarines Talent, Token* and *Sentinel* left the Island, followed by the RFA's *Fort Duquesne* and *Blue Ranger*. The following day HMS *Glasgow* in company with HM Ships *Saintes, St. Kitts, Barfleur, Gambia, Bermuda, Daring, Chequers, Cheviot, Chevron, Wrangler, Wakeful, Roebuck, Brigand,* and *Reggio,* sailed with the Mediterranean Fleet on passage to Gibraltar. A number of exercises which incorporated convoy escort duties, a simulated atomic attack, anti-submarine measures and air defence, involving aircraft from the carrier HMS *Eagle* and those based in North Africa and Gibraltar, were carried out en route.

The Home Fleet, under C-in-C Sir Michael M. Denny, KCB, CBE, DSO (who had played such an important part in the evacuation of King Haakon of Norway) in HMS *Vanguard* and the Mediterranean Fleet, arrived in Gibraltar on March 19.th Soon after arrival it was noted that the Reserve Fleet ships berthed along the Detached Mole were in a dilapidated state. Aware that Her Majesty the Queen Elizabeth II was due to visit the colony a decision was made that their appearance should be improved. Ships and squadrons of the Combined Fleets were each allocated a Reserve Fleet ship with instructions that they be made "tiddly". In two days they were all washed down and painted overall in what was to become known as "Operation Glamour." The crews having worked hard to smarten the

Reserve Fleet were rewarded with a programme of social and sporting activities.

On Thursday 25th March 1954, the F.S. *Gustav Zede*, flying the Flag of Vice-Admiral Rosset, arrived in Gibraltar just before the weather deteriorated so much so that by 3.0 pm those ships lying outboard of those secured alongside had to cast off and put to sea to avoid damage. Having endured a storm swept night outside in the Bay the ships were able to return to more comfortable positions in the harbour again.

At this time a civilian Comet aircraft G-ALYP had crashed into the sea off Elba and a portion of the stricken plane had been recovered from the seabed. This was brought into Gibraltar aboard HMS *Whirlwind* pending its transfer onto HMS *Vanguard* for transportation back to England for examination by the Civil Aviation accident investigation team. While on passage *Whirlwind* answered a distress call from a Spanish trawler the *Cabo Corona* off Cape Palmos. Although hampered by the wreckage from the Comet on her upper deck the warship managed to take the Spanish vessel in tow until salvage tugs arrived from Cartegena.

March concluded with the fire and subsequent foundering of the troop transport *Empire Windrush* off Algiers. On 28th March an explosion occurred in the engine room of the vessel which started a fire resulting in the passengers and crew being ordered to abandon ship. HM Ships *Saintes* and *St Kitts* were dispatched from Gibraltar to assist. The two warships raced to the scene but on arrival all the passengers and crew had been picked up by merchant ship and taken into Algiers. HMS *Saintes* valiantly took the *Empire Windrush* in tow but the fire had an uncontrollable hold and the troop transport foundered and sank shortly after midnight of 29th/30th March.

The Fleets then began to disperse to take part in *"Medflexable"*, a large scale NATO exercise in which French and British Fleets took part. The exercise which aimed to test anti submarine and air defence capabilities of the participating ships also coincided with another NATO exercise *"Shield One"* during which American, French and Italian aircraft engaged in "attacking" the surface forces. These exercises coincided with possible trouble brewing in the area around the Suez Canal and ships were put to a state of short notice standby. In the event the perceived danger proved to be a false alarm.

It was during exercise "Shield One" that Lord Louis was able to out manoeuvre the commanders of the American ships, much to their annoyance. The C-in-C Mediterranean issued orders to the captains of the British warships that sets of all-round green lights over all round white, were to be rigged on the Quarterdecks of their ships. As darkness fell the order "Darken ship" was issued, whereupon all navigation lights apart from those indicating port and starboard were extinguished, and the green and white lights were turned on. Lord Louis's ships took on the appearance of a large fishing fleet. The Americans fooled by the dupe failed to recognise their "enemy" and sailed on! Mountbatten then gave orders for the British ships to revert back to their regulation lighting profiles and the Americans were caught "with their trousers down."

On 2nd April the Mediterranean Fleet, involved in "*Medflexable*," were manoeuvring near Elba, not far from the crash site of Comet G-ALYP, and those aboard the *Glasgow* were able to witness the difficulties experienced by the salvage crews in the recovery of wreckage. The salvage vessel the *Sea Salvor* was able to recover a major part of the plane, the fore end, and by the time the operation was complete well over 90% had been retrieved.

On 3rd April the *Glasgow*, in company with H.M.S. *Surprise*, arrived at Toulon and fired a national salute. Admiral Lambert, the Prefet Maritime, Admiral Mariani, the Admiral d'Escadre at Toulon, M. Eudier, Sous-Prefet of the Var and Maitre Lebellegou, Mayor Depute of Toulon were later received aboard the warship.

Toulon, a commercial and industrial city in south-eastern France, lies on the Mediterranean Sea approximately 30 miles east of Marseilles. The harbour serves as the primary naval base for the

Toulon 1954   (RP)

French Mediterranean fleet. In November 1942, much of the French fleet was scuttled in the harbour to prevent its seizure by the Germans. After its occupation by the enemy it served as a German submarine base. It was extensively damaged, by Allied bombing in 1943 and 1944, before being retaken by the French in August of 1944, since when most of it has been restored but the charm of the old section north of the harbour remains unspoilt.

Three days later a preliminary critique of Medflexable was held aboard the British cruiser after which, on 8th, she proceeded to Naples where she arrived on 10th April. As *Glasgow* approached the Italian port the ship's piper stood on the top of B turret playing his set of bagpipes. 'Lord Louis' knowing that the Italians disliked the sound took advantage of every opportunity to upset them by ordering the piper to play whenever the cruiser entered an Italian port.

Once in the Italian port however the ship and her crew were well received and the Royal Marine Bands of the Fleet, including that from HMS *Glasgow*, beat a Retreat in the Piazza Plebiscity much to the delight of the local crowds. During the *Glasgow's* stay in Naples the Italian Naval authorities made arrangements for crew members to visit a number of places of interest including Capri, Pompeii. On Tuesday 13th April 1954 the Fleet departed from Naples to exercise, en route to Malta, in preparation for the impending visit of Her Majesty the Queen Elizabeth II, who had recently completed her Commonwealth Tour, in May. To greet the royal couple, as they approached in HMY *Britannia*, the C-in-C practised a spectacular manoeuvre. The Fleet advanced at twenty-five knots, twice the speed of *Britannia* , then turned inwards and swept past the Royal Yacht, sailing so close that some of the ships splashed water over her decks. The exercise was perfectly safe provided no mistake was made, but even the slightest deviation of course could have caused a disastrous accident. He certainly impressed the royal party!

HMY Britannia arrives (RP)
in Malta in May 1954

Her Majesty the Queen, arrived in Malta, where she was greeted by ship's crews assembled on the decks of warships anchored in Valletta Harbour.

HM Queen Elizabeth II welcomed aboard HMS Glasgow 5/5/1954   (RP)

The C-in-C made the necessary arrangements to meet her Majesty and HMY *Britannia* came alongside *Glasgow* to enable him transfer by Jackstay to join her Majesty.

Following the arrival of the Royal Yacht in Malta Her Majesty Queen Elizabeth II, accompanied by His Royal Highness Prince Philip, was welcomed aboard HMS *Glasgow* and took the salute from the Quarterdeck.

Early in 1954 a decision had been taken to alter the traditional square rig jumper, which was to incorporate a concealed zip. On the occasion of Her Majesty's visit a small number of the seamen were paraded wearing the new style jumpers and her opinion was sought as to whether or not it was to her liking. Having taken the salute Her Majesty inspected the Royal Marine Guard of Honour before being introduced to the Divisions of the ship's company in turn.

At the conclusion of her visit Her Majesty, together with the Duke of Edinburgh, agreed to be included in the photograph of the ship's company taken on the fo'c'sle. This is believed to be unique.

Her Majesty Queen Elizabeth II inspects the Royal Marine Guard of Honour (RP)

Her Majesty Queen Elizabeth II meets the Chief Petty Officers (MC)

The Royal Marine 'A' Team. (Racing Whaler) (MC)

Also proudly displayed was the silver "Cock of the Fleet" trophy which had been won by the royal Marines 'A' crew racing team.

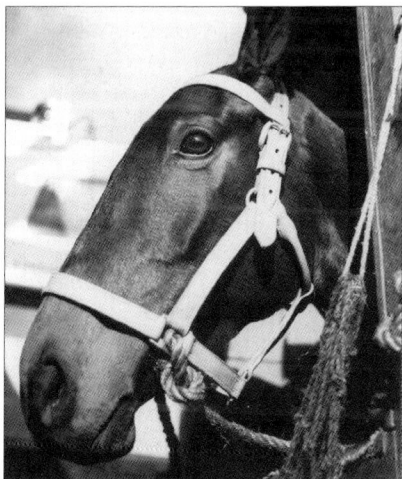

Lord Louis' Polo Pony (RP)
on its way back to England at the end of the commission

Her Majesty departed from the ship to continue her inspection of the remainder of the Fleet before returning to the UK, via Gibraltar, in the Royal Yacht escorted by *Glasgow* at the completion of her tour.

Earl Mountbatten, aware that *Glasgow* was returning to the UK took advantage of the fact by having his polo pony transported back aboard the cruiser. The horse was accommodated on the top deck amidships and one of the crew volunteered to look after it. This was one of the perks of high rank!

285

Ship's Company of HMS Glasgow with HM Queen Elizabeth II
5th May 1954

Captain P.Dawnay, MVO, DSC, RN

After an uneventful voyage *Glasgow* returned to Portsmouth where, on 19th of May 1954, Captain P. Dawnay, MVO, DSC, RN. assumed command of the cruiser. (Captain Dawnay joined the ship from The Signal School HMS *Mercury* having qualified as a Signal Officer in 1929.)

Glasgow decommissioned on 20th May and the Royal Marine detachment marched off the cruiser with the band playing, proceeded round the corner out of sight of the ship and embarked on lorries which took them back to Eastney Barracks.

The 1954 Commission march through the dockyard 20/5/1954 (DR)

That same day *Glasgow* re commissioned and as soon as the new draft was settled in, the cruiser departed from Portsmouth bound for Portland where she worked up before making her way back to Malta via Gibraltar. *Glasgow* arrived in Gibraltar on 1st June where she remained for three days during which the Royal Marine Detachment Beat Retreat in the Main Square. On 4th she sailed for Malta to arrive on 7th June for more working up exercises.

Glasgow sailed again for Gibraltar on 17th July to take part in the celebrations held for the 250th anniversary of the taking of Gibraltar and arrived at her destination three days later.

HMS Glasgow tied up alongside Sheerlegs Jetty Gibraltar (RP)

Gibraltar occupies a strategic position at one of the world's cross-roads and because of this has been fought over on many occasions in the past. In 1462 it became a Spanish protectorate after the Moors had been defeated in battle. Gibraltar remained a Spanish possession until the beginning of the eighteenth century when it became a pawn in the War of Spanish Succession when there were two claimants to the throne of Spain. One of the claimants was the Austrian Archduke Charles ("Charles III") who gained the support of an Anglo-Dutch force, who captured the "Rock" on behalf of the Archduke in 1704. The Treaty of Utrecht which ended the conflict ensured that the Crown of Great Britain was granted possession "for ever." During the nineteenth century, Gibraltar developed into a Fortress of renowned impregnability and became the "Crown Colony of Gibraltar." In both the 1914-1918 and 1939-1945 wars Gibraltar was a key point in the anti-submarine campaigns. Patrols kept the Straits clear of enemy shipping, and the Bay became an important assembly point for convoys. During the Second World War, the "Rock" underwent dramatic changes which resulted in extensive tunnels being dug in the limestone to create an underground city and the construction of an airfield. After the war there was a demand for self-government by certain factions of the population, while Spain continues to press for the colony to be re-integrated into her territory.

The celebrations arranged for the 250th anniversary of the taking of the "Rock" included the Ceremony of the Keys which took place on 24th July, the date of the original battle in 1704.

This impressive ceremony, witnessed by many interested residents of the "Rock" was held on a lovely bright summer's day, and involved the Royal Marine Detachment and Band.

Royal Marine Detachment from HMS Glasgow at Ceremony of Keys

Two days later *Glasgow* slipped from her berth and returned to Malta for shoots and additional working up exercises. This was the pattern of daily routine until she sailed, on August 13th, for Port Said to evacuate 45 Commando from the Canal Zone. On 16th August the cruiser arrived in Port Said and commences the embarkation of the Royal Marine Commandos.

Royal Marine Commando transport is loaded aboard HMS Glasgow at Port Said.
16/8/1954

The principal problem encountered was transferring men and stores in as short a time as possible. Three days after her arrival the job was completed and *Glasgow* steamed back to Malta with additional crew aboard. The return passage was without incident and upon her arrival back in Grand Harbour on 23rd the process of disembarking the "bootnecks" and their equipment began.

Within hours of the ship's return to Malta the 'Royals' had left for barracks and *Glasgow* prepared to set sail once again the next day, on this occasion bound for Benghazi, with the C-in-C aboard. After a three-day passage the *Glasgow* arrived in Tripoli on 27th August 1954.

While the ship was in Tripoli trips were arranged for the crew to visit ancient sites at Sabratha and Leptis Magna.

Glasgow returned once again to her base in Malta on 28th August where she remained until September when she began her summer cruise which took her first to Palmas Bay in Sardinia where a fleet regatta was organised to take place on 10th and 11th of that month.

On 14th September 1954 the cruiser sailed for Calvi in Corsica, Calvi, jewel of the Balagne and birthplace of the explorer and navigator Christopher Columbus, impresses with the variety of its beauty: an imposing Genoese citadel with cheerful and colourful alleys at its foot, a high town full of self assurance and serenity and a beach which stretches languorously along its pinewood clad coastline.

290

The Ruins at Sabratha *(DR)*

Calvi

From Calvi the ship sailed, on 19th, westwards through the Bonifacio Straits between Corsica and Sardinia before changing course to head south-east in order to meet up with other units of The Fleet and carry out evolutions with them.

Glasgow then pressed on past Stromboli to steam between Scylla and Charybdis in the Messina Straits to "Show the Flag" in Yugoslavia. First port of call in Yugoslavia was Melzine Bay near Kotor where a pleasant afternoon was spent cruising in the area. The weather, however, was not too good. Although the sun shone the clouds hung low when the ship arrived in Dubrovnik on 23rd September.

Stromboli

The inner, as well as the exterior, characteristic features of Dubrovnik were built under the propitious influence of a growing prosperity. Strong fortified walls encircle the city; the facades of pub-

Dubrovnik   *(DR)*

lic buildings and private homes in her squares and narrow mediaeval streets display the Roman and Gothic styles of the days of their
origin. Cars are not permitted to travel on the roads, which have no
pavements, and have been worn smooth by countless generations.

   After a visit lasting two days *Glasgow* sailed, on September 25,th for
Korcula Island further up the coast, where however, there was little
to do. Some of the more hardy spirits thought it time to get closer to
nature by forsaking the comforts of the ship for the rigours of camp
life ashore. Their needs satisfied, the intrepid modern day Robinson
Crusoes' returned to the ship and she sailed for Split, an ancient
town which is almost wholly based on the Palace of the Roman
Emperor Diocletian, on September 27th . Reg Gossage was impressed
with the beauty of the coastline and the old fashioned atmosphere of
Dubrovnik and Split remembering in particular the Island of
Churches in the middle of the Kotor Inlet. He recalls " our leisurely
cruise around the Kotor Inlet brought out all the budding photogra-
phers on board. The mediaeval towns were a photographer's delight
being surrounded by high walls."

Split (DR)

From Split the cruiser sailed towards Malta, engaged in Fleet Exercises as she did so, and entered Grand Harbour on 4th October 1954.

Shortly after the arrival of the Mediterranean Fleet in Malta *Glasgow* went to sea again and on 8th October 1954 engaged in Fleet Manoeuvres including the "Gridiron" and a ceremonial steam past carried out in honour of His Imperial Majesty Emperor Haile Selassie of Ethiopia who was on route to a State Visit to England.

HMS Glasgow enters Grand Harbour Valletta (JM)

Reg Gossage who was on board at the time recalls "to witness two lines of ships a few cables apart at full speed and at a given signal turning towards each other is quite a spectacle. No wonder it is called the 'Gridiron.' It was certainly a day to remember what with varying exercises and manoeuvres concluding with a steam past HIM Haile Selassie taking the Fleet salute aboard *Glasgow.*"

His Imperial Majesty Emperor Haile Selassie of Ethiopia takes salute.

Mediterranean Fleet steam past as Salute to
HIM Emperor Haile Selassie of Ethiopia 8th October 1954

On October 18th HMS *Glasgow* entered the dockyard at Ghajn Tuffeiha for a refit which was to last nearly two months. As the year came to a close Earl Mountbatten relinquished his position as C-in-C, and on 10th December 1954 in accord with naval tradition was rowed ashore by six Admirals, representing the six Allied Navies under his command in the Admiral's Galley. On April 18th the following year he became the First Sea Lord.

Lord Louis leaves the Mediterranean Fleet (DR)

Four days later the ship's company were able to see the first performances of the traditional Christmas Ship's Concert, which was held in the Carradino Canteen Cinema over a three day period.

S.O.D.S. perform at Carradino Canteen

Poland Welcomes Glasgow

While the ship was in the Maltese Dockyard parties, from the ship's company went to the south-west side of the island to engage in weapon firing and assault course training.

Ratings on the Range receiving instruction in small arms

On 4th January 1955, the day before the ship's refit was completed, members of the crew organised a children's party, aboard, for local orphans. These children greatly appreciated not only being entertained but also the lovely selection of food they were given. For their part those crew members who gave up their free time were also rewarded by the obvious pleasure experienced by the children who attended.

After coming out of the dockyard the ship needed re-painting, and was re-stored and re-ammunitioned. An Admiral's inspection followed, after which the ship joined in Combined Fleet exercises with

Crew entertain local children at party given 4th January 1955, Malta

The Crew re-provision and re-ammunition Ship after refit

the Home Fleet, who were to re-enter Malta with *Glasgow* for a few days.

On 13th January the ship proceeded to sea to exercise before returning to harbour where, on January 25th 1955, a conference, attended by Field Marshal Montgomery, C-in-C Mediterranean, FO 2 and His Excellency the Governor of Malta was convened aboard HMS *Glasgow*.

On February 6th the ship was dressed overall, as were the other ships in harbour, to celebrate the anniversary of the accession to the throne of Her Majesty Queen Elizabeth II. Later that same month the ship engaged in exercises in the Mediterranean and was subject to an Admiral's Inspection. A lot of detailed forward planning, went into

Captain P. Dawnay, MVO, DSC, welcomes Field Marshal Lord Montgomery of Alamein aboard

preparing for an Admiral's inspection often lasting for weeks and on some occasions months. This preparation often occupied a dis- proportionate amount of the Captain's and Executive Officer's time to the detriment of other matters. The pending inspection was neither spontaneous nor unpredictable as to its date or the form it would take. Furthermore the ship's company assumed that it was intended as an encouragement-cum-threat to keep them on their toes at a stage in the commission when they might be getting stale. After the Admiral had scrutinised the cruiser's state, which had been brought up into a pristine condition above and below decks by the time the inspection was carried out, a succession of high-speed harbour drills would be ordered by staff officers. These drills were predictable and therefore well rehearsed often requiring such things as weighing anchor by hand, rigging sheer-legs, fire and emergency drills, laying a Dan buoy and in an attempt to introduce a little light relief, sending the ship's cooks away in a sea boat to deliver two live cockroaches, to the flagship. The outcome of a flag officer's inspection was of little significance to the men on the lower decks unless it was so unsatisfactory that a re-scrub had to be ordered. This rarely occurred and the inspection had a bigger impact on an officer's annual report than on the matelots and marines. Had the inspection been undertaken without prior warning it would undoubtedly have been more effective in terms of a true test of efficiency.

During the early part of March 1955 HMS *Glasgow* was engaged in Fleet exercises near Naples before travelling to undertake courtesy visits to Villefranche on the French Riviera.

HMS Glasgow off Villefranche

The cruiser anchored off Villefranche on 28th March and after the mayor had paid his official visit to the ship the gangway was opened to libertymen. Although viewed from the ship there did not appear to be much there, the town turned out to be well stocked with pavement bars and cafes. After a five day visit *Glasgow* left Villefranche on April 2nd, and headed for the Moroccan port of Tangiers where the ship made a brief two day stop before crossing the Straits to enter Gibraltar for Easter on 7th April.

A week later the C-in-C Mediterranean, Sir Guy Grantham, boarded the ship and she set course and speed for the two day voyage to Algiers in north-west Africa.

Here in Algeria, where the Sahara Desert takes up the southern four fifths of the country and temperatures can climb to 49° C, most of the people live in cities in the north where, separated from the remainder of the country by the Atlas Mountains, the land is green and the climate more bearable. Elsewhere it is a vast area of empty desert — a harsh landscape of rock, gravel and sand.

The Market Place Tangier

Looking down on Algiers Harbour and Dockyard

Four days later, on 17th April, *Glasgow* departed from Algiers to cross the Bay of Biscay and return to Pompey, arriving there on 22nd April 1955. After an all too short a leave period the cruiser left Portsmouth for Portland Bay, where she exercised for two days, in advance of heading northwards to steam under the Forth Bridge to dock at Rosyth where self-maintenance was undertaken.

On 6th June *Glasgow* sailed from Rosyth for Invergordon where the Home Fleet Athletics competitions were held.

Four days later she was on the move again to take part in the Fleet Regatta which was held at Scapa Flow.

Cox of PO's All-Comers whaler goes for swim aided by Yeoman Brown

After a short stay there she resumed her passage and made for Amsterdam where she arrived on 17th June.

HMS Glasgow in Amsterdam 17th June 1955

Having completed her courtesy visit to the Dutch port, *Glasgow* returned to British shores to visit Southend in the east of England.

Towards the end of the month the cruiser set sail for the Polish port of Gdynia, where a large number of the local inhabitants turned out to welcome *Glasgow's* entry into the port.

Welcome to HMS Glasgow-Gdynia Poland 1955

A Polish Naval Guard of Honour had formed up on the quayside and having presented arms were able to witness Captain Dawnay berth alongside. Captain Dawnay, who on every occasion spurned the services of local pilots, manoeuvred the cruiser into her allotted space with little room for error and the minimum of fuss to secure alongside with about four feet behind her stern. The Polish naval representatives were suitably impressed with the display and wanted to know "what was under the bonnet?" What they didn't know was that the ship was experiencing problems with one of the starboard engines steam glands which effectively reduced the available power and so it was pure luck that brought about the polished performance!

During the British ship's visit the required protocol was observed and Polish dignitaries were entertained aboard. For their part the Polish Navy proved to be admirable hosts, organising tours and holding lunches for *Glasgow's* officers and men.

HMS Glasgow in Gdynia

In a moving ceremony attended by service personnel from both the Royal Navy and the Polish Navy, Captain Dawnay laid a wreath at the memorial at Westerplatte, where the first shots of the 1939-45 war were fired against a Polish Army garrison.

Captain Dawnay lays wreath at Westerplatte

At the completion of her three-day visit HMS *Glasgow* returned to Rosyth before travelling south to visit Sunderland. Shortly after her arrival in the port the ship's company gave a party for a group of children from a local orphanage. The wide-eyed children were welcomed aboard by their 'Pirate' hosts and led to a playground, which had been constructed specially for the occasion. Here, the delighted youngsters played games and shrieked with laughter as they slid down the slide which the crew had rigged up. Eventually it was time for tea and the hungry children were ushered towards the Main Dining Hall, where they proceeded to devour a veritable feast. Tired but happy they left the ship and the 'pirates' were able to relax, knowing that they had brought a lot of pleasure to a group of less fortunate children.

Children's Party in Sunderland 1955

The cruiser returned briefly to Portsmouth for Summer leave before sailing in turn to Invergordon and Trondheim, where on 30th September, the ship was dressed overall as His Royal Highness the

Crown Prince Olav of Norway made a nostalgic visit to the ship. *Glasgow* remained in Norway for a few days where her crew was able to enjoy the hospitality extended by a grateful population, re-enforcing the bond that had been forged during the Second World War.

Her visit over, *Glasgow* returned to Rosyth on 12th October 1955. Shortly after her return to Scotland she made a courtesy visit to the City of Glasgow, where the association with the city and bonds of friendship were renewed. Her ties renewed, the cruiser departed and steamed northwards to round the British Isles before turning southwards to return to Rosyth.

On 10th November 1955 she returned to Portsmouth where command of the vessel was assumed by Captain C.D. Bonham-Carter, RN, with *Glasgow* wearing the Flag of Vice-Admiral Richard G. Onslow CB, DSO***, FOFHF.

The Last Commission

On 11th November 1955 Captain C.D. Bonham-Carter, joined the ship and assumed command. That day, at the Royal Marine barracks in Eastney, HMS *Glasgow's* Royal Marine Detachment formed up, and led by the Band marched through the streets of Portsmouth before passing through the naval dockyard gate.

Perfectly in step they passed Nelson's Flagship, HMS *Victory* and carried on to where the cruiser was berthed at the South Railway Jetty. Seamen and naval officers arrived from their respective barracks and the new ship's company formed up on the jetty facing the ship. Captain Bonham-Carter welcomed the crew and at the conclusion of his address read out the Commissioning Warrant.

The new crew was dismissed, and they went aboard with their kit to find "new homes" on the mess decks below. For many it was the first time they had been aboard a warship, and for a while they frequently lost their way as they made journeys to the heads or the main dining hall. Often they asked for directions from a shipmate, who like them was equally lost and with a lot of swearing and cursing they eventually found the place they sought.

For the first few days the routine was reasonably relaxed but this came to an end when the lower deck was cleared and the Captain informed the ship's company as to her programme, as he knew it.

On 22nd November 1955, orders were given "Make ready for sea". An exigent nerve-racking clamour sounded throughout the ship. Signal flags of many colours stood away from the ship in the stiff breeze. These were rapidly hauled down to make way for others.

Captain Bonham-Carter gave the order "Let go forward. Let go aft". The hawsers, which had secured the ship to the quayside, now splashed into the grey dirty water of Portsmouth Harbour. There was a trembling throughout the ship. Everybody could feel it and hearts beat faster. The Parsons geared turbines throbbed, driving the screws and from the funnel came a cloud of dancing gasses, like the fire-breathing snort of a dragon. The last hawser fell hissing into the water and suddenly, at 9.46 am all touch was broken between the men and their wives, their sweethearts, their mothers, their parents and their friends on shore. As *Glasgow* proceeded down the Solent towards the English Channel a 17-gun salute to the C-in-C was fired. Once into the Channel she headed towards the south coast of Devon to begin a period of "working up".

On reaching the Channel, the engine room telegraphs clanged to show "Full Speed Ahead", and the cruiser's speed increased, and the head wind began to increase, whistling and howling in the deck structures. The wind itself had risen and there was a strong breeze blowing. Behind the stern, the water bubbled and frothed as though balls of cotton wool had been thrown overboard. *Glasgow* was rolling heavily now and the men who as yet had not found their sea legs began to wonder dismally whether anyone could possibly feel as they did and still live on.

The working up period, which went on day after day and often into the night as well, was taken up with exercises, which included night shoots, torpedo runs and high speed manoeuvring. The schedule was arduous and long hours were worked by the ship's company who looked forward to returning to their Hampshire port for a rest.

Eventually *Glasgow*'s captain was satisfied that the officers and crew were able to function efficiently as a unit and that the ship could take its place with the Fleet. Orders were given and the cruiser sailed back to Portsmouth to enable Christmas and New Year seasonal leave to be taken.

When the men had returned from their long seasonal leave, prepa-rations were made for the cruiser to visit Gibraltar and on 16th January 1956 she left Pompey for Portland, where more exercises and speed trials were carried out. Often "Action Stations" would sound during the night and almost immediately half-dressed sailors and Royal Marines, finishing dressing as they ran, would tumble out of hammocks and run to their "action station".

Four days later, on 20th January 1956, HMS *Glasgow* departed from Portland Bay and set course and speed for Gibraltar. However, halfway across the Bay of Biscay a storm blew up and the cruiser's course was altered to enable her to go to the assistance of an LCT which had got into difficulties. As she put her bows into the seaway the giant swells caused *Glasgow* to roll uncomfortably and the thoughts of her crew turned towards the conditions being experienced by those aboard the smaller vessel. Several of the ship's company felt decidedly unwell as the cruiser settled down on to her new course and corkscrewed. It was not long before the Commander (E) expressed his concern about the performance of the ship's propellers and *Glasgow's* speed was reduced, adding further to the misery of those suffering the effects of seasickness. At the moment visual contact was made the LCT had regained power rendering further assistance unnecessary and *Glasgow* was able to regain her former course and with it a little relief for those whose retching stomachs had no more to give up. At 8.47 am on 25th January the British warship arrived safely in Gibraltar.

The following day *Glasgow* sailed out into the Straits to carry out more speed trials, and as she made her way through the water, on the 27th, a problem was identified with the starboard outer screw. The cruiser returned to harbour where arrangements were made for her to enter dry dock to examine the propeller. While awaiting entry into the dry dock *Glasgow* ventured out again into the Straits, on 1st February, to exercise her guns, before steaming northwards to Tangier. Her arrival on the 2nd was heralded by the firing of a 21-gun salute to the Sultan of Morocco.

Tangier, set upon a spectacular bay, has been called the 'Gateway to Morocco' and overlooks the Straits of Gibraltar with a view of Spain's southern coast.

The Sultan's Palace Tangier (DO)

During the Second World War Tangier was completely controlled by Spain, reverting back to international authority in 1945, finally gaining independence. Soon after *Glasgow's* visit it became a fully integrated part of the Kingdom of Morocco.

Before going ashore the crew was warned of the dangers of pickpockets and venereal disease, although the Surgeon Commander was overheard in the Wardroom to say "the men are more likely to get a dose in Brighton than they are here." Once ashore groups of men tended to keep together, believing there was safety in numbers, and thus were able to effectively deal with those Arabs who continually pestered them with offers of trinkets and sexual favours. For many of the young men it was the first time in their lives they were to be exposed to the delights of "erotica" as they were enticed into bars where 'exhibitions' were organised for their pleasure.

On 5th April *Glasgow* returned to Gibraltar before sailing the next day to Cape St Vincent. A day later she returned from exercising to enter the dry dock to undergo an examination of the starboard propeller.

Apart from the Royal Marine Detachment, the remainder of the crew was able to take advantage of the dockyard routine and relax, many of them sunbathing on the upper deck or sight seeing around the 'Rock'. The "Royals", however, were drilled on the quayside in preparation for an inspection by His Royal Highness Prince Philip, the Duke of Edinburgh. Because it was not officially 'Summer Time' the "bootnecks" were dressed in their blue serge uniforms with high collars as they practised complicated drill movements in the high temperatures that prevailed, albeit in February. (It was hot enough to fry an egg on the gun turrets!). In some discomfort they practised daily, marching up and down to perfect the required drill movements. Eventually the day arrived when the Royal Yacht, with His Royal Highness Prince Philip aboard, arrived in Gibraltar. The Royal Marines formed up on the quayside and marched off to form the Guard of Honour.

The Duke of Edinburgh arrived and the squad came to attention. With the Detachment at the 'present' Captain Richards raised, lowered and raised his sword again in salute. The Duke of Edinburgh quickly passed along the ranks of the assembled Guard of Honour giving little more than a cursory glance to each rank as he did so, before moving on to fulfil another engagement. Several of the younger members of the guard later expressed an opinion that the inspection had seemed to provide little reward for the discomfort suffered and the effort made.

HRH The Duke of Edinburgh inspects the Royal Marine Guard (DO)

Relieved from ceremonial duties the Royal Marines were, like the matelots, able to relax and enjoy the attractions of Gibraltar.

Returning aboard from shore leave 'drunk and incapable' was a common offence, though some officers of the day were more prone than others to turn a blind eye, provided that the inebriated reveller was closely supported by a relatively sober mate to keep him upright, and to see him safely below. One of the attractions of visiting the 'Rock' was being able to purchase duty free goods, including alcohol, and many of the crew visited the bars that line the Main Street.

For the author this was an experience in itself. Coming from a village in Norfolk where teenage drinking was hardly encouraged he soon succumbed to the local liquor, aided by some of his "seasoned" messmates. Subconsciously aware that he must not be 'adrift' he left the bar and picked his way precariously through the dockyard to where *Glasgow* was berthed, somehow avoiding the dangers of falling into a dry dock. Somehow, he found his way back and climbed the gangway to reclaim his watch-card before going to the heads where he passed out, only to be found and taken below to the mess deck to sober up. The following morning, sober and much wiser, he was eternally grateful to the officer of the watch for not having him put in the 'brig'.

When a warship is in a foreign port a "Quayside Sentry" is posted to patrol the quayside for the length of the ship, armed with a rifle, to deter strangers from coming aboard the ship. The author recalls that while patrolling along the Sheerlegs Jetty during the Middle Watch he heard someone singing. He looked around but failed to see anyone in the immediate vicinity. The singing continued and appeared to be coming from on high. Puzzled and straining his eyes against the light he was able to pick out the outline of a sailor at the top of the 'Sheerlegs'. These are the tallest in the world and miraculously the matelot had managed to climb all the way to the top without falling to his death. Everyone breathed a sigh of relief when the drunken sailor was persuaded to return to the ground, which he did unaided!

Sheerlegs Gibraltar (RP)

On 24ᵗʰ March 1956 *Glasgow* left Gibraltar and steamed through the Straits into the Bay of Biscay, which she crossed without incident, and arrived in Portsmouth three days later on the 27ᵗʰ at 12.03 pm. After a month in her home port *Glasgow* sailed for Portland on 1ˢᵗ May 1956 and she anchored in Weymouth Bay.

Weymouth was a dreary run ashore, with the town shrouded in a grey mist as rain fell heavily for the next two days from a leaden sky. Libertymen going to and from shore in an MFV huddled together, seeking whatever shelter they could find on the leeward side of the boat to escape being drenched to the skin. Three days after her arrival off the Dorset coast *Glasgow* sailed on 3ʳᵈ May bound for Cherbourg.

The French port, which lies along the English Channel, north west of Paris and situated at the mouth of the small Divette River to the north shore of the Cotenin peninsula, had been rebuilt during the years following the bombardment of 1944. The remarkable harbour, well sheltered except to the north, was now cleared of the debris of war and open again to the great maritime routes that criss-cross the English Channel. As HMS *Glasgow* entered harbour, on 4ᵗʰ May, those on her upper decks were greeted by the sight of the *Queen Mary* berthed alongside the jetty, towards which the British cruiser was moving. Captain Bonham-Carter, aware that the eyes of passengers aboard the liner were watching every move, ensured his ship entered the harbour slowly and with care. Gracefully, the warship went alongside the jetty and with the aid of French dock workers was quickly secured.

HMS Glasgow with the Queen Mary in background at Cherbourg (GB)

313

Gangways were lowered and Captain Bonham-Carter went ashore to fulfil his official duties.

Libertymen going ashore to sample the local liquor were not conscious of any ill feeling existing amongst the local population as the result of *Glasgow's* involvement in the action taken by the Allies twelve years earlier. Two days later, assisted by tugs, the *Queen Mary* majestically left her berth, turned about and set sail to continue her voyage to America.

The following day, on 7th May, whilst returning from a run ashore after midnight Chief Engineering Mechanic Robert Henry Fowler and Chief Engineering Mechanic Ernest Victor Venables heard cries for help coming from the dock. On investigation they saw a lady struggling in the water and although neither man was young they didn't hesitate over what action they should take. CEM Venables quickly jumped from the jetty into the water in an attempt to rescue her but soon got into difficulties. CEM Fowler, aware his friend was in trouble followed him into the water and together they managed to get the lady back to her boat. The lady, a British subject, later identified as Lady Phipps, had fallen into the water while on her way back to the yacht *"Crissa-Queen"*. After Lady Phipps was safely aboard a crew member was sent to get a doctor but returned instead with a Gendarme and Lady Phipps was then taken ashore for treatment. For their gallantry both members of *Glasgow's* crew were awarded "Medaille de bronze" pour actes de courage et de devouement" by the French Government.

On 9th May 1956 *Glasgow* sailed from Cherbourg for Invergordon where she was berthed for five days following her arrival in the Scottish base on the 12th. There followed a twenty-four hour period of exercising in Dornoch Firth before she returned again to her berth.

A week later *Glasgow* sailed north around the top of the British Isles before turning south to anchor in Loch Eriboll on 26th May. Using the Loch as a base *Glasgow* weighed anchor on the 28th to exercise her main armament in the waters nearby over a period of two days, before returning again to anchor in the sheltered inlet.

On 29th May over the tannoy came the message "Royal Marines muster on the Quarterdeck in full battle kit with weapons". Below, on their mess decks the "bootnecks" scrabbled and jostled with each other to get 'kitted out' before finally emerging to assemble aft. The Sergeant and Corporals quickly called out the men's names before reporting to the Captain RM "All present and correct, Sir". Each man received a "Haversack Ration" which included 'Tiddy Oggies' and hard-boiled eggs. These were tucked safely away into ammunition pouches before the order was given to embark. The Royal Marines clambered over the ship's sides, using scrambling nets, to embark in the cruiser's boats, which took them away to the nearby shores where they were landed.

Dressed in tin helmets and battle-dress with full packs the "Royals" practised simulated attacks on hidden positions. The weather was hot for the time of year and in a short time, as they crawled through the bracken and heather, perspiration blended with camouflage cream to create feelings of great discomfort as the combined mixture found its way into their eyes. Crawling through the heather to reach their objectives did little to improve the quality of the "bootneck's" lunch, and when it was time to take a break they were lucky to be able to salvage anything worth eating!

One of the "Royals", nicknamed 'Jumbo' for obvious reasons was known to be greedy and had been given an extra large "Tiddy oggy". It was only when he bit into it that he found it had been filled with old tea leaves and wire pot-scourers!

Having spent an exhausting day romping about in the Scottish countryside the tired men returned to the ship and it was while climbing back up the scramble nets to board *Glasgow* that Marine Davis let go of his weapon, a "bren" gun, which hit the water below and disappeared. Royal Marine Davis had some explaining to do later.

On 1st June 1956 *Glasgow* weighed anchor again and sailed for Invergordon where she arrived to secure on Buoy 23 the following day. Routine maintenance was carried out by the crew in preparation for her impending visit to Den Helder. On 11th June *Glasgow* left Invergordon and crossed the North Sea, making for the Dutch naval base. After a passage lasting two days the British cruiser arrived in the Netherlands on the 13th, where she exercised with destroyers from the Dutch Navy. Next on the agenda was a visit to Rotterdam and *Glasgow* slipped on 15th June to make the short voyage to the Dutch port, arriving there later that same day.

The city of Rotterdam has officially been in existence since 1328 when Count Willem III granted "City Rights" to the town that had been developing around a dam in the river Rotte. Thereafter it became known as Rotte-dam. Initially it was just a small, quiet fishing harbour in a bend of the Rotte but over the years, because of its position close to deep water it thrived and became important.

Following the outbreak of World War II the Germans subjected the Netherlands to a 'Blitzkrieg' strategy and on 14th May 1940 an extensive bombardment, using blockbusters and firebombs, laid the heart of the city to waste. The casualties were numerous and the Dutch Government was forced to capitulate in order to avoid further bloodshed. No city in Holland suffered as greatly as Rotterdam and after the German surrender in 1945 the process of rebuilding began. The Russian-French sculptor Ossip Zadline, seeing the wasteland that had once been the heart of Rotterdam was inspired to create his statue "The Razed City".

The "Razed City" Statue in Rotterdam   *(DO)*

The finished statue was erected in the centre of an otherwise empty square, as a symbol of the bombed out wasteland which had a single building left standing. For those of *Glasgow's* crew that saw it the statue brought home the wartime suffering endured by the Dutch people.

During her ten day visit a great bond of friendship existed between the Dutch people and *Glasgow's* crew. Much hospitality was extended with the local population organising a ship's dance and trips to visit places of interest including the Parachute Regiment's Cemetery at Oosterbeck, the museum dedicated to the disastrous Arnhem operation "Market Garden", the town of Marken and the Island of Vollendam. For the more adventurous the city of Amsterdam beckoned and it was here, as they strolled along the streets bordering the canals, that young men were able to negotiate openly with prostitutes who sat in the bay window of the canal-side houses exhibiting their 'attributes'. A number of the crew succumbed to temptation believing that the girls in Amsterdam were a safer bet that those in UK! All too soon it was time to leave, and orders were piped: "Close all X doors and scuttles". "Special sea duty men to your stations". "Fo'c'sle men on the fo'c'sle". "Quarterdeck men on the Quarterdeck" "Stand by for leaving harbour". The formality of leaving harbour on 25th June was observed by the crew in rig of the day - Number 3's- standing to attention as they made their way out past other ships, but once the ship was well clear of the harbour entrance formality was discarded and off-duty men got their heads down or settled to a routine of writing to parties ashore.

The cruiser headed north, skirting around Cuxhaven to enter the Kiel Canal, at Brunsbuttelkoog (on the North Sea, at the mouth of the Elbe River) as she made her way to visit Malmö in Sweden. The German Nord-Ostsee-Kanal (North Sea-Baltic Sea Canal) is a waterway, which extends eastwards for a distance of 61 miles to Holstenau (at Kiel Harbour on the Baltic Sea, in northern Germany). Along its length it is spanned by seven bridges, about 140 feet high, and constitutes the safest, most convenient, shortest, and cheapest shipping route between the two seas. Since the First World War the canal has been in the state of Schleswig-Holstein, and is subject to conditions determined by the Treaty of Versailles, which guarantees freedom of navigation. The canal remains an important route for ships heading for the Baltic.

Having successfully negotiated the Canal, *Glasgow* steamed through the Baltic Sea to berth alongside the jetty in Malmö harbour on 26th June 1956. The following day the ship was open to visitors and a large number of local residents, including some very attractive girls turned up to look round the ship. The sight of these nubile young ladies gladdened the hearts of the crew, officer and seaman alike.

Ornamental Fountain in the King's Park Malmö (DO)

The city was a beautiful place to sightsee, with its royal parks, architecture and ornamental statues. However, the cost of living was high and the ship departed a week later, on 2nd July, with its crew short of money and eagerly looking forward to the next pay-day.

The next four days were spent at sea before *Glasgow* berthed at Rosyth on 6th July where general maintenance was undertaken before she left on the 11th for Whitby, on the north Yorkshire coast.

Whitby, which stands on a steep wooded inlet of the river Esk, has been a port for more than 1,000 years, still remaining a seafarer's town. Its narrow streets and picturesque houses stand on the steep slopes, and dominating the harbour are the ruins of an abbey, originally founded in 657 AD. In its heyday the port was a centre for whaling and herring fleets. It is the port from which Captain James Cook was to set sail as he embarked on his historic voyages. In fact, his ships the *Resolution* and the *Endeavour* were built in the local shipyards. Even the town's darker corners have been immortalised in the classic Victorian novel "Dracula".

Glasgow was unable to dock in the harbour for the visit and dropped anchor offshore where she rode uncomfortably in the swell. Libertymen wishing to go ashore were transferred from the ship, by liberty boats, to land alongside one of the jetties. On the second night of the visit the crew was able to attend a dance, which had been organised by some of the local residents. The music was provided by Chris Barber and his jazz band together with Lonnie Donegan and was well attended. Having enjoyed the hospitality and the local brew, several of the crew wended their way back to the jetty, inebriated, to be picked up for the return to the cruiser. The transfer was difficult, particularly at night, because of the tidal surge from the sea into the harbour, which caused the liberty boat to rise and fall by as much as ten feet. Two of the seamen misjudged the distance between jetty and boat and disappeared beneath the water, before surfacing again, a little more sober but minus their caps which bobbed gracefully up and down before being gradually swept out to sea. The men were plucked out of the harbour to take their places in the liberty boat, suffering as they did so the ribald comments of their grinning companions.

The following day, 15th July, the weather deteriorated and in the shallow coastal waters *Glasgow* began to drag her anchors. The courtesy visit was cut short and she weighed anchor before setting course for the Sussex resort of Brighton, where again she anchored off shore. The problems associated with Whitby were not present here on the South Coast and libertymen were able to go ashore relatively easily. Brighton, where the emphasis was on relaxation, became a popular 'run ashore' and the crew was able to experience the delights of the town. The holiday season was well underway and bikini-clad girls sunbathed on the beach. This gave Jack ample opportunities to use his chat-up lines. A week later, which was all too soon for some of the more virile members of the ship's company, the *Glasgow* left to head back to Portsmouth.

From the end of July until the beginning of September that year the cruiser remained in Portsmouth where her crew attended to routine maintenance. On 4th September the cruiser slipped from her berth and headed for Portland. During the following ten days *Glasgow* steamed up and down the Dorset coast engaged in exercises with "D" class destroyers and the Royal Marines exercised ashore.

On 17th September 1956 the British cruiser left Portland to return to Invergordon, arriving there two days later. Invergordon was to be the venue of the Home Fleet cross-country championship and *Glasgow's* team trained hard for the event. The effort paid off when the cruiser provided the individual winner and also took the team title. The author is proud to have been a member of the winning team.

HMS Glasgow making her way through the Kiel Canal

A month later on 12th October 1956, *Glasgow* left Invergordon to visit the German port of Kiel and she sailed slowly along the Firth of Forth heading for the open sea. A two-day passage across the North Sea followed before *Glasgow* berthed alongside the Sud Mole in Tirpitz Haven, Kiel. The city of Kiel itself which, like Plymouth, was grievously damaged during the Second World War, was being rebuilt into a fine modern port with the spire of its ancient church of St Nicholas, patron saint of seafarers, dominating the skyline. In its beautiful setting of Kiel Bay, it seemed to spell out a message of the futility of Europe's wars fought in the 20th century.

In the German port the ship was open to visitors for two days during the afternoons and a large number of local people were attracted to look round the warship. Although barely eleven years had passed since the German surrender there was little evidence of ill- feeling existing between the ship's crew and the residents. It was considered to be a good 'run ashore' and having tasted the local beers some of the crew were to become future lager drinkers.

Centre of the city of Kiel

The *Glasgow* left Kiel on 24th October for Den Helder, arriving there the following day. For the next two days *Glasgow* exercised with ships of the Dutch Navy before leaving the Dutch coast to steam towards Pompey. On 30th October 1956 HMS Glasgow entered Portsmouth harbour flying her decommissioning pennant.

As she lay alongside the Railway Jetty news of the Suez Crisis reached the crew, which led to much speculation as to what was likely to happen. The "buzzes" were further fuelled when "Z" class Royal Marine Reservists embarked and the ship went to a state of readiness, which would allow her to sail at four hours notice. The Royal Marine mess decks became crowded as the reservists tried to find spaces to sleep and shore leave was restricted to the town of Portsmouth. It was a period of great uncertainty and the crew was relieved when tension in Suez eased following the landings by Royal Marine Commandos and the Parachute Regiment.

321

HMS Glasgow entering Portsmouth for last time

Eventually, normal routine was restored and the ship 'paid off' on 12th November 1956. The ship's company assembled on the quayside of the Railway Jetty and formed up ready to march away to their respective barracks to await re-posting. Led by the Royal Marine Band, the Royal Marine Detachment and Seamen marched through the dockyard and out through the Dockyard gates. A few administration staff remained on board to complete the paperwork and shortly afterwards, her duty done, the "old lady" was mothballed.

In March 1958 a decision was made that she be put on the disposal list and on 4th July 1958 she was towed from Portsmouth to the yard of Hughes Bolkow at Blyth where the breaking up process began four days later.

Epilogue

Although HMS *Glasgow*, the subject of this book is no more her name lives on in her successor, a Type 42 destroyer, who has as her sister ships HM Ships *Newcastle, Birmingham, Cardiff, Exeter, Southampton, Nottingham, Liverpool, Gloucester, Manchester, York* and *Edinburgh.* This eighth ship to bear the name HMS *Glasgow* was built at Wallsend launched in 1976 and commissioned in 1979. On board the ship has a complement of 206 men and women who staff the four main departments – Operations, Supply and Secretariat, Weapons Engineering and Marine Engineering – where each person is an expert in his/her own field, and in a modern, complex warship such as this, the emphasis is increasingly placed on technical skills. The destroyer routinely carries a Lynx helicopter and is equipped, as part of her weapons system, with a 114mm 'anti-missile' Phalanx gun, Sea Dart missiles and torpedoes.

Unlike her predecessors the destroyer is air-conditioned, carries large quantities of fuel, spares and stores and has an electrical desalination plant aboard which provides fresh water which enables the ship to be self sufficient at sea for long periods. As with most of the Royal Navy's latest warships the most recent HMS *Glasgow* is propelled by marine gas turbine engines, is highly manoeuvrable and has a top speed in excess of 30 knots. She has already seen action in a theatre of war, the Falklands War in 1982, during which she came under attack from the enemy and sustained damage to her engine room. HMS *Glasgow* continues to enjoy the good fortune of those ships bearing her name.

To a sailor a ship is a living thing with a life and character of its own, and there are ships that seem sombre and even malevolent, just as there are people whose personalities lack vitality and warmth.

HMS *Glasgow*, the subject of the book, definitely had a soul. She always seemed a happy ship, and her spirit pervaded the whole crew, giving rise to a certain fierce pride, which was felt by all old *Glasgow* men from the Captain down to the humblest rating.

Petty Officer F. D. Bunt, typical of many who served aboard the cruiser stated, in a press release; "the *Glasgow* was the finest ship I've had the honour to serve in"

Just before he died in December 2000 Mike Cobbold wrote, in an extract from the 1952-54 commission for the author, " she was a very happy ship, it had her ups and downs, what ship does not? We were very proud of our ship and constantly strove to prove it."

Les Darnell wrote, "We were all very lucky to serve aboard her. She was such a happy ship."

Vic Smith recently stated "she was a lucky ship".

———————————

In peacetime, both pre-war and post-war, HMS *Glasgow* was able to visit many foreign ports with outstanding success. Her respective ship's companies can be justifiably proud of the highly successful contribution they made to the peacetime role of the Royal Navy, namely "Showing the Flag." During wartime her crews fulfilled their duties with great fortitude, humour and dedication, with many being decorated for their bravery.

There is no pain in death; the pain is in the waiting. You can spend every day of a whole lifetime fearing something, which will come only once and, when it does, be gone in a moment. Why waste our lives fearing something over which we have no choice.

We have only one really important choice and that has nothing to do with dying; it's all about living. How long we have is of little consequence, what we do with it is everything. That's what makes facing death difficult, the regrets. The things you've done or, even worse, the important things you've left undone.

Glossary

Throughout this book I have used terms used by those serving in the Royal Navy and Royal Marines. These may seem foreign to anyone not aquainted with naval life and I hope the definitions below will help the reader understand the unique vocabulary of the Royal Navy.

These definitions come from a variety of sources including my own.

AB:	Able Seaman
ACTU:	Asdic Control Training Unit.
Action Stations:	Places of duty from which to fight ship.
Adrift:	Absent without leave
Aggie Westons:	Sailors homes set up by Dame Agnes Weston, providing cheap overnight accommodation in the main naval towns
Aground:	Stuck on seabed; potential court martial situation
Akkers:	cash
Andrew:	Royal Navy
Angle of vanishing stability:	Angle of roll beyond which a ship will capsize
Arse Bandit:	Homosexual
ASW:	Anti- submarine warfare
Badger:	see Stripey
Banyan:	Naval picnic/ outing ashore
Barge:	Senior officer's personal motor boat.
Beetle crushers:	Drill Boots
Belay:	Stop
Bible Bosun:	Padre
Bible Puncher:	Padre
Board Admiralty Board;	RN's most senior people.
Bosun's Mate:	QM's assistant
Bottom:	Seabed.
Brass monkeys:	cold weather (the term cold enough to freeze the balls off a brass monkey comes from days of sail when iron cannon balls contracted so much they came loose in their brass tracks "monkeys" and so fell off around the deck).
Brightwork:	anything brass or bronze
Broadside:	Guns fired simultaneously
Brow:	Gangway between ship and shore
Brown Hatter:	Passive Homosexual
Buff stoker:	Second class stoker lowest Engineering Branch rating
Buffer:	Chief Bosun's Mate.
Bulkheads:	the ship's walls
Bumfluff:	a poorly growing beard

Bunting Tosser:	Yeoman
Buoy Jumpers:	Men who secure a ship's cable to a mooring buoy.
Burton, gone for a:	Killed
Buzz:	Rumour about the latest news.
Cable:	Measure of distance;200 yards.
Caboosh:	Small compartment or den.
Can spanner:	in opener
Carley floats:	a type of liferaft
CEM:	Chief Engineering Mechanic.
Chief Bosun's Mate (CBM):	Senior seaman who is responsible for upper deck maintenance and seamanship.
Chief Buffer:	Seaman Chief Petty Officer in charge of the upper deck being responsible for all three Divisions - each of which were headed by a Petty officer and a Chief Petty officer
Chief Yeoman:	Senior Signals rating on board.
Chokka:	Fed up exasperated
CO:	Commanding Officer /Captain.
Colours:	Ceremony performed during which the Royal Ensign is hoisted.
Cottage:	Old hands name for a mess
Crusher:	Master at Arms Regulating Petty Officers; So called because in early days the Jaunty or RPO was up and about rousing crew crushing cockroaches underfoot as he did so.
Cuddy:	Admiral's or Captain's day cabin.
Cutter:	Naval rowing boat;32 feet long.
CW:	Commissioned Warrant Officer
Damager:	NAAFI canteen manager
Desert Chicken:	Corned Beef
DF's:	duty free cigarettes
Dhobi:	Washing
Director:	
Ditty box:	receptacle for odds and ends
Divisions:	muster of the crew
Dockyard matey:	dockyard worker
Dogger Bank Pheasant:	Kipper
Doggo:	ugly
Dose:	venereal disease
DR:	Dead reckoning; a simple method of calculating a ship's navigational position.
Draught:	Vertical measurement between the waterline and the lowest part of a ship's keel.
Drip:	To moan or complain.
Duff:	Pudding
Duck pond:	A sector of the sea artificially calmed by a ship turning sharply into the wind with the helm turned hard over.
Ebb tide:	Tidal movement running to seaward.
Echo sounder:	Acoustic device for measuring depth of water below the keel.

EP:	Estimated position, a more accurate navigational plot of the ship's position.
ERA:	Engine Room Artificer, a skilled technician.
Errol Flynn:	someone who fancies himself with women. Also nickname given to anyone with surname Flynn.
Fanny:	Oblong Receptacle made of steel and polished for containing liquid i.e. rum
Fanny Rat:	promiscuous womaniser
Fathom:	Measurement of water depth ; 6 feet.
First Lieutenant:	Second in command of a small warship.
Flags:	Admiral's personal staff officer ; Flag Lieutenant.
Foc's'le:	The working deck in the most forward part of the ship; Forecastle.
Gannet:	greedy person.
Gash Bucket:	Receptacle for Rubbish.
Gash:	Rubbish.
General Drill:	Short exercises and evolutions.
GI:	Gunnery Instructor.
Goffa:	A soft drink made with water and flavoured juice e.g. lime, raspberry
Goffa Bar:	Bar on Board where soft drinks could be purchased
Golden Rivet:	a legendary rivet in the ship's hull, far below decks which older hands were supposed to entice younger men to see, so they could be seduced
Gondola:	hammock; Also name for American warship which had a configuration like that of a slung hammock
Goolies:	testicles
Grippo run:	an invitation to a party or outing usually by a civillian ashore
Gunroom:	Very junior officer's messroom.
Gut, the:	Straight Street Malta the Valetta red light area
Guzz:	Slang for Devonport/Plymouth.
Have a Bastard/ Cob on:	be in a temper
Hawse pipe, Through the:	an officer who has come up through the ranks
Heads:	Lavatories.
Herrings in:	Traditional naval delicacy; Herrings in tomato sauce.
Hook, on the:	at anchor
Hooky:	see Killick
Ikkey:	ice in the Arctic
Jack:	Sailor.
Jacob's ladder:	a ladder suspended over the ship's side for climbing in and out of boats
Jankers:	punishment
Jar:	pint of beer or ale

Jaunty:	Master at Arms/policeman from Gendarme
Jimmy/ Jimmy	
the One:	First Lieutenant/ Executive officer
Josser:	Master at Arms
Jumping ladder:	A rope and wood ladder slung down the ship's side.
K.R.&A.I.	King's Regulations and Admiralty Instructions.
Kai:	A hot cocoa drink issued to hands often during the Middle watch.
Killick:	Leading Hand./ Hookey (From Anchor Badge worn on left arm) Equivalent to the rank of corporal
Kite:	A device for submerging sweep wires.
Knee trembler:	stand up sex
Knot:	A measurement of speed at sea; 1 nautical mile per hour.
Lee:	Position or area away fom the direction of the wind.
Legless:	Drunk; incapable of walking properly.
MAA:	Master at Arms; Senior rating responsible for maintaining discipline aboard ship.
Matelot:	Sailor.
Mick:	Hammock.
Nap hand:	to have gonorrhoea and syphilis at same time
Nelson's Blood:	After he died Nelson's body was placed in a barrel of brandy (falsely thought to have been rum) on board HMS Pickle a fast frigate to preserve it on its way to Plymouth.
Number:	(x) Uniforms in descending order of quality. Medicines number nine was a laxative, Punishments in descending order of severity.
Nutty:	any kind of sweets/chocolate
Oggie/Tiddy Oggie:	West Country pasty
Oggin:	the sea (Ocean)
OOD:	Officer of the Day
OOW:	Officer of the Watch.
OP:	Observation Point.
Oppo:	Opposite number; mate, friend, chum.
OTC:	Officer in Tactical command.
Party:	steady girl friend
Pavement pounder:	fried liver
Peado:	Pea soup.
Pierhead Jump:	Re-appointment at very short notice/ Last minute draft to a ship about to sail
Pig's Orphan:	Petty Officer
Piggery:	The Wardroom/Officer's Mess
Pigs:	Officers
Pipe:	an order over the ship's tannoy system
Pipe Down:	order to turn in to sleep

Pipe s out:	order to return to work
Pit:	hammock/sleeping berth
Plumber:	Slang for Engineer officer.
Pompey Lil:	a legendary whore in Portsmouth
Pompey:	Portsmouth
Pot – mess:	Stew.
Prat:	inconsequential fool
Pusser:	anything belonging to the Admiralty/ RN
Pusser's Dirk:	Jack Knife issued as part of kit
Quarterdeck:	Furthermost working deck aft/ after end of the upper deck of a ship.
Quartermaster (QM):	Senior rating guarding access to the ship.
RAS:	Replenishment at sea.
Rattle, in the:	under punishment
RINS:	Royal Indian Naval Service
RM:	Royal Marine(s).
Rose Cottage:	venereal disease clinic in rn barracks taking its name from the rose like sores which are a symptom of syphilis
Rounds:	An inspection of the ship by the Captain or his second in command
Sally Ann:	Salvation Army
Scran:	Food
Scranbag:	untidy person
Scuttle:	porthole
Shiny Sheff:	HMS Sheffield
Sick Bay Tiffy:	Sick-berth Attendant/ Male Nurse (SBA)
Sin Bosun:	Padre
Skin:	good looking young man
Sky Pilot:	Padre
SODS:	Ship's Operatic and Dramatic Society responsible for organising concerts to entertain the crew, hence expression SODS Opera.
Slick method	
Sparks:	Telegraphist
Special Sea Dutymen:	These were considered to be special and were called upon when entering and leaving harbour.
Spithead Pheasant:	Fish
Splice the Mainbrace:	Double issue of rum issued when enemy ship sunk, Sovereigns birthday celebrated or before collecting the dead from the sea.
Springs:	Hawsers used to berth a ship, preventing movement of the ship fore and aft when secured to a jetty.
SRE:	(Sound Recording Equipment)
Stand easy:	a ten minute break off work in the forenoon and in the afternoon
Starshell:	An illuminating round fired high to illuminate a target.
Station card:	on board identity card

Subby:	sub lieutenant
TAS:	Torpedo and Anti submarine.
TI:	Torpedo Instructor
Tiddly:	shipshape / good looking
Tiffy:	Engine room Artificer.
Tot:	Rum ration; abolished in 1970.
Townie:	Someone from the same town or City
Train Smash:	sausage and tomato
TS:	Transmitting Station
Ukkers:	a game played on a ludo board
VHF:	Very high frequency radio transmission.
Wanker:	a weakling; not to be relied on
Wardroom:	Naval officers mess.
Watch Card	See Station Card

Watches:

Midnight	to 0400hrs	Middle.
0400hrs	to 0800hrs	Morning.
0800hrs	to 1230hrs	Forenoon.
1230hrs	to 1600hrs	Afternoon.
1600hrs	to 1800hrs	First Dog.
1800hrs	to 2000hrs	Second Dog.
2000hrs	to Midnight	First.

Went Adrift:	Went absent without permission.
Winger:	a special friend
Wings:	an address to someone usually younger
Working Up:	Period of hard sea training to bring the ship to maximum working efficiency.
Yaffle:	to eat

Why is a Ship called She?

A ship is called a she because there is always a great deal of bustle around her; there is usually a gang of men about, she has a waist and stays; it takes a lot of paint to keep her good looking; it is not the initial expense that breaks you, its the upkeep; she can be all decked out; it takes an experienced man to handle her correctly; and without a man at the helm, she is absolutely uncontrollable. She shows her topsides, hides her bottom and, when coming into port, always heads for the buoys.

Bibliography

The Narvik Campaign   **Johan Waage**
George G. Harrop and Co Ltd.

The Invasion of Norway   **Herman K. Lehmkhul**

Norway 1940   **Francois Kersandy**
Collins 8 Grafton Street London W1

Cruisers of World War Two.
An International Encyclopaedia.   **M.J.Whitley**
Brampton Press. London.

The D-Day Ships   **John de S. Winser**

The Royal Navy. An Illustrated History.   **Anthony J. Watts**
Brockhampton Press 20 Bloomsbury Street London WC 1B 3QA

War at Sea   **Edward Smithies with Colin John Bruce**
Constable and Co Ltd 3 The Lancasters, 162 Fulham Palace Road London W6 9ER

A Pictorial History of the SEA WAR 1939-1945.   **Paul Kemp**.
Brockhampton Press 20, Bloomsbury Street. London WC1B 3QA

Jane's Fighting Ships. Studio Editions. Princess House, 50 Eastcastle Street,
London W1 N 7AP

The Royal Marines 1919 – 1980   **James D. Ladd**
Jane's Publishing Co. Ltd. 238 City Road, London EC1V 2PU

The Penguin Atlas of D-Day
and the Normandy Campaign   **John Man**
Penguin Books Ltd 27 Wrights Lane London W8 5TZ

Engage the Enemy More Closely   **Correlli Barnett**
Hodder and Stoughton

Surface Warfare Magazine May/June 1986 OP-03AX.1300 Wilson Boulevard. Room
782. Arlington. VA 22209-2388

Defiance at Sea   **Jon Guttman**
Arms and Armour Press Cassell Group Wellington House 125 Strand London WC2R
0BB

Convoys to Russia 1941-1945   **Bob Ruegg and Arnold Hague**
World Ship Society 28, Natland Road, Kendal. LA9 7LT England

A Sailors Odessey   **AB Cunningham**
(Viscount Cunningham of Hyndhope KT GCB OM DSO) Admiral of the Fleet
Hutchinson and Co Publishers Ltd

Narvik Battles of the Fjords   **Captain Peter Dickens**
Ian Allan Ltd Shepperton Surrey.

Heart of Oak   **Tristan Jones**
Waterline Books Airlife Publishing Ltd 101,Longden Road Shrewsbury SY3 9EB

Hearts of Oak.
A Collection of Royal Naval Anecdotes Edited by   **P.McLaren**
Fernhurst Books 33, Grand Parade, Brighton, East Sussex. BN2 2QA

Convoy! Drama in Arctic Waters   **Paul Kemp**
Brockhampton Press 20, Bloomsbury Street. London WC1B 3QA

Jane's War at Sea 1897 – 1997   Harper Collins Publishers
77-85 Fulham Palace Road Hammersmith London W6 8JB

Visitors Guide to the Normandy Landing Beaches Published by Moor Farm Road
West, Ashbourne. Derbyshire DE6 1HD

The Navy 1939 to the Present Day   **Max Arthur**
Holder and Stoughton

Mountbatten. The Official Biography   **Philip Zeigler**
Collins 8 Grafton Street London W1

Artic Convoys   1941-45   **Richard Woodman**
John Murray

Seafaring 1939-45 as I saw it   **Captain R.F. McBrearty, MN**
The Pentland Press

"Sparks" RN – A charmed Life   **W.D. Newman, RN.**
Bill Newman 1 Hanover Court Highbury Street
Old Portsmouth Hampshire PO1 2 BN

Lloyds War Losses Second World War Vol.1 page 382

Records held by the Public Record Office, of which there are many.

Diaries and Accounts held by the Royal Naval Museum

HMS Glasgow – Technical Data

This was the seventh ship to bear the name of HMS *Glasgow*, the first being launched in 1707.

HMS *Glasgow* was a Southampton Class British cruiser of which there were 8 ships in 1936/1937:

1) *Southampton* (ex *Polyphemus*) Built Clydebank
2) *Newcastle* (ex *Minotaur*) Built V.A.Tyne
3) *Sheffield* Built V.A. Tyne
4) *Birmingham* Built Devonport
5) *Glasgow* Built Scotts
6) *Gloucester* Built Devonport
7) *Liverpool* Built Fairfield
8) *Manchester* Built Hawthorn

These ships were built in response to the Japanese cruisers *Mogami* and *Mikuma*, which had twelve six; inch guns fitted as part of their armament. Originally the first two were built, armed, like the Japanese ships, with twelve six-inch guns. At the end of 1934 another two were laid down, with the remaining four in 1935.

Glasgow was ordered on December 17th 1934, with construction commencing on April 16th 1935 at the shipyard of Scotts and Engineering Company Limited (Greenock). The company had slips for eight large vessels; fitting out basin; and a graving dock, with the capability to build cruisers, destroyers, submarines, etc. It also made heavy oil engines.

Glasgow was launched on 20th June 1936 and completed on September 8th 1937. Overall the ship had a length of 591 feet 6 inches, being 558 feet at the waterline. The beam was 61 feet 6 inches and the draught was 17 feet (mean). Oil capacity for the ship was 1,970 tons and her displacement was 9100 tons, (12,400 tons full load). The ship had armour plating, which was 1"- 2"thick for the turrets, 4" -3"thick for the sides, 4"thick at the Conning tower, and 2"thickness for the decks.

The power for the ship came from 8 Admiralty 3 drum oil fired boilers. These were linked to Parsons geared turbines to generate 75,000 Shaft Horsepower (S.H.P) via four shafts to propellers, each weighing twelve and a half tons, enabling the ship to have a full speed of 32 knots.

Upon completion the armament provided consisted of 12 Mark XXIII six-inch breach loading guns in four turrets. Each turret weighed 135 tons, with the guns weighing approximately seven tons each. The weight of each piece, without its breach mechanism, was 6tons 14cwts 2 qtrs. The centre gun of each turret was mounted slightly further back than the other two, 30 inches, to reduce interference between the shells in flight. The calibre of the bore was 6" with each barrel being 45 calibre's in length and could be elevated to 45 degrees. Each shell fired weighed 100 lbs. With a full charge the muzzle velocity generated was 2,750 feet per second. Weight of Full charge was 27 1/8lbs.

In addition to the six-inch armament the ship was fitted with 8 MARK XVI four-inch anti-aircraft guns, in twin shielded Mark XIX mounts. Two of which were mounted on each beam abaft the after funnel. These were light, breach loading, quick firing guns, which used fixed ammunition. The bore calibre was 4" with the barrels being 40 calibre's in length. The weight of each gun, without its breach mechanism, was 1ton 6cwts 0 qtrs. The weight of the projectile was 31 lbs. The weight of charges 5 1/6 lbs. The muzzle velocity generated was 2,100 feet per second. The cruiser was also fitted with a 3.7-inch howitzer, 4 x three pounders and 16 smaller guns, oerliokens and 0.5 inch machine guns.

Six twenty-one inch torpedo tubes, tripled, were fitted to enable the standard twenty one-inch heater type torpedo to be fired. These were carried on the upper deck between the four-inch guns and completed the armament.

Originally it was intended that the ship carried five aircraft, however, this was reduced to three, which were launched by use of a steam-operated catapult fixed athwart-ships. The two separate hangers, one on either side of the fore funnel, were incorporated at the aft end of the forecastle and could each accommodate a Walrus amphibian aircraft.

The ship was also fitted with HACS on port and starboard sides, with a third added on the centre line aft.
In the early summer of 1940 radar type 286 was fitted together with 2 UP mountings. Two years later quadruple 0.5 inch machine guns were removed to be replaced by nine single 20mm (Oerlikens).

Types 273,281,282 and 285 replaced the radar type 279. Two years later,in December 1942, five single 20mm guns (Oerlikens) were removed and eight twin 20mm were fitted, The armament was further supplemented, by the fitting of two more single 20mm guns, in the autumn of 1943.

The ship's armament was changed further by April 1944 when her outfit consisted of eight power-operated twin 20mm and seven singles. During the carrying out of repairs and a refit between June 1944 and May 1945 the six inch gun X turret was removed, together with two twin and four single 20mm guns. Radar type 273 was removed leaving her with radar types 281,274 and 293.

The aircraft fittings were also removed and the armament was reinforced by the provision of two quadruple 2 pounders and four single 2 pounder pom-poms on completion of her refit.

The armament available had also changed: - 9x six inch guns, 8x four inch anti aircraft, 8 to 16 – 2 pounder pom-poms, 16-22x 40mm anti aircraft (Bofors), 15-17x 20mm anti aircraft (Oerlikons). The six, twenty-one inch, torpedo tubes, tripled, were still fitted.

The boilers had been replaced and were now 4 Admiralty oil fired 3 Drum type.

Special ventilating trunks were installed, with openings on either side of the hull at the break of deck level abreast of "B" turret

By 1942 the *Gloucester, Manchester,* and *Southampton* had been lost to enemy action.

Between 1950 and 1951 the ship had a refit and had an aircraft homing beacon fitted on the starboard side abaft the after funnel, which distinguished her from H.M.S. Sheffield. By this time the original aircraft hangers were used for cafeteria style messing, for the ship's company, and also doubled up as a cinema.

The ships complement in peacetime was 809-833, with a Royal Marine Detachment of 60 plus Band 18. In wartime the detachment of Royal Marines was raised to 90.